Cracknell's
Law Students' Companion

EQUITY AND TRUSTS

SECOND EDITION

BY

J. G. RIDDALL, M.A.

of the Inner Temple, Barrister;
Lecturer in Law at the University of Leeds

LONDON
BUTTERWORTHS
1974

ENGLAND: BUTTERWORTH & CO. (PUBLISHERS) LTD.
LONDON: 88 KINGSWAY, WC2B 6AB

AUSTRALIA: BUTTERWORTHS PTY. LTD.
SYDNEY: 586 PACIFIC HIGHWAY, CHATSWOOD, NSW 2067
MELBOURNE: 343 LITTLE COLLINS STREET, 3000
BRISBANE: 240 QUEEN STREET, 4000

CANADA: BUTTERWORTH & CO. (CANADA) LTD.
TORONTO: 14 CURITY AVENUE, 374

NEW ZEALAND: BUTTERWORTHS OF NEW ZEALAND LTD.
WELLINGTON: 26–28 WARING TAYLOR STREET, 1.

SOUTH AFRICA: BUTTERWORTH & CO. (SOUTH AFRICA) (PTY.) LTD.
DURBAN: 152–154 GALE STREET

ISBN 0 406 56791 3

Printed in Great Britain by
Chapel River Press, Andover, Hants.

PREFACE TO THE SECOND EDITION

THIS edition contains sections from statutes enacted since the first edition and a number of fresh cases, in particular those making up the *Re Baden* saga. The index has been presented in a new form.

I am grateful to the publishers for permission to use material from the All England Law Reports, to Mrs. G. S. Plowright, Solicitor, for suggestions about cases to be included, and to my wife who typed the text of all the new material for this edition.

December, 1973.   J. G. RIDDALL

EXTRACT FROM THE PREFACE TO THE FIRST
VOLUME OF THE SERIES

THIS work is not intended to compete with other legal textbooks, but it is hoped that it will be of use as a companion to textbooks, lecture notes and correspondence courses. It is intended primarily for the student who does not have access to or time to take full advantage of a law library and finds it difficult to ascertain the facts of cases or the working of Acts of Parliament to which he has been referred in the course of his studies. Other students are more fortunate in so far as they have the opportunity to make full use of a law library, but it is thought that even they might find it to be of assistance to have this work at hand, especially when revising for examinations.

July, 1961.   D. G. CRACKNELL

PREFACE TO THE FIRST EDITION

THIS book is for students studying equity and trusts, and more particularly for those who do not have access to a law library.

Cases in equity cover a wide field and impinge on other branches of law, for example land law and contract, which are usually studied as separate subjects. In this book cases have not been included if they fall to be dealt with more properly in one of the other books in the series. Thus, cases on equitable mortgages have not been included, nor cases on the administration of assets; these will be covered in the books on Real Property and on Succession respectively.

I am most grateful to Mr. M. L. S. Passey, M.A. (Cantab.), Solicitor, for preparing the Glossary.

I should also like to express my thanks to my mother and father for their help and encouragement in the preparation of this book, and in particular for undertaking that most tedious of jobs, the reading of the proofs.

June, 1967   J. G. RIDDALL

CONTENTS

CASES

Abbott Fund Trusts, Re, Smith v. Abbott, [1900] 2 Ch. 326   **[1]**

A fund was raised by subscription to support two distressed ladies and to enable them to live in lodgings in Cambridge. On their death a surplus remained in the hands of the trustees. *Held*, it was not the intention of the subscribers that the money should become the absolute property of the ladies (with the result that on the death of the survivor the property would have passed to the survivor's estate) and it followed that the trustees held the balance on a resulting trust for the subscribers.

Abdulla v. Shah, [1959] A.C. 124 (Privy Council)   **[2]**

A. contracted with S. to sell him three shops in Nairobi. These were let to three tenants at rents controlled under the local rent restriction legislation. After the date of the contract but before completion, one of the tenants surrendered his tenancy. Without consulting S., A. relet the vacated shop to another tenant at the same maximum controlled rent. It was shown that, owing to shortage of building, the value of the premises with the vacated shop unlet was 18,000/- more than with the shop let. S. claimed specific performance of the agreement and compensation by way of an abatement of the purchase price for the loss resulting from the reletting. *Held*, the obligations imposed on the vendor by legislation applicable in Kenya were substantially the same as those imposed on a vendor under English law, by which a vendor has no right, without consultation with the purchaser, to diminish the value of the property by reletting it. S. was therefore entitled to a decree for specific performance and an abatement of 18,000/- from the purchase price.

Aberdeen Town County Council v. Aberdeen University   **[3]**
(1877), 2 App. Cas. 544 (House of Lords)

The Aberdeen Town Council held land on trust for certain professorships in Aberdeen University. The Council obtained a grant from the Crown of the salmon fishing opposite the land and applied the income from this to municipal purposes. *Held*, the Council held the income from salmon fishing on trust for the beneficiaries.

Ackroyd v. Smithson (1780), 1 Bro. C.C. 503   **[4]**

A testator gave land in Leeds to trustees on trust to sell it and out of the proceeds pay specified legacies to fifteen persons, and to divide the residue between the same fifteen persons in proportion to the legacies given to each. Two of the legatees died during the testator's life-time and their shares were claimed by the testator's next-of-kin. The claim was contested by the testator's heir-at-law. *Held*, the shares of the deceased legatees should rank as realty and therefore go to the testator's heir-at-law.

Adams, Re, Gee v Barnet Group Hospital Management   **[5]**
Committee, [1967] 3 All E.R. 285 (Court of Appeal)

A testatrix who died in 1964 gave her residuary estate on trusts which included a provision that in the events which had happened, one half of the residuary estate should be applied " in endowing beds for paying patients " in the Finchley Memorial Hospital in memory of the testatrix's husband. The Finchley

1

Memorial Hospital had seventy-six beds, of which twelve were amenity beds, which, under the National Health Service Act 1946, were made available to patients who undertook to pay partially for their accommodation; and there were also ten private beds, provided under the same Act, which were set apart for patients who paid the whole cost of their accommodation. There was unlikely to be any demand for further amenity beds or private beds at the hospital. There was fresh evidence before the Court of Appeal of a number of ways in which the income of the share of the residuary estate could be used for providing improvements for the benefit of paying patients. *Held,* the phrase " endowing beds " included in its scope the investing of the endowment and the application of the income of the investments in improving the services provided, and was not limited to the provision out of capital of the cost of an additional bed or beds. The further evidence showed that there were amenities that could properly be provided for paying patients, and since there was nothing unlawful in providing them for patients who paid their way, the share of the testatrix's residuary estate given for the benefit of the Finchley Memorial Hospital was bequeathed on valid charitable trusts.

Adams and the Kensington Vestry, Re (1884), 27 Ch.D. 394   [6]
(Court of Appeal)

A testator left property "unto and to the absolute use of my wife Harriet Smith, . . . in full confidence that she will do what is right as to the disposal thereof between my children, either in her lifetime or by will after her decease". *Held,* no trust for the children had been created, and the wife took the property beneficially.

Alcock v. Sloper (1833), 2 My. & K. 699   [7]

In his will a testator gave all his residuary estate, which included certain annuities, to trustees on trust "to permit my wife, Catharine Hudson, to receive the rents, profits, dividends and annual proceeds thereof, to and for her own sole use and benefit, during her life", and directed that on his wife's death all his property real and personal should be sold and the proceeds distributed according to directions in the will. The question arose as to whether the trustees were bound to convert the annuities under the rule in *Howe* v. *Dartmouth,* or whether the widow was entitled to receive the income from the annuities *in specie. Held,* as there was evidence that the testator intended the widow to receive the income from the annuities *in specie,* operation of the rule in *Howe* v. *Dartmouth* was excluded.

Allcard v. Skinner (1887), 36 Ch.D. 145 (Court of Appeal)   [8]

When Miss Allcard was about 35 years of age she felt a desire to devote her life to good works. She became associated with the Sisters of the Poor and after a few years became a professed member of that sisterhood and bound herself to observe the rules of poverty, chastity and obedience. The rule as to poverty required a member to surrender all her property either to her relatives, the poor or to the sisterhood itself. The rules also provided that no sister should seek advice from anyone outside the order without the consent of the lady superior. Within a few days of becoming a member Miss Allcard made a will bequeathing all her property to Miss Skinner, the lady superior, and in succeeding years made gifts to the value of about £7,000 to the same person. When Miss Allcard left the sisterhood about eight years later she immediately revoked her will but waited a further six years before commencing an action to recover what was left of the money given to Miss Skinner. *Held,* if she had sued to recover the amount of her gifts which had not been expended on the fulfilment of the purposes of the sisterhood at an earlier date she would have succeeded on the ground of undue influence, but as it was her acquiescence rendered her claim barred by laches.

Allen-Meyrick's Will Trusts, Re, Mangnall v. Allen-Meyrick,   [9]
[1966] 1 All E.R. 740

By clause 3 of her will, a testatrix who died in 1960 provided " I give all my property . . . to my trustee . . . to hold the residue upon trust that they may apply the income thereof in their absolute discretion for the maintenance of my said husband and subject to the exercise of their discretion upon trust for my two godchildren . . . in equal shares absolutely." At the time of her death both the testatrix and her husband were undischarged bankrupts and her husband remained so. The testatrix had a power of appointment over a settled fund and her will was effective to exercise it. The trustees had exercised their discretion under the will by paying the rent of the house in which the husband lived, but they had retained the rest of the income in their hands and, apart from paying certain debts of the husband, were unable to agree whether to apply further income for his benefit. *Held*, (1) the court would not accept from trustees the surrender for the future of such a discretion as that conferred, *viz.*, a discretion which involved considering from time to time changing circumstances and which could not be exercised in advance; though the court would be prepared to give directions how trustees should act in particular circumstances put in evidence before the court. (2) As and when income accrued and became distributable the trustees should decide within a reasonable time, their decision having to be unanimous if it were to be effective, to what extent they would apply the income for the maintenance of the husband; insofar as income was not so applied within a reasonable time, the trustees' discretion in relation to it was at an end, and the trust in favour of the testatrix's godchildren attached to it.

Ames' Settlement, Re, Dinwiddy v. Ames, [1946] 1 All E.R. 689   [10]

A father covenanted to pay trustees £10,000 by a settlement in contemplation of the marriage of his son. Under the settlement the son was to take a life interest. If no issue of the marriage attained a vested interest the money was to be held on trust for the persons who would have been entitled if the son had died intestate and without ever having been married. The marriage took place and the father paid the money to the trustees. The son and his wife lived together until 1926 when the marriage was annulled. The father died in 1933. The son continued to receive the income until his death in 1945. The trustees sought direction as to whether the trust money should be paid to the father's estate or to the son's next-of-kin. *Held*, the marriage having been void *ab initio*, there was a total failure of consideration and it followed that the trustees held the fund on a resulting trust for the father's estate.

Armitage's Will Trusts, Re, Ellam v. City and County of   [11]
Norwich, [1972] 1 All E.R. 708

By her will a testatrix bequeathed her residuary estate to Sheringham Urban District Council (" the council ") and Norwich Corporation, instructing her executors to give to those bodies " equal annual payments of £200 or £300 to nursing homes for elderly women. Preference to be given to those who can prove they saved for old age but lost savings through natural catastrophes or national affairs beyond their control. Payments to continue as long as capital lasts." The power of the council to accept and administer gifts of property was contained in s. 268 (1) of the Local Government Act 1933. That power was subject to the provision in s. 268 (3) that the section " shall not authorise the acceptance by a local authority of property which, when accepted, would be held in trust . . . for an eleemosynary charity ". It was contended that the council had power to receive the gift since it was not a gift for the relief of poverty and therefore did not constitute an eleemosynary charity within the meaning of s. 268 (3). *Held*, (1) the expression " eleemosynary charity " covered all charities directed to the relief of individual distress, whether due to poverty, age, sickness or other similar afflictions: accordingly the council

3

had no power to accept the gift.   (2) However, since the language of the will did not indicate that the personalities of the appointed trustees were essential to carrying out the intention of the testatrix, whose mind was directed essentially to the relief of elderly women, no part of the residuary gift failed.

Associated Distributors, Ltd. v. Hall and Hall, [1938]   [12]
1 All E.R. 511 (Court of Appeal)

A hire-purchase agreement in respect of a tandem bicycle made provision for its determination by the hirer and, in the event of the hirer's default, by the owner. Clause 7 of the agreement stipulated that in the event of its determination for any cause whatsoever there would be payable by the hirer " by way of compensation for depreciation . . . such sums as with the amount previously paid for rent shall make up a sum equivalent to not less than one-half of the total amount". The hirer elected to terminate the hiring and the court was asked to decide whether the sum which the owners claimed under clause 7 was liquidated damages or a penalty. *Held*, the hirer had exercised an option on the terms of clause 7 and the question whether sums payable under that clause constituted liquidated damages or a penalty did not arise.   It followed that the hirer had to pay the amount which he had made himself liable to pay under that clause.

Astor's Settlement Trusts, Re, Astor v. Schofield, [1952]   [13]
1 All E.R. 1067

In 1945 Lord Astor settled property on trust to apply the income during a speci-fied period for a number of non-charitable purposes which included the "mainten-ance . . . of good understanding . . . between nations", the "preservation of the independence and integrity of newspapers ", and "the protection of newspapers . . . from being absorbed or controlled by combines". *Held*, the trust failed (1) because the objects of the trust were void for uncertainty, and (2) because the trust was not for the benefit of individuals but for a number of non-charitable purposes which no one could enforce [*i.e.* the trust was a trust of "imperfect obligation"].

A.-G. v. Mathieson, [1907] 2 Ch. 383   [14]

In 1876 W began mission work to the Jews.   His work was supported by voluntary contributions from those interested in his work.   To start with the property and funds of the mission, which was called the Mildway Mission to the Jews, were vested solely in W, who carried on the work without any formal rules or regulations, and without any formal expression of the purposes for which the property and funds were held.   But W. published annual reports and accounts.   In 1884, a gift of £1350 from a contributor who specified no special object for the gift, was applied in the purchase of a building, Cromwell Lodge, for use as a home and school for Jewish children.   In 1885, the income and property of the mission having assumed considerable proportions, W. thought it right that there should be some formal declaration of trust, and a deed was accordingly prepared on his instructions.   The deed, dated September 28th, 1885, conveyed the trust property including Cromwell Lodge, to eight trustees on trust for the maintenance of the institution known as the Mildway Mission to the Jews, the objects of which were described as being to " To preach the Gospel . . . to Jews . . . , employing in the prosecution of the work medical missions, convalescent homes, inquirers' homes, homes for destitute children, . . . sewing classes for women . . . and for promoting the salvation of their souls ".   In 1906, the trustees contracted to sell Cromwell Lodge with a view to using the proceeds to buy a more suitable building.   Before the purchase was completed the Charity Commissioners intervened claiming, in an action brought by the Attorney-General, a declaration that the trustees were not entitled to sell without their consent.   The Commissioners based their claim on s. 29 of the Charitable Trusts Amendment Act 1855, which provided that charity trustees were not entitled to sell trust land which formed part of the permanent endowment without the consent of the Charity Commissions. In reply the trustees argued (1) that s. 29 did not apply as exemption from the section was provided by s. 62 of the Charitable Trusts Act 1853, which gave exemption to charities " . . . wholly maintained by voluntary contributions ", and that the mission was so maintained; or in the alternative (2), that (a) as the money with which Cromwell Lodge had been bought had not been given for any particular object the purchase of the building was to be regarded not as part of the permanent endowment but rather in the nature of an " investment "; (b) the purchase of the building having been made before 1885, the execution of the trust deed in that year did not alter the manner in which the building was to be regarded as being held (*i.e.* as an " investment "); (c) as it was not part of the permanent endowment, s. 29 was not applicable to the sale of the building.

Held, as to (1) a charity could not be said to be " wholly maintained by voluntary contributions " if it had freehold premises used for the purposes of the charity, and the fact that these premises produced no actual income was immaterial; thus the charity did not fall within s. 62 which therefore provided no protection.   As to (2), " When money is given by charitable persons for somewhat indefinite purposes, a time comes when it is desirable, and indeed necessary, to prescribe accurately the terms of the charitable trust, and to prepare a scheme for that purpose.   In the absence of evidence to the contrary, the individual or the committee entrusted with the money must be deemed to have implied authority for and on behalf of the donors to declare the trusts to which the sums contributed are to be subject.   If the individual or the committee depart from the general objects of the original donors, any deed of trust thus transgressing reasonable limits might be set aside by proper proceedings instituted by the Attorney-General, or possibly by one of the donors.   But unless and until set aside or rectified, such a deed must be treated as in all respects decisive of the trusts which, by the authority of the donors, are to regulate the charity.   And it is irrelevant to urge that the donors did not originally give any express directions on the subject, or that it might have been competent to the individual or the committee to have dealt with the sums contributed as income ". (*per* COZENS-HARDY, M. R.). [Thus the provisions of the trust deed of 1885 " related back " to contributions made before the execution of the deed.]   Since Cornwell Lodge was treated as part of the permanent endowment of the charity in the trust deed, it was to be regarded as such (and not as an " investment ") from the time of its purchase.   As part of the permanent endowment it was subject to s. 62, and thus the trustees were obliged to seek the consent of the Charity Commissioners before the property was sold.

A.-G. v. Plowden, [1929] All E.R. Rep. 158   [15]

A testatrix gave her residuary estate to trustees on trust to found an institution to be called "The Beaumont Animals Benevolent Society" whose objects should be the protection of animals and birds and the support of anti-vivisection. *Held,* although a trust for the protection and benefit of animals might be charitable if its execution necessarily involved a benefit for the community, the trust in question was not beneficial to the community and was thus not charitable and consequently failed.

Attenborough v. Solomon, [1913] A.C. 76 (House of Lords)   [16]

A testator in his will appointed A. S. and J. S. executors and trustees of his will, and gave his residuary estate to the trustees on trust for sale for certain beneficiaries. After the testator's death part of the residuary estate, consisting of plate, was retained by A. S. in his own possession pending the ultimate division of the trust estate. Fourteen years later A. S., without the knowledge of J. S., pledged the plate with a pawnbroker as security for a loan, and used the money advanced for his own purposes. On the death of A. S. the transaction was discovered. J. S. and R. C., who had been appointed a trustee of the will in place of A. S., brought an action against the pawnbroker to recover the plate. *Held*, at the date of the pledge, the executors had assented to the trust dispositions taking effect, and held the plate not as executors but as trustees; therefore, A. S. had no power to pledge the plate and the existing trustees were entitled to recover it.

Baden's Deed Trusts, Re, Baden v. Smith (No. 1),   [17]

[1967] 3 All E.R. 159 (Chancery Division); [1969] 1 All E.R. 1016 (Court of Appeal): *sub nom. McPhail* v. *Doulton*, [1970], 2 All E.R. 228 (House of Lords)

By deed dated July 17th, 1941, a fund was established for the benefit of officers and employees, etc., of a company. Clause 9 of the trust deed, provided " (a) the trustees shall apply the net income of the fund in making at their absolute discretion grants to or for the benefit of any of the officers and employees or ex-officers or ex-employees of the company or to any relatives or dependents of any such persons in such times and on such conditions (if any) as they think fit . . . (b) the trustees shall not be bound to exhaust the income of any year or other period in making such grants as aforesaid." By clause 9 (c) the trustees were empowered to realise " any investments representing accumulations of income and [to] apply the proceeds as though the same were income of the fund ". Clause 10 provided " all benefits being at the absolute discretion of the trustees, no person shall have any right title or interest in the fund otherwise than pursuant to the exercise of such discretion, and nothing herein contained shall prejudice the right of the company to determine the employment of any officer or employee ". The class eligible for benefit under clause 9 (a), namely " the officers and employees or ex-officers or ex-employees . . . or any relatives or dependants of any such persons " was so large as to be almost certainly incapable of exact ascertainment. *Held*, in Chancery Division, in view of the facts (i) that clause 9 (a) merely directed grants to be made and did not contain any direction to distribute income and (ii) that the trustees were not bound to exhaust income, the deed on its true construction created (notwithstanding the imperative words " shall apply " in clause 9 (a)) a power of appointment and not a trust. [The disposition was therefore not void for uncertainty, as it would have been (under the rule in *I.R.C.* v. *Broadway Cottages Trust (post)*) if it had been a trust.]

Held, in Court of Appeal, (1) if clause 9 (a) constituted a trust in favour of a class whose members were incapable of exact ascertainment, the deed would be void for uncertainty, whereas if the clause constituted a mere power of appointment the deed would be valid if the donees of the power could say with reasonable certainty of any applicant for a benefit, that he or she were a member of that class. (2) The considerations in favour of construing the provisions of clause 9 (a) as creating a trust for the class mentioned were so evenly balanced by those in favour of construing them as creating a mere power, that the court should construe them as creating a power and so give effect to the intentions of the settlor. (3) Clause 9 (a), being construed as creating a power, was therefore valid.

Held, in House of Lords, (1) clause 9 (a) was mandatory and constituted a trust. (2) The test to be applied in determining whether a trust had certainty of objects should be that approved in *Re Gulbenkian's Settlement Trusts (post)* for powers of appointment, namely that the trust was valid if it could be said with certainty that any given individual was or was not a member of the class of beneficiaries designated (and no longer that applied in *I.R.C.* v. *Broadway Cottages Trust (post)*); (3) The case was remitted to the Chancery Division for determination as to whether, on the basis of the correct test, clause 9 was valid or void for uncertainty.

Baden's Deed Trusts, Re, Baden v. Smith (No. 2),   [18]

[1971] 3 All E.R. 985 (Chancery Division) (referred from the House of Lords in *McPhail* v. *Doulton*, [1969] 1 All E.R. 1016), [1972] 2 All E.R. 1304 (Court of Appeal)

Held, in Chancery Division, applying the test established by the House of Lords for determining the validity of a trust, (1) the inclusion of the word " dependants " did not invalidate clause 9 since the trustees or the court could come to a conclusion in any given case whether or not a particular person could properly be described as a dependant; the description of a person as wholly or in part dependant on the earnings of an employee or former employee conjured up a sufficiently distinct picture for the purposes of the trustees or the court. (2) Regarding the word " relatives ", although it could never be said with certainty that a person was not a relative of another person and thus not a member of the class (save where either was known to have illegitimate ancestry) in practise the use of the word relative could not cause any difficulty since a supposed relative to whom a grant was contemplated would be bound to prove his relationship. (The only uncertainty which could be said to exist arose only from the difficulty of proving a totally irrelevant negative). Thus the inclusion of the " relative " did not invalidate clause 9 (a). (3) clause 9 was therefor valid.

Held, in Court of Appeal, (1) regarding the word " relatives ", (i) (a) (*per* SACHS, L. J.) in applying the test laid down by the House of Lords for determining the validity of a discretionary trust it was necessary to distinguish between conceptual uncertainty and evidential difficulty. It was conceptual uncertainty to which the test whether a person " is or is not a member of the class " refers. The court would not be defeated by evidential uncertainty. Once the class of persons to be benefited was conceptually certain and the trustees were able to make a survey of the range of objects such as to provide a sufficiently accurate enumeration of numbers in the class to enable them to appreciate the width of the field from which the beneficiaries might be drawn, it then became a question of fact to be determined on evidence whether any particular person came within the class. Thus the fact that it might be impossible to prove that a person was not a relative of any employee or ex-employee did not make the expression too uncertain. The inclusion of the word relative therefore did not render clause 9 void for uncertainty. Alternatively, (*per* MEGAW, L. J.) (b) a trust for selection would not fail because the whole range of objects could not be ascertained. In the present case the trustees could ascertain, by investigation and evidence, many of the objects. The test of certainty was satisfied if, as regards at least a substantial number of objects, it could be said with certainty that with certainty that they fell within the trust. Validity or invalidity depended on whether one could say of any individual that he was or was not a member of the class for only then could one make a survey of the range of objects. If the word " relatives " was treated as meaning descendants from a common ancestor, a trust for distribution among them would be invalid since a survey of the range of objects would certainly be incomplete. The word " relatives " was not, however, to be given that meaning but was to be construed as meaning next-of-kin or " nearest blood relations "; in that sense the class of beneficiaries was clearly defined and there was no difficulty in determining whether a given individual was within or without it. The inclusion of the word " relative " therefore did not render clause 9 void for uncertainty. (2) Regarding the word " dependants ", there was no conceptual or linguistic uncertainty in the use of the word " dependants ". The word meant a person who was wholly or in part dependant on the means of another. Any difficulties which might arise in determining whether an individual was a dependant were evidential and raised questions of fact, not law. (3) Thus clause 9 of the deed was therefore not void for uncertainty by reason of the inclusion of the words " relatives or dependants ".

Bahin v. Hughes (1886), 31 Ch.D. 390 (Court of Appeal) [19]

A testator left £2000 to Miss E. H., Mrs. B. and Mrs. E. on trust to invest in specified securities, for Mrs. Bahin for life with remainder to her children. E. H. invested the money in an unauthorised security. The security proved insufficient and a loss to the trust fund resulted. Mrs. Bahin brought an action against the trustees seeking to make them liable to make good the loss. (As Mrs. E. had died the action was brought against her husband.) Mr. E. and Mrs. B. claimed to be indemnified by Miss E. H. on the ground that Mr. E. had instigated the purchase of the investment, and had represented the security as a proper and sufficient one. *Held*, the trustees were jointly and severally liable to make good the loss and Mr. E. had no right of indemnity against Miss E. H. Where the management of a trust is left in the hands of one out of several trustees, and the acting trustee commits a breach of trust, the innocent trustee is not entitled to an indemnity from the acting trustee, unless special circumstances exist, as where the acting trustee is the solicitor to the trust, or has obtained personal gain from the breach of trust.

Baker v. Archer-Shee, [1927] A.C. 844 (House of Lords)   [20]

A testator, a United States citizen, left the residue of his property on trust 1or his daughter for life. The trustees paid the income from the property into an account in the daughter's name at a bank in New York. The Commissioners of Income Tax claimed that tax on the income was payable on the grounds that under rule 16 (i) of the Income Tax Act 1918 "The profits of a married woman living with her husband shall be deemed the profits of the husband, and shall be assessed and charged in his name, and not in her name or the name of the trustee"; and under Schedule D, case 5, r. 1 of the Act "The tax in respect of income arising from stocks, shares and rents in any place out of the United Kingdom shall be computed on the full amount thereof . . . whether the income has been or will be received in the United Kingdom or not . . ." The wife's husband, Archer-Shee, contended that tax was not payable on the grounds that under rule 2 of the Act, "The tax in respect of income arising from possessions out of the United Kingdom . . . shall be computed on the full amount of the actual sums annually received in the United Kingdom . . ." and that no such sums had been received. (The Income Tax Act 1918 is now replaced by the Income Tax Act 1952.) *Held*, the daughter being specifically entitled in equity to the income from the trust fund during her life, her husband was liable for tax on such income whether it was remitted to the United Kingdom or not.

Baldry v. Feintuck, [1972] 2 All E.R. 81   [21]

The objects of Sussex University were defined in the charter as being to advance learning and knowledge by teaching and research and to enable students to obtain the advantages of university education. Under subsequent provisions of the charter there was to be established a students' union. The union was duly established in accordance with the charter. Its objects were defined in its constitution and were exclusively for charitable educational purposes. The union was treated by the Inland Revenue authorities as being a charity. At the annual general meeting in 1971 the union approved the adoption of a new constitution, under which the aims and objects of the union were expressed as being " the promotion of any matter whatsoever of interest to its members ". Following the adoption of the new constitution the meeting was adjourned. At the adjourned meeting a budget was adopted authorising the payment of £500 to " War on Want ", a charitable (but non-educational) organisation, and £800 towards a political campaign of protest against the government's policy of ending the supply of free milk to schoolchildren. A member of the union sought to restrain the use of the union's funds for those purposes. *Held,* (1) the objects of the union were confined to charitable educational purposes; the amendment to the union's constitution was invalid insofar as it purported to authorise the use of funds for the purpose of promoting any object which might happen to interest members regardless of whether it was charitable and educational or not and accordingly the objects as defined in the original constitution continued to apply; alternatively, if the amendment were valid, the objects must be construed in the context of the educational purposes of the university and so were confined to charitable purposes, (2) Although part of the educational process was research, discussion, debate and reaching a corporate conclusion on social and economic problems, it did not follow that the provision of money to finance the adoption outside the university of that corporate conclusion formed part of the educational process; the proposed payments were, therefore, contrary to the union's constitution since (a) War on Want, although a charity, was not an educational charity and it was not open to one charity to subscribe to the funds of another charity unless the recipient charity was a purpose or object of the donor charity, and (b) the milk campaign fund was a political and not a charitable purpose. Accordingly the relief sought was granted.

Banfield, Re, Lloyds Bank, Ltd. v. Smith, [1968] 2 All E.R. 276   **[22]**

By her will, a testratrix gave half her residuary estate to the Pilsdon Community House. There was no trust deed or other written instrument establishing or regulating the Pilsdon Community House. A pamphlet and various letters written by the first defendant from time to time showed that the object and purpose was to found a community where persons would lead a simple pious life together. The court found that the community was a religious community existing to do the will of God in practical Christianity. The community was open to persons of all creeds and to those who had none. It received and tended the needs of those members of the public who needed help for a variety of reasons e.g. drug addiction, drink, having been in prison, or loneliness; and members went out to offer help where required. *Held,* the gift was charitable for the following reasons: (1) because it was a gift for the furtherance of the work and purposes of the community, not a gift to the community itself, and the purposes of the community were in law charitable purposes, as being for the advancement of religion, and as having the requisite public element. (2) Even if the purposes of the community were not for the advancement of religion, they were charitable purposes as being within the fourth class of the classification in *Pemsel's case* (see *Commissioner of Income Tax v. Pemsel, post*), *viz.*, other purposes beneficial to the community.

Bannister v. Bannister, [1948] 2 All E.R. 133 (Court of Appeal)   **[23]**

The plaintiff and the defendant made an oral contract by which the plaintiff agreed to buy two cottages—30 and 31 Maryland Cottages, Mountnessing, Essex— from the defendant, and to allow the defendant to live rent free for as long as she desired in number 30. The conveyance made no mention of this undertaking. Subsequently, with the defendant's consent, the plaintiff occupied the whole of number 30, with the exception of one room which the defendant continued to occupy. In an action for the recovery of possession of that room the plaintiff claimed that the defendant had been occupying it as a tenant at will and that her tenancy at will had been determined by notice to quit. *Held,* the purchaser held the cottage on trust for the vendor for as long as she desired to occupy the cottage and subject thereto on trust for himself. "It is, we think, clearly a mistake to suppose that the equitable principle on which a constructive trust is raised against a person who insists on the absolute character of a conveyance to himself for the purpose of defeating a beneficial interest, which, according to the true bargain, was to belong to another, is confined to cases in which the conveyance was fraudulently obtained. The fraud which brings the principle into play arises as soon as the absolute character of the conveyance is set up for the purpose of defeating the beneficial interest, and that is the fraud to cover which the . . . Law of Property Act 1925 [s. 53] cannot be called in aid in cases in which no written evidence of the real bargain is available" (*per* SCOTT, L. J.).

Banque Belge v. Hambrouck, [1921] 1 K. B. 321   **[24]**

A. obtained, by fraud or forgery, cheques drawn on his employer's account at a bank. A. paid the proceeds into his own bank and withdrew large sums which he gave to his mistress. The employer's bank claimed £315, traceable to the money fraudulently obtained by A., standing in the mistress' account at another bank. *Held*, as the money was traceable the plaintiff bank could recover it.

Barclays Bank, Ltd. v. Quistclose Investments, Ltd.,   **[25]**
     [1968] 3 All E.R. 651 (House of Lords)

Q. Ltd., loaned R. Ltd. £209,179 on the agreed condition that R. Ltd. would use the money to pay a dividend which R. Ltd. had declared. Q. Ltd's cheque was sent to R. Ltd. with a covering letter dated 15 July which stated " we would like to confirm the agreement reached with you this morning that this amount will only be used to meet the dividend due . . . " Q. Ltd.'s cheque was paid into a separate account opened specially for the purpose with B. Ltd.'s bank, which knew that the money had been borrowed and which agreed with R. Ltd. that the money would only be used for the purpose of paying the dividend. Before the dividend had been paid R. Ltd. went into voluntary liquidation. *Held*, (1) since (a) the transaction of loan, giving rise to a legal action of debt, did not of itself exclude the implication of a trust enforceable in equity (for legal and equitable rights and remedies can co-exist in one transaction); (b) it was clear from the terms of the loan that the money was not intended to become part of the assets of R. Ltd., but was to be used only for the payment of a dividend, and that if for any reason the dividend were not paid, the money was to be repaid to Q. Ltd.; (c) there was no reason why the law should not give effect to the clear intention to create a secondary trust for the benefit of Q. Ltd. which would arise if the primary trust (to pay the dividend) could not be carried out; the terms of the loans were such as to impress on the money a trust in Q. Ltd.'s favour in the event of the dividend not being paid. (2) Even if it were necessary to show that B. Ltd., had notice of the trust (or of the circumstances giving rise to it) at the time when they received the money, the letter of July 15 and a prior phone call from R. Ltd. explaining the arrangement constituted sufficient notice, and they accordingly had such notice of the trust as to make it binding on them. [Since B. Ltd. hold the money on trust for Q. Ltd., B. Ltd. was therefore not entitled to set off the £209,719 against the overdrafts on R. Ltd.'s other account at the B. Ltd. bank].

Barnes v. Addy (1874), 9 Ch. App. 244   **[26]**
     (Court of Appeal in Chancery)

A settlor settled a fund on trustees, one of whom was A., on trust as to one moiety of the fund on A.'s wife and children, and as to the other moiety on B.'s wife and children. A. was the sole surviving trustee. In exercising a power of appointing new trustees A. appointed B. sole trustee of half the fund, taking an indemnity from him, and retained the other half in his own name. In appointing B. sole trustee A. acted against the advice of his solicitor, Duffield, who prepared the deeds of appointment and indemnity. The solicitor employed by B., Preston, warned B.'s wife of the risk of a sole trustee being appointed, but after obtaining her written consent to this, settled the deed of indemnity. B. later misapplied the moiety of the fund transferred to him and became bankrupt. The children of B. sought to make A. liable for a breach of trust in appointing B. sole trustee, as a fraud on the power of appointing new trustees, and in transferring the stock to B. They sought also to make both solicitors responsible for the fund which had been lost. *Held*, the estate of A., who had died two years previously, was liable to make good the loss. As regards the solicitors ". . . strangers are not to be made constructive trustees merely because they act as the agents of trustees in transactions within their legal powers, transactions, perhaps, of which a court of equity may disapprove, unless those agents receive and become chargeable with some part of the trust property, or unless they assist with knowledge in a dishonest and fraudulent design on the part of the trustees" (*per* LORD SELBOURNE, L. C.). The solicitors were not liable.

Barney, Re, Barney v. Barney, [1892] 2 Ch. 265   **[27]**

In his will a testator left his business as a miller to his wife on trust for the wife for life with remainder to his children in equal shares: he gave no direction as to the carrying on of the business. On his death the widow decided, with the advice of her husband's friends, to carry on the business. Two of the friends, M. and A. agreed to assist her. A banking account was opened in her name, and the bankers were instructed by her not to honour her cheques unless they bore certain initials, which were in fact the initials of M. and A., but neither of them had any authority to draw on the account. The business was carried on and M. and A. supplied goods to the business for which they received payment. There was no suggestion of fraudulent or unfair dealing on the part of either of them. The business eventually made a loss and some of the children brought an action seeking to make M. and A. liable, as trustees *de son tort*, for any trust property received and applied by them for purposes contrary to the trust and for any such property employed by them for purposes of the business. *Held*, a beneficiary may proceed against an agent of his trustee where the agent has not confined himself to the duties of an agent, but by accepting a delegation of the trust, or by fraudulently mixing himself up with a breach of trust has himself become a constructive trustee. But to become a trustee the agent must have trust property vested in him, or so far under his control that he is in a position to require that it be vested in him. The fact that the widow could not draw money from the bank without the concurrence of M. and A. did not give M. and A. such control over the money as was necessary to establish a case against them as constructive trustees. Further, they were not constructive trustees of the money received by them for goods supplied to the business.

Belchier, *Ex parte*, (1754), Amb. 218   **[28]**

An assignee in bankruptcy employed a broker to sell by auction some tobacco which formed part of the bankrupt's estate. The broker sold the tobacco and retained the proceeds. Ten days later the broker died insolvent. *Held*, the assignee in bankrupty was not liable for the loss as a trustee may employ an agent where this is necessary "or conformable to the common usage of mankind" and is not answerable for consequent losses.

Bennet v. Bennet (1879), 10 Ch.D. 474   **[29]**

A son needing £3000 and not having security of his own to borrow this amount, his mother borrowed this sum from an insurance office on security of certain of her interests. The mother paid the £3000 over to the son, who himself paid the insurance office the interest on the loan during his life. The son died insolvent during his mother's life, and the insurance office called on her to pay the interest on the loan. The mother claimed the £3000 against the son's estate. *Held*, when a mother makes an advancement to her child, whether the father is alive or not, there is no presumption that it is a gift [*i.e.*, there is no "presumption of advancement".] In the present case there was evidence to show that a gift and not a loan was intended. The mother was therefore, entitled to prove for the £3000 against the son's estate.

Berry v. Berry, [1929] 2 K. B. 316   **[30]**

By a deed of separation a husband agreed to pay his wife a certain allowance. The parties purported to vary the terms of the deed by an agreement in writing. *Held*, the written variation would be enforced in equity.

Berry v. Green, [1938] A.C. 575 (House of Lords)   [31]

A testator directed his trustees to accumulate income until the death of the last of several annuitants, and subject thereto, and to the payment of certain legacies, he gave the whole of his property to the Congregational Union of England and Wales. The Church, which wanted immediate possession of the fund, argued that as the estate was amply sufficient to satisfy all the annuities and legacies, they were entitled at once to call a halt to the accumulation. *Held*, the Church was not entitled to immediate possession. As the testator died in 1925, the trust for accumulation could not legally continue beyond the expiry of the statutory period in 1964. The surplus income, from then until the death of the last surviving annuitant, realised by the operation of s. 164 of the Law of Property Act, must pass according to the rules of intestacy, and the estate could, therefore, only be handed over to the Church authority at the expense of a violation of the rights of those entitled under those rules.

Best, Re, [1904] 2 Ch. 354   [32]

A testator bequeathed residue to trustees on trust to apply the property for "such charitable and benevolent institutions in the city of Birmingham . . ." as the trustees should determine. *Held*, "the testator intended that the institutions should be both charitable and benevolent; and I see no reason for reading the conjunction 'and' as 'or'" (*per* FARWELL, J.). Thus the gift was a valid charitable gift, and was therefore not void for uncertainty.

Beswick v. Beswick, [1967] 2 All E.R. 1197 (House of Lords)   [33]

By an agreement in writing P. B. assigned his business as a coal merchant to his nephew, J. B. In consideration J. B. agreed to employ P. B. as a consultant at £6 10s. 0d. a week for the rest of his life; and, further, to pay P. B.'s wife after his death an annuity of £5 a week for her life. P. B.'s wife was not a party to the agreement. After P.B.'s death, J. B. paid one sum of £5 to the widow, but refused to pay any further sum. The widow sought an order for specific performance of the agreement in her capacity as administratrix of her husband's estate and in her personal capacity. *Held*, although s. 56 of the Law of Property Act 1925, did not apply to this agreement and so enable the widow to enforce the agreement in her personal capacity, the widow as administratrix was entitled to enforce the agreement by an order for specific performance in her own personal favour.

Biscoe v. Jackson (1887), 35 Ch.D. 460 (Court of Appeal)   [34]

A testator left property on trust for "the establishment of a soup kitchen for the parish of Shoreditch, and of a cottage hospital adjoining thereto, in such manner as not to violate the Mortmain Acts". It was impossible to carry out the trust as no suitable land could be found in the parish. *Held*, the will showed a general charitable intention to benefit the poor of the parish and the trust should therefore be executed *cy-près*. A scheme was directed accordingly.

Bishop, Re, National Provincial Bank, Ltd. v. Bishop, [1965]   [35]
    1 All E.R. 249

In 1946 a husband and wife opened a joint bank account into which they both paid, in unequal amounts, out of their own resources, and out of which they both drew for their own requirements, for housekeeping and for the purpose of purchasing investments. In some instances investments of similar amounts were purchased in the names of the husband and wife separately. In other instances the husband or wife purchased investments in his or her name without any purchase being made in the name of the other. On the husband's death in 1959 the trustees sought to determine the extent of the wife's interest in the investments purchased in the husband's name and in the wife's name, and in the balance in the joint-account at the husband's death. *Held*, where a joint account was opened for a husband and wife on the terms that either could draw on it, then in the absence of evidence of intention to contrary, each spouse could draw on it not only for the benefit of them both, but also for his, or her, individual benefit. Accordingly, if one of them purchased a chattel for his own benefit or made an investment in his own name, that chattel or investment belonged to the person in whose name it was purchased or the investment made. Thus, the husband was the beneficial owner of the investments purchased in his name and the wife was beneficial owner of those purchased in her name. On the husband's death the balance standing to the credit of the joint account accrued beneficially to the wife. (See also *Jones* v. *Maynard*).

Biss, Re, Biss v. Biss, [1903] 2 Ch.D. 40 [36]

J. B. was the yearly tenant of a house in Westminster where he carried on a profitable business as a lodging-house keeper and in 1900 he died intestate. The widow took out administration to her husband's estate, and she and the two adult children, one of whom was a son, continued to carry on the business under the existing tenancy. The widow applied to the lessor for a new lease for the benefit of the estate, which he refused to grant, but, having determined the yearly tenancy by notice, he granted to the son "personally" a new lease for a further three years. The widow, as administratrix, applied to the court to have the new lease treated as having been taken by the son for the benefit of the estate. *Held*, no constructive trust arose and the son could keep the lease for his own benefit, as any hope of renewal of the lease to the estate had been extinguished by the refusal of the widow's application; and also on the grounds that the son had in no way abused his position, nor stood in a fiduciary position to the other persons interested in the estate.

Blackwell v. Blackwell, [1929] A.C. 318 (House of Lords) [37]

A testator in a codicil to his will gave £12,000 to five persons on trust "for the purposes indicated by me to them". The testator gave instructions to C. orally regarding the application of the money, and the object of the trust was known in outline and accepted by the other four before the execution of the codicil. On the same day as the execution of the codicil, though a few hours afterwards, C. signed a memorandum containing the instructions given to him by the testator. *Held*, a valid trust had been established. [A "half secret trust".] Section 9 of the Wills Act 1837 did not interfere with the exercise of a general equitable jurisdiction, even in connection with secret dispositions of a testator, ... The effect, therefore, of a bequest being made in terms on trust, without any statement in the will to show what the trust is, remains to be decided by the law as laid down by the courts before and since the Act and does not depend on the Act itself. ... It is the communication of the purpose to the legatee, coupled with acquiescence or promise on his part, that removes the matter from the provisions of the Wills Act and brings it within the law of trusts, as applied in this instance to trustees, who happen also to be legatees" (*per* VISCOUNT SUMNER).

Blandy v. Widmore (1716), 1 P. Wms. 323 [38]

H. covenanted with his wife's trustees that his executors should pay his wife £620 within three months after his death. H. died intestate. The wife became entitled by the Statutes of Distribution to a moiety of the personal estate which amounted to more than £620. *Held*, the amount received under the intestacy was to be deemed to be in performance of the covenant, and the wife could not claim performance of the covenant in addition to the amount received under the intestacy.

Boardman v. Phipps, [1966] 3 All E.R. 721 (House of Lords) [39]

A testator who died in 1944 left his residuary estate to be divided, subject to an annuity to his widow, between his children. The trustees of the will were, in 1956, the testator's widow (who was then senile), a married daughter, N. and an accountant, F. B. was a solicitor who acted for the trustees and for a son of the testator, P. The residuary estate included 8000 shares in a private company which had an issued share capital of 30,000 shares. In 1956 F. and B. decided that the position of the company was unsatisfactory and that something must be done to improve it. Towards the end of 1956 B. and P. attended the company's annual general meeting with proxies obtained from N. and F. They attended as representing the estate. Shortly after this meeting B. and P. decided, with the knowledge of N. and F., to endeavour to obtain control of the company by themselves purchasing shares. The trustees had no power to invest trust monies in shares of the company. B., purporting to act on behalf of the trustees as shareholders, obtained information from the company concerning the price at which shares had changed hands. The negotiations for acquisition of shares were prolonged. Between April 1957 and October 1958 B. obtained much information from the company by purportedly acting on behalf of the trustees. In November 1958 the widow died. Ultimately, in March 1959, an agreement for the sale of £14,567 shares of the company to B. and P. was signed and by the end of July 1959 they had acquired, with other purchases, 21,986 shares of the company. A considerable profit subsequently accrued from capital distributions on these shares. B. and P. had acted honestly throughout. A son of the testator, J., who was entitled five-eighteenths of the estate, claimed that B, and P. held five-eighteenths of the profits they had made on trust for him. *Held,* (1) (a) the mere use of knowledge or opportunity coming to a trustee or agent in the course of the trusteeship or agency did not necessarily render him accountable for profit from its use. (b) In the present case, as both the information which satisfied B. and P. that the purchase of the shares would be a good investment and the opportunity to bid for them came to B. and P. as a result of B.'s acting or purporting to act on behalf of the trustees for certain purposes (though not for the particular purpose of bidding), B. and P. were constructive trustees of five-eighteenths of the 21,986 shares in the company for J. and were liable to account to him for the profit thereon. (2) There should be an inquiry as to what sum should be allowed to B. and P. for their work and skill in obtaining the shares and profits thereon. As B. and P. had acted openly, albeit mistakenly, payment to them should be on a liberal scale.

Bowden, Re, Hulbert v. Bowden, [1935] All E.R. Rep. 933   [40]

In 1868 a daughter purported to assign to trustees any property to which she might become entitled on her father's death under his will, to hold upon specified trusts. The settlement was voluntary. The father died in 1869 and during the years 1871–1874 his executors transferred the property to which the daughter would have been entitled to the trustees of the settlement. In 1935 the daughter requested the trustees to transfer the trust funds to her as her absolute property. *Held,* whilst at law and in equity a voluntary assignment of an expectancy is ineffective, where the assignor allows the assignee to receive the property, the assignor will not be able to recover it. The original trustees had received the daughter's share under a valid authority which had not been revoked and the property was thus subject to the trusts of the settlement.

Bowen, Re, Lloyd Phillips v. Davies, [1893] All E.R. Rep. 238   [41]

A testator who died in 1847 bequeathed two sums of money to trustees upon trust to establish a day school in certain parishes in Wales. He directed that if at any subsequent time the government established a " general system of education " the trust should cease and he bequeathed the trust money " in the same manner as I have bequeathed the residue of my personal estate". He appointed his three sisters to be his residuary legatees. After the passing of the Elementary Education Act 1870, the personal representatives of the residuary legatees took out an originating summons to determine whether the legacies had fallen into residue. *Held,* the principle in *Re Tyler* (that a gift over from one charity to another is valid notwithstanding the fact that the gift over is to arise upon an event which need not necessarily occur within the perpetuity period) has no application where a gift to a charity is followed by a gift to private individuals. The bequest to the residuary legatees was therefore void as infringing the rule against perpetuities.

Bowes, Re, Earle of Strathmore v. Vane, [1896] 1 Ch. 507   [42]

B., a tenant for life of settled land, left money in his will to be spent on the planting of trees on the estate of which he had been tenant for life. On B.'s death the land passed to S. for life. On S.'s death it would pass to G. in tail. S. and G. asserted that since the planting of trees was a disadvantageous way of spending the money, they should be entitled to receive the money. *Held*, (1) the money was held on trust. (2) By executing a disentailing assurance with S.'s concurrence, G. could bar the entail; S. and G. would then be capable of dealing with the estate as they liked; in that case they would, between them, be absolutely entitled to the land. (3) the gift in the will was intended to improve the estate for the benefit of the persons absolutely entitled. (4) the persons absolutely entitled to the estate were entitled to the money, whether it was actually laid out on the planting of trees or not. (5) On the execution of a disentailing assurance by G., a declaration would be made that S. and G. were entitled to receive the money.

Boyes, Re, Boyes v. Carritt (1884), 26 Ch.D. 531   [43]

A testator instructed his solicitor to draw up a will leaving all his property to the solicitor himself. He told the solicitor that he wished him to hold the property according to directions which he would communicate to him. The solicitor agreed to this and a will was prepared accordingly. No directions were given by the testator to the solicitor, but on the testator's death an unattested paper was found addressed to the solicitor in which the testator stated that he wished that Nell Brown should receive the property. *Held*, as the testator had failed to communicate the object of the trust to the solicitor during his lifetime, no valid trust in favour of Nell Brown had been constituted. "... no case has ever yet decided that a testator can, by imposing a trust upon his devisee or legatee, the objects of which he does not communicate to him, enable himself to evade the Statute of Wills by declaring those objects in an unattested paper found after his death" (*per* KAY, J.). The solicitor held the property on trust for the testator's next of kin.

Brandon v. Robinson (1811), 18 Ves. 429   [44]

A testator left property on trust for sale for his children in equal shares. He directed that the share of his son Thomas should be invested and that the income "should be paid ... into his own proper hands ... to the intent that the same should not be grantable, transferable, or otherwise assignable, by way of anticipation of any unreceived payment or payments thereof, or of any part thereof", with remainder over. After the death of the testator, Thomas became bankrupt. The assignee in the bankruptcy claimed that he should receive the income. *Held*, although a limitation until bankruptcy or attempted alienation is valid [see *Rochford* v. *Hackman*], a life interest with a condition that it is not to be alienated or that it is to be forfeited on bankruptcy is void. The condition in the will was therefore void and the assignee in the bankruptcy was entitled to receive the income.

Bristow v. Warde (1794), 2 Ves. Jun. 336   [45]

J. B., the donee of a power of appointment, had power to appoint certain property to his children, to whom the property was to go in default of appointment. In his will J. B. appointed part of the property to the children, but the rest he appointed to strangers. *Held*, the father not having left the children any property of his own, the children were not put to their election as to the property appointed to strangers, and could retain the property appointed to them and, as the persons entitled in default of appointment, take the property appointed to strangers.

Brockbank, Re, Ward v. Bates, [1948] 1 All E.R. 287   **[46]**

W. and B. were trustees of a will under which a testator settled his residuary estate on trust for his widow for her life and after her death for his children. W. wished to retire as trustee. The widow and the children desired that a bank should be appointed trustee. B. was unwilling to join with W. in exercising the statutory power vested (by s. 36, of the Trustee Act 1925) in himself and W. in order to appoint the bank trustee, as he considered that the bank's fees would impose an unnecessary charge on the trust property. W., the widow and the children took out a summons asking that B. should be directed to concur in appointing the bank trustee. *Held*, dismissing the summons, that beneficiaries who are together absolutely entitled to trust property are not entitled to control the exercise by their trustees of the power of appointing new trustees. Such beneficiaries must either put an end to the trust; or, if the trust is continued, the trustees must be those appointed according to the original instrument or under s. 36 of the Trustee Act 1925, and not persons selected by the beneficiaries.

Brooker, Re, Brooker v. Brooker, [1926] W.N. 93   **[47]**

A testator left residuary property on trust for conversion, with power to postpone conversion, for persons in succession. The property included leaseholds. *Held*, having regard to sections 28 (2) and 205 (1) (ix) of the Law of Property Act 1925, the tenant for life was entitled, in the absence of any indication to the contrary, to receive the income from the leaseholds *in specie*, until conversion.

Buchanan-Wollaston's Conveyance, Re, Curtis v. Buchanan-   **[48]**
Wollaston, [1939] 2 All E. R. 302 (Court of Appeal)

B.-W., C., S. and B. held a piece of land at Lowestoft as joint tenants. In 1928 the four joint-owners entered into a deed of covenant by which it was agreed, *inter alia*, that "Any transaction in connection with the . . . land . . . must be unanimously agreed to by all the parties hereto". In 1930 S. transferred her interest in the land to C. In 1932 B. died. C. later wanted the land to be sold and the proceeds of sale divided. B.-W. and B.'s executors refused to concur in selling the land. In 1938 C. took out a summons under s. 30 of the Law of Property Act 1925, seeking an order by the court ordering B.-W. to concur in selling the land. *Held*, the court would not aid C. to break his contractual obligations by ordering, on his application, a sale of the land under s. 30 of the 1925 Act.

Burdick v. Garrick (1870), 5 Ch.App. 233   **[49]**

In 1858 P. E. Garrick authorised D. Garrick and Monckton to sell his real and personal property and to invest the proceeds in the name of trustees on his behalf. D. Garrick and Monckton sold the property and invested part of the proceeds but retained a considerable sum in their own hands. In 1859 P. E. Garrick died and in 1867 his widow took out letters of administration. She claimed from D. Garrick and Monckton the proceeds of sale of her husband's property for which they had not accounted. D. Garrick and Monckton replied that the claim was barred by the Statute of Limitations. *Held*, (i) D. Garrick and Monckton, although agents of P. E. Garrick, were in a fiduciary position with regard to the money entrusted to them, and were therefore not able to set up the Statute of Limitations against the claim; (ii) they should be charged with simple interest at 5 per cent for the period during which the funds had been misappropriated.

Burrough v. Philcox (1840), 5 My. & Cr. 72   **[50]**

A testator gave property to his two children for their lives and empowered the survivor to dispose of the property by will "among my nephews and nieces or their children, either all to one of them, or to as many of them as my surviving child shall think proper." *Held*, a trust had been created in favour of the testator's nephews and nieces, subject to a power of selection and distribution vested in the surviving child. The surviving child having failed to exercise the power, the property was to be divided equally among the relatives specified by the testator, i.e. his nephews and nieces and their children.

Cannon v. Hartley, [1949] 1 All E.R. 50 [51]

In a separation agreement a husband covenanted with his wife and daughter to settle one half of certain after acquired property on trust for himself for life, with remainder to the wife for life, with remainder to the daughter absolutely. The husband failed to settle property acquired by him subsequently. The daughter sued the husband, her father, for damages for breach of covenant. *Held*, the daughter was entitled to succeed since, although a volunteer, she was not only a party to the deed but also a direct covenantee under the covenant. She did not require the assistance of equity to enforce the covenant as she had a right to do so at common law.

Carpenters Estates, Ltd. v. Davies, [1940] 1 All E.R. 13 [52]

The plaintiffs bought some land from the defendant for building purposes and the defendant covenanted that he would construct certain roads and sewers. The defendant made the roads but neglected to make the sewers. The plaintiffs claimed specific performance of the defendant's promise. *Held*, an order for specific performance would be made as an award of damages would not be a sufficient remedy.

Carrington, Re, [1931] All E.R. Rep. 658 [53]

In his will made in 1911, C. bequeathed certain shares to J. He left the residue of his property to trustees on trust for sale for S. for life with remainders over. In 1927 C. granted H. an option to purchase the shares, to be exercised within one month of C.'s death. C. died in January, 1930. In February of that year H. notified C.'s personal representatives that he intended to exercise the option to purchase. *Held*, the bequest of the shares to J. was adeemed by the exercise of the option, and the purchase money passed as residue.

Caunce v. Caunce, [1969] 1 All E.R. 722 [54]

In 1959 a husband (H.) and wife (W.) bought a house, W. contributing £479 to the purchase price. The house was conveyed into H.'s name alone. While the H. and W. were living in the house, H., without W.'s knowledge, raised three sums of money on the security of the house by means of three mortgages with a bank. In July 1966 H. left the matrimonial home. W. continued to live there without him. Shortly afterwards H. was adjudicated bankrupt. W. claimed that she had a beneficial interest in the house, and that this beneficial interest had priority over the mortgages to the bank. *Hèld*, (1) W. had an equitable interest in the property. (2) (a) The bank ought not reasonably to have been expected to enquire into the details of W.'s account at the bank. (b) Since the husband and wife were both living in the house at the time of the mortgages to the bank, the wife was not in apparent occupation or possession of the property. (c) The presence of the wife in the house at the time of mortgages by H. to the bank was not inconsistent with H having sole title. (d) The mere fact that the house was the matrimonial home was not sufficient to fix a purchaser or mortgagee with constructive notice of a spouse's equitable interest in the property. (e) There were no special facts that should have given the bank notice of W's equitable interest. For these reasons the bank did not have constructive notice of W.'s equitable interest. (3) As, (a) the bank had acted *bone fide*; (b) by virtue of s.87 (1) of the Law of Property Act 1925, the bank had the same protection as if it had obtained the legal estate; (c) the bank did not have notice, actual or

constructive of W.'s equitable interest, the bank took the mortgages free of
W.'s equitable interest.

Caus, Re, Lindeboom v. Camille, [1934] Ch. 162   [55]

A testator, a Roman Catholic priest, who died in 1931, by his will bequeathed
£1000 for " Masses, foundation and others—for my four houses at Great Holme
Street [Leicester] I leave for one foundation Mass to be said for my soul, and
the souls of my parents and relatives, during the space of twenty-five years,
and the property to revert to the parish of St. Peter's Roman Catholic Church
for extension purposes ".   Evidence showed that by " foundation mass " was
meant a Mass the saying of which was to be paid for out of interest from an
invested fund.   If the gift was not charitable, it would thus be void as infringing
the rule against inalienability.   *Held,* because the gift (1) enabled a ritual act,
central to the religion of a large proportion of Christian people, to be performed
and (2) assisted in the endowment of priests whose duty it was to perform the
act, the gift was for advancement of religion and, as such, was charitable.   (But
see *Re Coates, post*).

Cave v. Cave (1880), 15 Ch.D. 639   [56]

Charles Cave was the sole trustee of a marriage settlement.   In 1872 he used the
funds, in breach of trust, to purchase land in the name of his brother Frederick
Cave.   In 1873 Frederick Cave created a legal mortgage in favour of Philip Chaplin
and subsequently created an equitable mortgage in favour of John White.   In 1879
Frederick Cave became bankrupt and beneficiaries under the marriage settlement,
the plaintiffs in the action, claimed priority over the mortgages created in favour of
Philip Chaplin and John White, the defendants.   *Held,* as Philip Chaplin did not
have notice that the land was trust property, as a *bona fide* purchaser for value of a
legal estate without notice, his legal mortgage took priority over the interests of the
beneficiaries.   As between the equitable interests of the beneficiaries and the equitable mortgage of John White, under the principle *qui prior est tempore potior est
jure* (he who takes earlier in time is stronger in law), the interest of the beneficiaries
took priority over the equitable mortgage held by John White.

Central London Property Trust, Ltd. v. High Trees House,   [57]
Ltd., [1947] K.B. 130; [1956] 1 All E.R. 256

The plaintiffs leased to the defendants a block of flats at a rent of £2500 p.a. from
September 1937.   Owing to the outbreak of war the defendants were able to let
only a few of the flats and in 1940 the plaintiffs agreed in writing to accept a lower
rent of £1250 from the beginning of the lease.   The defendants paid the reduced rent
agreed.   By 1945 the flats had become fully let and in September 1945 the receiver
of the plaintiff company informed the defendants that the full amount of rent
originally agreed must be paid, and claimed arrears amounting to £7916.   In order
to test the legal position the plaintiffs claimed the difference between the rent
originally agreed and the reduced rent for the last two quarters of 1945.   *Held,*
(i) where a promise is made with the intention of creating legal relations, and where,
to the knowledge of the person making the promise, the promise is going to be
acted on by the person to whom it is made, and where it is in fact so acted on, the
courts will refuse to allow the party making the promise to act inconsistently with
it; (ii) the promise by the plaintiff that the rent should be reduced to £1250 was
intended "as a temporary expedient while the block of flats was not fully, or substantially fully let, owing to the conditions prevailing" and when the flats became
fully let, early in 1945, the reduction ceased to apply; (iii) the promise by the
plaintiffs was binding on them until early in 1945, but ceased to apply thereafter.
The plaintiffs were thus entitled to succeed in their claim for the full rate of rent
for the last two quarters of 1945.

Chapman v. Chapman, [1954] 1 All E.R. 798 (House of Lords)   **[58]**

By a settlement made in 1944, P. and his wife Q. declared that certain land or the proceeds of sale thereof and such further assets as might from time to time be brought into the settlement (" the trust premises ") should be held by trustees, subject as thereinafter by clause 3 provided, for all or any child of R., who should attain the age of twenty one years or die under that age leaving issue and if more than one in equal shares. By clause 3 it was provided: " . . . that until the youngest child of [R.] shall have attained the age of twenty-five years . . . the trustees shall retain the trust premises and shall apply such part as they in their discretion shall think fit of the income thereof for or towards common maintenance education or other benefits of the children of the said [R.] for the time being living whether minors or adults. In order to save estate duty on the deaths of the settlors it was proposed that the trustees should with the sanction of the court advance their funds to the trustees of a new settlement which was to contain similar trusts, but omitting the provision for common maintenance contained in clause 3. *Held,* it could not be said that the court had unlimited inherent jurisdiction to modify or vary trusts provided only that (a) all persons interested who were *sui juris* consented, and (b) the modification or variation was clearly shown to be for the benefit of all persons interested who were not *sui juris* (including unborn persons). The jurisdiction of the court was limited to cases in which the court (i) effects changes in the nature of an infant's property or (ii) allows trustees of settled property to enter into some business transaction which was not authorised by the settlement; or (iii) allows maintenance out of income directed to be accumulated; or (iv) approves a compromise on behalf of infants and possible after-born beneficiaries (a compromise in this connection meaning an agreement relating to disputed rights); and, therefore, there being in this case no dispute as to rights, the court had no jurisdiction to sanction the scheme on behalf of infants and unborn persons.

Chardon, Re, [1928] Ch. 464   **[59]**

A testator bequeathed £200 to trustees on trust to invest the money and to pay the income to a cemetery company for as long as the company maintained two specified graves. The testator directed that if the company failed to maintain the graves, the trustees should pay the income to the persons entitled to the residuary estate. *Held,* "the cemetery company and the persons interested in the legacy . . . could combine tomorrow and dispose of the whole legacy. The trust does not, therefore, offend the rule against alienability. The interest of the cemetery company is a vested interest; the interests of the residuary legatee . . . are also vested. All the interests therefore created in this £200, legal and equitable, are vested interests and, that being so, the trusts do not offend the rule against perpetuity" (*per* R<small>OMER</small>, J.). The trust was therefore valid.

Chaytor, Re, Chaytor v. Horn, [1905] 1 Ch. 233   **[60]**

A testator left residuary personalty to trustees on trust to sell and convert, with power to postpone conversion as long as the trustees thought proper and to retain any investments subsisting at his death, whether of the kind authorised by the will or not, and out of the proceeds of sale to pay debts and legacies, and to invest the residue and to hold the investments purchased on trust for his wife for life and on her death for his children. At his death the testator held shares in a coal mining company which were not authorised by the investment clause in the will. The shares produced a high dividend. Pending conversion the trustees paid the widow, not the full dividend produced by the shares, but a percentage of the value of the shares at the testator's death. The widow claimed that she should be paid the full income from the shares, *i.e.* that she should receive the income *in specie*. *Held,* in the absence of any express or implied gift of the income, pending conversion the widow was not entitled to receive the income *in specie*, but only to 3% of the value of the shares at the testator's death. [The percentage since *Re Beech*, [1920] 1 Ch.

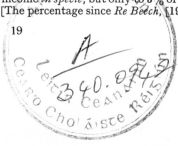

40 has been 4%]. The balance of the dividends were to be treated as capital and invested.

Chesham (Lord), Re, Cavendish v. Dacre (1886), 31 Ch. 466   [61]

A testator left certain chattels to his two younger sons, and the residue of his property to his eldest son C. The chattels were, in fact, heirlooms settled on trust to be held with a certain mansion house of which C. was the tenant for life. The younger sons claimed that C. should be put to his election to take under or against the will, and that if he elected to take under the will, he should compensate them out of the residue to the extent of the value of his interest in the settled chattels. *Held*, C., having only a limited interest in the chattels, was not put to his election. He could therefore take the residue and retain his interest in the chattels without compensating the younger brothers.

Chesterfield, Earl of, Trusts, Re (1883), 24 Ch.D. 643   [62]

A testator left residuary personalty to trustees on trust for conversion, with power to postpone conversion, for persons in succession. The property included a mortgage debt with arrears of interest. The trustees postponed conversion, and a number of years later the debt, with interest, was repaid. *Held*, the money was to be apportioned between capital and income by calculating what sum invested at the date of death at 4% compound interest, after deducting income tax, would have yielded the sum actually received. The sum so calculated was capital and the balance was income which should be paid to the tenant for life.

Chichester Diocesan Fund and Board of Finance (Incorpor-   [63] ated) v. Simpson, [1944] 2 All E.R. 60 (House of Lords)

A testator directed his executors to apply the residue of his estate "for such charitable or benevolent object" as they should select. *Held*, the use of the word "or" resulted in the trust being not *exclusively* charitable. It could therefore not be charitable and, as a private trust, it failed for uncertainty.

Chillingworth v. Chambers, [1896] 1 Ch. 685 (Court of Appeal)   [64]

P. and D., the trustees of a will, advanced sums of trust money on the security of mortgages of certain property. Such a form of investment was not authorised by the will. P., while a trustee, later became entitled as a beneficiary under the trust. More trust money was advanced by P. and D. on mortgage after P. had become a beneficiary. The value of the properties mortgaged proved, when realised, to be inadequate security, and there was a deficiency of £1580. P. and D. were declared jointly and severally liable to make good the loss. The whole loss was made good out of P.'s share of the trust fund (which exceeded the amount of the loss). P. claimed contribution from D. *Held*, the normal rules as to the right of contribution as between trustees all or both of whom were to blame for a breach of trust and of whom one has made good the loss, does not apply where the trustee who has made good the loss is also a beneficiary. P. therefore had no right to contribution from D. in respect of any part of the loss.

Civilian War Claimants Association v. The King, [1932]   [65] A.C. 14 (House of Lords)

By the Treaty of Versailles 1919 Germany undertook to pay compensation for damage to civilian populations and property in the countries against which it had fought during the 1914–1918 war. The British Government required civilians having claims for war damage to submit claims to the Government for presentation to Germany. When Germany had made a payment to the British Government in respect of the British claims the plaintiffs, an association of persons who had made such claims, sought a declaration that the money received from Germany was held by the Crown as trustee for them. *Held*, the Crown did not hold the money as the trustee of those who had submitted claims, because (i) the Crown had showed no intention of accepting the position of trustee in respect of the money, and (ii) " the terms of the treaty were that Germany should pay the sum necessary to satisfy the claims of the various people who had suffered, and it was left to the Governments themselves, as between them and their nationals, to determine how that money was to be distributed " (*per* LORD BUCKMASTER.)

Clayton's Case, Devaynes v. Noble(1816), 1 Mer. 529, 572   **[66]**

D. was the senior partner in a firm of bankers, of whom C. was a client. When D. died, C. continued to do business with the firm, but later the firm went bankrupt and C. claimed against D.'s private estate for the amount owing to him by the firm at the time of D.'s death. The amounts which C. had since received from the firm were more than sufficient to satisfy the balance due at D's. death, but C. argued that these amounts could be appropriated by him to the subsequent moneys paid in by him to his account at the bank, leaving the earlier items still unpaid. *Held,* a debtor might at the time of payment exercise his option as to how the payment was to be appropriated; and if the debtor did not elect, the creditor had the option of doing so at any time subsequently, but that in the case of a current account, such as a banking account, where there was a continuation of dealings, then in the absence of express declaration at the time of payment, there was a presumption that the payments made were appropriated to the various debts in the order that they were incurred. [The Rule in *Clayton's Case* is summed up by the phrase "first in, first out", the first payment in being set against the first payment out, and *vice versa.*]

Coates, Re, Ramsden v. Coates, [1955] 1 All E.R. 26   **[67]**

A testator directed: " If my wife feels that I have forgotten any friend I direct my executors to pay to such friend or friends as are nominated by my wife a sum not exceeding £25 per friend with a maximum aggregate payment of £250 . . . I have forgotten H., F. and J. but my wife will put that right." *Held,* the power conferred on the wife was a power collateral (a " pure power ") and not a power coupled with a duty (a " trust power "). It was therefore not essential to its validity that the whole class of beneficiaries should be ascertainable. It was sufficient if it was possible to postulate whether any given person came within the class. There would be no difficulty in determining whether a given person had been " a friend " of the testator and so was a proper object of the power. Thus the power did not fail for incertainty.

Cockburn, Re, [1957] 2 All E.R. 522   **[68]**

T. appointed three persons to be executors and trustees of his will. Two predeceased him and one renounced probate and never acted as trustee. Two Administrators with the will annexed were appointed. They paid the funeral and testamentary expenses and the testator's debts and death duties. They then asked whether they were the trustees of the will and at liberty to exercise the powers conferred on trustees by the will. *Held,* when personal representatives, whether executors or administrators, have completed the administration they became trustees, holding 1or the beneficiaries and are bound to carry out the duties of trustees. They have power under s. 36 to appoint new trustees in their place.

Cole, Re, Westminster Bank Ltd. v. Moore, [1958] 3 All E.R. 102   **[69]**
(Court of Appeal)

A testator, who died in 1955, devised two freehold houses on trust, " to apply the income arising therefrom . . . for the general benefit and general welfare of the children for the time being in [S. House] . . . I desire that the superintendent for the time being of [S. House] should be consulted with a view to ascertaining his views as to the allocation of the before mentioned income ". S. House was a home provided and maintained by a local authority pursuant to s. 15, the Children Act 1948, for the accommodation of children in its care. The home provided accommodation for up to thirty children of either sex between the ages of five and fifteen. A child might remain there for periods ranging from a few weeks to about two years. The cost of maintaining the children was provided partly from grants of money by Parliament and partly from contributions received from parents. The classes of children admissible by virtue of the two Acts included orphans, or children abandoned by their parents, children committed to the local authority as a " fit person ", including children found guilty of offences punishable in the case of an adult with imprisonment and children exposed to moral danger or beyond the control of their parents. The question arose whether the devise was for a charitable purpose. *Held*, while a gift for the endowment or maintenance of S. House might be charitable, the present gift " for the general benefit and general welfare " of the children for the time being in S. House was not charitable because the terms of the gift permitted the application of income for non-charitable objects, *e.g.* the purchase of a television set for the benefit of delinquent or refractory children.

Combe, Re, [1925] Ch. 210   [70]

A testator left residue to trustees on trust for his wife for life, with remainder to his son for life, with remainder " In trust for such person or persons as my said son . . . shall by will appoint but I direct that such appointment must be confined to any relation or relations of mine of the whole blood ". There was no gift over on default of appointment. The son took out a summons to ascertain what would be the result of his releasing the power of appointment. *Held*, the power of appointment was a pure power (a " power collateral ") and not a trust power, as there was nothing in the will to indicate an intention on the part of the testator to create a trust in favour of the objects. Thus if the son released the power the property would be held on (a resulting) trust for the testator's next-of-kin.

Combe v. Combe, [1951] 1 All E.R. 767 (Court of Appeal)   [71]

A wife had obtained a decree nisi and her solicitors wrote to the husband's solicitors to ask them to confirm that he would allow her £100 *p.a.* and they confirmed that this was the case. The wife did not apply to the court for maintenance and the husband did not observe his promise to pay her £100 *p.a.* *Held*, as the husband had not requested the wife to refrain from making an application to the court there was no consideration for his promise; even if he had made such a request there would have been no consideration, as the wife's promise not to apply for an order would not be binding on her so as to preclude her from applying for an order for permanent maintenance. The principle stated in *Central London Property Trust, Ltd.* v. *High Trees House, Ltd.* must be "used as a shield and not as a sword" (*per* BIRKETT, L. J.).

Commissioner of Income Tax v. Pemsel, [1891] A.C. 531   [72]
(House of Lords)

Land was conveyed in 1813 to trustees on trust to apply a proportion of the rents and profits for missionary establishments commonly known as the Moravian Church, of which Pemsel was the treasurer. It was claimed that the gift was for "charitable purposes" under the Income Tax Act 1842, and hence exempt from income tax. *Held*, since the trust contemplated purposes which had no relation to the relief of poverty, the purposes were not "charitable" within the meaning of the 1842 Act and thus income tax was payable. [Note: This case is noteworthy chiefly because of the definition of charity given by LORD MACNAGHTEN: "How far then, it may be asked, does the popular meaning of the word 'charity' correspond with its legal meaning? 'Charity' in the legal sense comprises four principal divisions: trusts for the relief of poverty; trusts for the advancement of education; trusts for the advancement of religion; and trusts for other purposes beneficial to the community, not falling under any of the preceding heads.'']

Compton, Re, Powell v. Compton, [1945] 1 All E.R. 198 [73]
(Court of Appeal)

By her will a testatrix gave money on trust for the education of children of C., P. and M. who were under twenty-six years of age. There were twenty-eight descendants of these persons eligible. *Held*, a class of persons determined by reference to a personal relationship was not a sufficient section of the public to satisfy the requirement that (with the exception of trusts for the relief of poverty) to be charitable a trust must be for the public benefit. The exception to this rule which applied in the case of trusts for the relief of poverty was not to be extended to trusts for purposes other than poverty. The trust was therefore not charitable.

Cooden Engineering Co., Ltd. v. Stanford, [1952] 2 All [74]
E.R. 915 (Court of Appeal)

A hire-purchase agreement in respect of a motor car provided that upon the determination of the agreement by the owners the car should be returned and the hirer should pay the instalments which were outstanding at the date of such determination and, by way of compensation for depreciation, 40% of the instalments which had not yet fallen due. *Held*, this sum was a penalty and could not therefore be recovered.

Conolly, Re, Conolly v. Conolly, [1910] 1 Ch. 219 [75]

A testator bequeathed property to his sisters and stated: "I specifically desire that the sums herewith bequeathed shall . . . be specifically left by the legatees to such charitable institutions of a distinct and undoubted Protestant nature as my sisters may select, and in such proportions as they may determine". *Held*, no trust had been created, and the sisters took the property beneficially.

Cook's Settlement Trusts, Re, Royal Exchange Assurance v. [76]
Cook, [1964] 3 All E.R. 898

A father gave certain property, which consisted mainly of valuable pictures, to his son. The son covenanted that if any of the pictures were sold during his life time, he would settle the proceeds on specified trusts for specified beneficiaries, who were members of the son's family (but who did not include the father). The trustees took out a summons to determine what steps they ought to take if the pictures were sold during the son's life time. *Held*, following the normal rule that only parties to a contract could enforce it, as the beneficiaries had given no consideration, and were not to be treated as if they had given consideration (as were the issue of a marriage in the case of an ante-nuptial settlement), they were unable to enforce the covenant. The court made a declaration that the trustees ought not to take proceedings against the settlor to enforce his covenant. (See *Re Kay's Settlement, post.*)

Cooper's Conveyance Trusts, Re, [1956] 3 All E.R. 28 [77]

In 1864 certain property was conveyed to trustees on trust for the Orphan Girls' Home at Kendal, and on failure of the trust the property was to be held on trust for specified persons and "for no other trust or purpose whatsoever". In 1954 the Home was closed owing to lack of support. The trustees sought the direction of the court as to the disposition of the property. *Held*, the gift over to the individuals specified was void as infringing the rule against perpetuities. (See *Re Bowen*.) The gift over showed that the donor intended the gift to charity only for a limited time and for a limited purpose. This expression of intention was sufficient to exclude the operation of the *cy-près* doctrine. The trustees therefore held the property on a resulting trust for the estate of the donor.

Coulthurst's Will Trusts, Re, Coutts and Co. v. Coulthurst,   [78]
[1951] All E.R. 774 (Court of Appeal)

A testator, who died in 1949, by his will gave to his trustees a fund of £20,000 to be called the Coulthurst fund and provided: " At the expiration of every six months calculated from the date of my death (Coutt's Bank) shall pay or apply the income earned by the Coulthurst fund during such period of six months to or for the benefit of such one or more exclusively of the . . . widows and orphaned children of deceased officers and deceased ex-officers (of the bank) living at the expiration of such half-yearly period as the bank shall in its absolute discretion consider by reason of his or her or their financial circumstances to be most deserving of such assistance." *Held,* having regard to all the terms of the gift, it constituted a valid charitable trust for the relief of poverty. " Poverty, of course, does not mean destitution. It is a word of wide and somewhat indefinite import, and, perhaps, it is not unfairly paraphrased for present purposes as meaning persons who have to ' go short ' in the ordinary acceptation of that term, due regard being had to their status in life and so forth ". (*Per* SIR RAYMOND EVERSHED, M. R.)

Coxen, Re, MacCallum v. Coxen, [1948] 2 All E.R. 492   [79]

A testator gave property to trustees on trust " to pay or make over the same to the Court of Aldermen for the City of London . . . upon trust out of the income of the trust fund to apply once a year a sum not exceeding the sum of £100 . . . to provide a dinner to the Court of Aldermen when they shall meet to decide the business of this trust and to pay to each member of the committee hereinafter mentioned who shall attend during the whole time of any committee meeting the sum of £1 1s. 0d. for his attendance at such meeting and to apply the balance of such income for the benefit of . . . the orthopaedic hospitals of England and other hospitals or charitable institutions carrying on similar work . . . in such shares and proportions as the said committee shall from time to time think fit ". He directed that the committee should consist of six Aldermen. The trust fund amounted to more than £200,000. *Held,* the trusts for the annual dinner and attendance fees were capable of furthering the trust for the charitable purposes specified by promoting efficient management and therefore were themselves charitable.

Dalziel, Re, Midland Bank Executor and Trustee Co., Ltd. v.   [80]
St. Bartholomew's Hospital, [1943] 2 All E.R. 656

A testatrix gave £20,000 to the governors of St. Bartholomew's Hospital to add to an existing discretionary fund, on which the cost of the upkeep of a family mausoleum was a first charge, on condition that they should use the income as far as was necessary to maintain and, when necessary, rebuild the mausoleum and directed that "if they shall fail to carry out this request I give the said sum of £20,000 to such other of the charities named in this my will as my trustees may select . . ." *Held,* as the gift was not an absolute gift to the charity, but a gift on which a non-charitable purpose (the upkeep of the tomb) was charged, the trust was not charitable. Being private, the trust came outside the rule permitting a gift to charity subject to a gift over to another charity on the occurrence of an event, specified by the settlor, which might take place outside the perpetuity period. The gift to the Hospital therefore failed as infringing the rule against inalienability. (The court rejected the view that the gift was void only as to the amount required for the upkeep of the tomb and valid as to the residue, on the grounds that there was no means of determining what surplus, if any, would be left after the upkeep of the tomb was provided for.)

Dean, Re, Cooper-Dean v. Stevens (1889), 41 Ch.D. 552   [81]

A testator devised his land to trustees, subject to an annuity of £750 *p.a.* charged on the land payable to the trustees, on trust for the plaintiff for life with remainders over. The will then stated "I give to my trustees my eight horses . . . and also my hounds. . . . And I charge my said freehold estates . . . with payment to my trustees for the term of fifty years commencing from my death, if any of the said horses and hounds shall live so long, of an annual sum of £750. And I declare that my trustees shall apply the . . . sum . . . in the maintenance of the said horses and hounds . . . and in maintaining the stables, kennels . . . and any part remaining unapplied shall be dealt with by them at their sole discretion." *Held*, the annuity of £750 was not given to the trustees beneficially, but the gift created a trust for the maintenance of the animals. Although it was not charitable and its execution was not enforceable by any one [a trust of "imperfect obligation"] the gift nevertheless constituted a valid trust. The court left open the question whether any surplus not employed on maintaining the animals belonged to the devisee of the land, or to the testator's heir-at-law.

Dearle v. Hall (1823), 3 Russ. 1   [82]

In his will made in 1794 P. B. bequeathed his residuary estate to his executor on trust for sale and conversion for his son Z. B. for life. The interest payable to Z. B. amounted to £93 a year. In 1808 Z. B. assigned to Dearle an annuity of £37 a year, payable during the life of Z. B. The annuity was secured on Z. B.'s annuity of £93. Z. B. retained the right to receive his annuity of £93 a year, but if he failed to pay the annuity of £37 to Dearle, then the £93 was to be paid to Dearle, who was to take his £37 out of the £93 and pay the balance to Z. B. The executor, Unthank, was unaware of this assignment. In 1812 Z. B. sold his life interest to Hall, who had no notice of the earlier assignment to Dearle. Hall gave written notice of his assignment to Unthank. *Held*, the assignment to Hall took priority over the assignment to Dearle, as Hall had been the first to give notice. [Note: the rule in *Dearle* v. *Hall* is that when there are successive assignments of an equitable interest in any property, real or personal, the priority of those assignments follows the order in which the respective assignees give written notice of their assigments to the trustees of the settlement or trust under which the interest assigned subsists.]

Delius, Re, Emanuel v. Rosen, [1957] All E.R. 854   [83]

The testatrix was the widow of Frederick Delius, the composer. She died in 1935, having by her will bequeathed to her trustees all the copyrights of the musical works of Delius to which she was entitled, and by clause 12 of the will she directed the trustees to apply the income from the royalties and the income of her residuary trust fund " for or towards the advancement . . . of the musical work of [Delius] under conditions in which the making of profit is not the object to be attained . . . by means of (i) the recording upon the gramophone or other instrument for the mechanical reproduction of those works of [Delius] which in the opinion of my trustees and their advisers are suitable for reproduction (ii) the publication and issue of a uniform edition of the whole body of the works of [Delius] and (iii) the financing in whole or in part of the performance in public of the works of [Delius]." *Held*, (1) the purpose of the trusts being to spread and establish knowledge and appreciation of Delius's works among the public of the world, and having regard to the musical worth of the works, the trusts were charitable trusts for the promotion of the art of music. (2) The charitable nature of the trust was not vitiated merely because incidentally the reputation of the testatrix's husband would be enhanced.

Denley's Trust Deed, Re, Holman v. H. H. Martyn & Co. Ltd., **[84]**
[1968] 3 All E.R. 65

Land was conveyed to trustees who were directed in the trust deed to maintain the land for use as a sports ground " primarily for the benefit of the employees " of a certain company " . . . and secondarily for the benefit of such person or persons (if any) as the trustees may allow to use the same . . . ". The trust deed further directed that if the land ceased to be required or used by the employees as a sportsground or if the company went into liquidation or if one other contingency occurred, then the land was to go to the General Hospital Cheltenham. The trustees were given powers of sale over the land. *Held,* (1) the rule that non-charitable " purpose or object " trusts are unenforceable applies to those trusts where there is no trust beneficiary [i.e. applies to trusts of " imperfect obligation "]. But a trust which, though expressed as being for a purpose, is directly or indirectly for the benefit of an individual or individuals, is valid, provided the individuals are ascertainable at any one time and the trust is not otherwise void for uncertainty or for any other reason. (2) The disposition in favour of the employees constituted a trust. The employees were an ascertainable class and the trust was thus valid as regards certainty. (3) The disposition in favour of " such other person or persons (if any) as the trustees may allow . . . " constituted not a trust but a power [of appointment] which operated in partial defeasance of the trust in favour of the employees. The power satisfied the conditions as to certainty of objects applicable in the case of powers of appointment. The power was thus valid. (4) The trust was not made void by infringing the rule that a trust must be capable of being administered by the court (see *Morice* v. *Bishop of Durham, post*).

Dicey, Re, Julian v. Dicey, [1956] 3 All E.R. 696   **[85]**
(Court of Appeal)

In her will S. D. devised to J. J. two houses in Beresford Road, Walthamstow. To C. D. she gave a house in Higham Road, Walthamstow, and the residue of her property. S. D. was merely a life tenant of the houses in Beresford Road. On her death they passed to C. D., J. J. and C. J. as co-owners in the proportions a half, a quarter and a quarter respectively. On S. D.'s death J. J. claimed that C. D. must elect either under the will (and retain the house in Higham Road and the residue, but convey to J. J. the half share to which he, C. D., had become entitled in the houses in Beresford Road) or against the will (and retain his half share in the houses in Beresford Road, but compensate J. J. to the extent of the value of this half share). *Held,* the doctrine of election applied and C. D. must elect whether to take under or against the will.

Dingle v. Turner, [1972] 1 All E.R. 878 (House of Lords)   **[86]**

By his will a testator directed his trustees to apply the income of certain property " . . . in paying pensions to poor employees of [D. Ltd.] ". At the testator's death D. Ltd. had 705 full-time employees and 189 part-time employees and was paying pensions to 89 ex-employees. On the question whether the gift was charitable, *Held,* in the field of relief of poverty the dividing line between a charitable and a private trust depended on whether, as a matter of construction, the gift was for the relief of poverty amongst a particular description of poor persons or was merely a gift to particular poor persons, the relief of poverty amongst them being the motive of the gift. If the former, the gift was not prevented from being charitable by virtue of the fact that the description of the poor people was by reference to the employees of an individual or a company. The gift fell into former category and was therefore charitable.

Diplock, Re, Diplock v. Wintle, [1948] 2 All E.R. 318   **[87]**
  (Court of Appeal)

A testator directed his executors to apply the residue of his estate "for such charitable institutions or other charitable or benevolent object or objects in England" as they should select. The executors distributed a large part of the residue among various charities before the next-of-kin of the testator challenged the validity of the bequest. In *Chichester Diocesan Board of Finance* v. *Simpson,* the House of Lords held that the gift failed for uncertainty. The next-of-kin claimed the amounts paid to the charities from the executors and, with the approval of the court, these claims were compromised. The next-of-kin also claimed against various institutions which had received money·from the executors. The claims of the next-of-kin were of two main kinds: (a) claims *in personam* against the institutions which had received money; (b) claims *in rem* against the assets held by the institutions. *Held,* as to the claims *in personam*: (i) An unpaid or underpaid creditor, legatee or next-of-kin had an equitable right of the kind claimed against a recipient who had been paid more than he was entitled to receive or who was not entitled to any payment. (ii) The claim by the next-of-kin was not defeated by the fact that the payment to the recipient had been made under a mistake of law, rather than of fact. (iii) the next-of-kin's primary claim was against the personal representatives, and the claim against the charities was limited to the amount irrecoverable from the personal representatives. (iv) The amount for which the defendants were liable under this head was to be reckoned without interest. (v) The period of limitation applicable to the claim was twelve years under s. 20 of the Limitation Act 1939.

As to the claims *in rem*: (i) A person whose money had been mixed with that of another might trace his money into the mixed fund (or assets acquired therewith), notwithstanding that the fund (or assets) were held, or the mixing haa peen done, by an innocent volunteer, provided that: (a) there had been a fiduciary or quasi-fiduciary relationship between the claimant and the original holder of the money [*i.e.*, in this case, the executors], so as to give the claimant an equitable interest in the money; (b) the claimant's money was identifiable; and (c) the equitable remedy available, *i.e.* a charge on the mixed fund (or assets) did not work an injustice. (ii) Where the money had passed to an innocent volunteer, and there was no question of mixing, the innocent volunteer held the money on behalf of the true owner. (iii) Where the money had passed to an innocent volunteer, who had mixed it with money of his own, then the claimant and the innocent volunteer ranked *pari passu* with regard to the mixed fund. Where the money had been paid into an active banking account *prima facie* the rule in *Clayton's Case* applied. Thus, where the money received by a charity had been mixed by the charity with money of its own, the next-of-kin were entitled to recover *pari passu* with the charity (subject to a rateable reduction in respect of the amounts recovered from the executors under the compromise). But where the money received by the charity had been expended on the alteration or improvement of its assets, *e.g.* by the erection of new buildings on its land, or in discharging debts of the charity, then the equitable remedy of a charge would work an injustice; in such circumstances the money could no longer be traced, and the next-of-kin had no remedy "*in rem*"against the money or assets of the charity. (See also *Ministry of Health* v. *Simpson.*)

Docker v. Somes (1834), 2 My. & K. 655   **[88]**

W. S. bequeathed property to trustees on trust for his children and directed that if the trustees thought it advantageous for the trust, they might carry on his shipping business for a period of up to six years from his death. Any profits made were to be added to the trust property. The trustees carried on the business and later disposed of certain shipping property. They paid the proceeds into their own account at a bank where it became mixed with money employed in the trustees' own private business. They charged themselves with 5% on the sums so received and credited this to the trust fund. *Held,* the beneficiaries under the trust were entitled to receive, if they preferred it, that proportion of the profit made by the trustees attributable to the sums received by them as trust money and employed in their own business, instead of interest on the amount of trust money so employed.

Dominion Students' Hall Trust, Re, Dominion Students' Hall Trust v. A.-G., [1947] 1 Ch 183   [89]

The Dominion Students' Hall Trust was a company limited by guarantee. The memorandum of association provided that its object was to maintain a hostel for male students " of European origin " from the overseas dominions of the British Empire. The company had charitable status. It asked for confirmation of a special resolution deleting the words " of European origin " from its memorandum of association and for sanction for a scheme by which the charity might be administered for the benefit of all students from the dominions regardless of racial origin. *Held*, to retain the existing condition as to European origin might defeat the charity's main object of promoting community of citizenship among all members of the British Commonwealth. Unless the colour bar was removed, the intention of the charity could not be properly carried out. The existence of the condition therefore rendered the trust " impossible " (and so subject to the principles of *cy-près*). The special resolution was therefore confirmed and the scheme sanctioned.

Doering v. Doering (1889), 42 Ch. 203   [90]

Mrs. D. was executor and trustee of the will of her husband, D. By his will D. left his property to Mrs. D. on trust for Mrs. D. for her life with remainder to his nine children. Two of the children later assigned their interests to Mrs. D., and Mrs. D. assigned these interests to F. by way of mortgage for a loan. When Mrs. D. died insolvent it was found that she had appropriated £3921 out of the estate to her own use. *Held*, the beneficiaries under the will were entitled to have the beneficial interest of the trustee (Mrs. D.) impounded in order to make good the breach of trust. F. took subject to the rights of the beneficiaries against Mrs. D., not withstanding that the default was committed by Mrs. D. after the assignment to F.

Dover Coalfield Extension, Ltd., Re, [1908] 1 Ch. 65   [91]

The D. company purchased 5105 shares in the K. corporation, which were transferred into the names of the chairman and secretary of the D. company as trustees for the D. company. In order to look after the interests of the D. company in the affairs of the K. corporation, C., a director of the D. company, was elected a director of the K. corporation. Under the articles of the K. corporation a director had to hold £1000 of shares in the corporation. So that C. should satisfy this qualification the D. company transferred £1000 of the shares it held in the corporation to C., who held them on trust for the company. When the D. company was wound up the liquidator claimed that the remuneration which C. had received from the K. corporation for acting as a director of the corporation was the property of the D. company and not of C. personally. *Held*, the remuneration received by C. as director of the K. corporation was not a profit received by him from use of the property held by him on trust for the D. company, and C. was under no liability to account for that remuneration to the D. company.

Drummond, Re, Ashworth v. Drummond, [1914] 2 Ch. 90   [92]

A testator, who died in 1911, left (1) certain shares to trustees, the directors of a company, on trust for the purposes of contribution to the holiday expenses of the work people employed in the spinning department of the said company in such manner as a majority of directors should in their absolute discretion think fit; (2) his residuary estate on trust for sale for the Old Bradfordian's Club to be utilized as the Committee of the Club should think best in the interests of the club or the school. *Held*, regarding (1), since the work people in question could not properly be regarded as being " poor ", the trust was not charitable. As a private trust, it was void as infringing the rule against alienability. Regarding (2) the gift of residue constituted a gift to the members individually. The property was held by the committee on trust for such purposes as the committee should determine for the benefit of the old boys or members of the Club. Since there was nothing to prevent the committee spending the capital in any manner they might decide for the benefit of the class intended, the gift did not infringe the rule against alienability and was valid.

Dunlop Pneumatic Tyre Co., Ltd. v. New Garage and Motor   [93] Co., Ltd., [1915] A.C. 79 (House of Lords)

Dunlop's supplied motor car tyres to a dealer under an agreement by which the dealer was bound not to resell the tyres at less than the manufacturers' current list price, and to pay £5 by way of liquidated damages for every tyre sold in breach of the agreement. The dealer sold a tyre to a co-operative society below the list price. In an action for damages for breach of contract, the dealer claimed that the sum of £5 in the agreement was a penalty and not liquidated damages. *Held*, where a single sum was agreed to be paid as liquidated damages on the breach of a number of stipulations of varying importance, and the damage was the same in kind for every possible breach and was incapable of being precisely ascertained, the sum, provided it was a fair pre-estimate of the probable damage and not unconscionable, would be regarded as liquidated damages and not as a penalty. The sum of £5 in the agreement was liquidated damages.

Dupree's Trusts, Re, Daley v. Lloyds Bank, Ltd.,   [94] [1944] 2 All E.R. 443

A donor by deed of gift in 1932 recited that certain shares had been transferred to Lloyds Bank and declared that the Bank was to pay the income to trustees to be applied in promoting annual chess tournaments for the encouragement of chess playing, open to boys or young men under 21 resident in Plymouth. *Held*, since the encouragement of chess playing was of definite educational value, the gift was charitable, and valid.

Eastes, Re, Pain v. Paxon, [1948] 1 All E.R. 536   [95]

Property was left in a will to trustees to pay the income to the vicar and church-wardens of a parish to be used by them "for any purposes in connection with the said church which they may select, it being my wish that they shall especially bear in mind the requirements of the children" of the parish. *Held*, The gift to the vicar and churchwardens constituted a valid charitable gift. The addition of the words "for any purposes in connection with the said church which they may select" did not deprive the gift of its charitable nature as the words did not authorise the use of the gift for non-charitable purposes. The words "it being my wish that they shall especially bear in mind the requirements of the children" of the parish were precatory and therefore not legally binding.

Eaton, Re, Daires v. Eaton (1894), 70 L.T. 761   [96]

A testator left residuary property on trust for his wife for life with remainder to his nephew. There was no direction to convert. Part of the property consisted of gas stocks. *Held*, as the gas stocks were "possibly risky", a duty to convert arose under the rule in *Howe* v. *Dartmouth*. Pending conversion the widow was entitled to receive interest at 4% *p.a.* on the value of the stocks at the testator's death, any excess of interest actually received over the 4% paid to the widow being treated as capital.

Edis' Trusts, Re, Campbell Smith v. Davies,   **[97]**
   [1972] 2 All E.R. 769

In 1860 a regiment was formed as a volunteer defence unit. Land was subsequently acquired and a headquarters and drill hall were erected on the site by means of funds raised by public subscription. In 1898 the fee simple in the land became vested in the commanding officer and three other officers of the regiment who executed a declaration of trust to hold the premises on trust for the commanding officer of the regiment and his successors " to be held and disposed of as property belonging to [the regiment] as he or they shall or may from time to time direct ". Section 8 (1) of the Military Lands Act 1892 provided that if " a volunteer corps holding land under this Act is disbanded, the land shall . . . vest in the Secretary of State from the date of disbandment ". The regiment retained its identity until 1967, when the then existing units of the Territorial Army were disbanded and new units were raised to constitute the new Territorial and Army Volunteer Reserve. On the question as to destination of the proceeds of sale of the headquarters and drill hall, *Held,* (1) on the true construction of the declaration of trust the equitable fee simple was intended to become " property belonging to " the regiment within the meaning of the expression as used in contemporary statutes. A declaration that a particular asset was to be held as property of the regiment did not import an intention to give it to the members of the regiment beneficially. The regiment was not in the same position as an unincorporated association since the essential link between the members was not their contractual relationship inter se but their common military service to the Sovereign. Neither were the trustees to hold the property on trust for purposes of the regiment. Although a gift to an unincorporated association, without more, took effect as a purpose trust, the regiment was authorised by statute to hold property in the same way as if it were a corporation. (2) It followed, therefore, that when the regiment was disbanded in 1967 with no identifiable successor the premises vested in the Secretary of State for Defence under s. 8 (1) of the Military Land Act 1892, since the premises were correctly described as land held by a volunteer corps under the 1892 Act.

Edwards, Re, Macadam v. Wright, [1957] 2 All E.R. 495   **[98]**
   (Court of Appeal)

In her will Mrs. E. left a house in Hounslow and the residue of her property to be divided between seven relatives. After making the will Mrs. E. transferred the house to one of the relatives, Mrs. W. The question arose whether Mrs. W. was put to election [either to take under the will and accept a share of residue but transfer the house to the seven relatives (including herself), or retain the house, but compensate the other relatives out of the share of residue received by her]. *Held,* Mrs. W. was not put to election as the transfer of the house to her by Mrs. E. adeemed the devise. She could keep the house and the share of residue.

Endacott, Re, Corpe v. Endacott, [1959] 3 All E.R. 562   **[99]**

A testator, who died in 1958, bequeathed his residuary estate as follows: " Everything else I leave to the North Tawton Devon Parish Council for the purpose of providing some useful memorial to myself subject to the proviso that if my wife outlives me they must during the lifetime of my wife pay to my wife the interest which may accrue on the capital when properly invested by them ". *Held,* (i) as a matter of construction, the bequest was not an out-and-out bequest to the council; the words " for the purpose of providing some useful memorial to myself " imposed an obligation in the nature of a trust; (ii) the nature of a parish council's activities was not so clearly defined as being of a charitable character as to impose a charitable limitation on the words of the gift; (iii) the trust did not fall within the " anomalous " class of trusts of a public character which, although not charitable, were never-the-less trusts which the court would enforce (*e.g.* trusts for the maintenance of tombs); (iv) the gift, though specific, was too wide and uncertain to qualify as an enforceable trust [*i.e.* it failed for lack of certainty of objects]. The Council thus held the property on a resulting trust for the testator's next-of-kin.

Eustace, Re, [1911] 1 Ch. 561   **[100]**

In 1882 E. mortgaged a house to L. for £700 and in August 1897 E. conveyed the equity of redemption to M. in consideration for £200. Shortly afterwards E. died. M. notified L. of E.'s death and continued to pay interest to L. up to August 1910, after which no interest was paid. L. sought to have the mortgage realized and claimed that if the security was worth less than the £700 which had been advanced, then the difference should be made up by E.'s estate. The defendant beneficiary under E.'s will claimed that if the security had in fact diminished in value, this was the result of the plaintiff L.'s negligence and laches in not realizing the security at an earlier date and that it would be inequitable that he should be allowed to resort to the assets held by the defendant beneficiary under E.'s will. *Held*, L.'s claim had not been defeated by delay and his claim succeeded.

Evans' Will Trusts, Re, Pickering v. Evans, [1921] 2 Ch. 309   **[101]**

A testator left all his property to trustees on trust to pay the income to his wife, and after her death on trust to divide the property into three equal parts and to pay the income from these three parts to two sisters and a brother respectively, with remainder on the death of any one of these to his or her children. The testator's property included the copyright of certain books, and the benefit of certain agreements with publishers by which the testator received royalties as owner of the copyright. *Held*, the trust to divide the residuary estate into three equal parts on the determination of the wife's life interest was not a sufficient indication of intention to exclude the rule in *Howe* v. *Dartmouth* and in accordance with that rule, pending sale of the property, the trustees must value the property and pay the wife 4% of the value.

Faraker, Re, Faraker v. Durell, [1912] 1 Ch. 488   **[102]**

A testatrix, who died in 1911, by her will gave a legacy " to Mrs. Bailey's Charity, Rotherhithe ". There had been a charity in Rotherhithe known as Hannah Bayly's Charity, founded in 1756 by a Mrs. Bayly for the benefit of poor widows in the parish of St. Mary, Rotherhithe. In 1905 the Charity Commissioner approved a scheme under which the endowments of fourteen charities in Rotherhithe, including Hannah Bayly's Charity, were consolidated, trustees appointed, and trusts declared for the benefit of the poor of Rotherhithe. There was no mention of widows in the trusts declared in the scheme. The executors took out a summons to determine whether the gift lapsed. (No question was raised on the spelling of the name Bayly.) *Held*, that " Hannah Bayly's Charity is not extinct, it is not dead, and . . . it cannot die. Its objects may be changed, though not otherwise than in accordance with law . . . . Subject to that lawful alteration . . . Hannah Bayly's Charity . . . exists just as much as it did . . . in 1756, . . . and as it does today. Now it is to be remembered . . . that this legacy was not given to Mrs. Bayly's Charity for widows; it was simply given to a charity which is identified by name . . . " " . . . in my opinion a gift of that kind carries with it the application of it according to the lawful objects of the charity funds for the time being." (*per* COZENS-HARDY, M.R.) The legacy therefore went to the consolidated charities.

Farley v. Westminster Bank Ltd., [1939] 3 All E.R. 491.   **[103]**
(House of Lords)

By her will, a testatrix gave part of her residuary estate " to the vicar and churchwardens of St. Columba's Church, Hoxton (for parish work) ". *Held*, " In my opinion, upon the true construction of this will, the words in brackets mean that the gift is not a gift for ecclesiastical or religious purposes in the strict sense, but it is a gift for the assistance and furtherance of those various activities connected with the parish church which are to be found, I believe, in every parish, but which, unfortunately for the donees here, include many objects which are not in any way charitable in the legal sense of that word." (*per* LORD RUSSELL OF KILLOWEN) The gift was therefore not charitable.

Finger's Will Trusts, Re, Turner v. Ministry of Health,   [104]
    [1971] 3 All E.R. 1050

A testatrix, who died in 1965, by her will (made in 1930) gave her residuary estate in equal shares to eleven charitable institutions. One share was given to the " National Radium Commission ". The court construed this as being a gift to the Radium Commission, an unincorporated body set up by royal charter in 1929. After the establishment of the National Health Service it became apparent that there was no longer a need for the Commission, which was wound up in accordance with its charter, in 1947. The work previously undertaken by the Commission was thereafter carried on by the Minister of Health. Another share was given to the National Council for Maternity and Child Welfare. This was a corporate body which had been in existence at the time of making the will, but which had been wound up in 1948. The bulk of its assets were transferred to the National Association for Maternity and Child Welfare, an association having similar aims to that of the Council, and which thereafter continued the work previously undertaken by the Council. *Held*, (1) (a) a gift to an unincorporated body (*e.g.* the Radium Commission) was *per se* gift on trust for the purpose of the work carried on by that body; (b) if the body ceased to exist before the gift took effect, then provided (i) the work was still capable of being carried on and (ii) there was nothing in the terms of the gift to indicate that gift was dependant on the continued existence of the body, then the gift did not fail, and effect would be given to it by means of a scheme; (c) since these conditions were satisfied in the case of the gift construed as being to the Radium Commission, the gift was valid and the court ordered that a scheme should be settled for the administration of the gift. (2) (a) A gift to an incorporated body was not to be construed as being a gift on trust for the purpose of the work of the body unless there was something positive to indicate that such a trust was intended; (b) there was no such indication in the case of the gift to National Council for Maternity and Child Welfare; (c) the Council having ceased to exist before the death of the testatrix, the gift to the Council failed; (d) since (i) virtually the whole estate was devoted to charity, and (ii) the Council had merely been a co-ordinating body, and (iii) the testatrix regarded herself as having no relatives, it was possible to find a general charitable intention; (e) [since the gift was impossible *ab initio*, but a general charitable intention existed], the gift was applicable *cy près*. If the Attorney-General did not object, a scheme would be ordered under which the share would be paid to the National Association for Maternity and Child Welfare on trust for its general purposes.

Fletcher v. Asburner (1779), 1 Bro. C.C. 497   [105]

In his will J. F. left his house at Kendal and all his personal property to trustees on trust for his wife for her life, and on her death to sell it and divide the proceeds between his son and daughter, or if either should predecease his widow, the survivor was to take all. The daughter, and later the son, died during the widow's life time. On the widow's death, the son's heir-at-law claimed the house. The son's next-of-kin contested the claim, contending that the house, as realty, had been converted into personality by the trust for sale. *Held*, the property had been so converted and thus passed to the son's next-of-kin.

Fletcher v. Collis, [1905] 2 Ch. 24   **[106]**

Property was vested in a trustee on trust for a husband for life with remainders over. In 1885, at the request of the husband's wife, and with the concurrence of the husband, the trustee sold the property and gave the proceeds to the wife, who spent it. The remainder men brought an action against the trustee but the proceedings were stayed on the trustee undertaking to make good the trust fund. When the trustee died in 1902, the trust fund had been replaced and there was a considerable surplus representing income. The personal representative of the deceased trustee claimed the surplus as part of the trustee's estate, on the grounds that it represented a partial indemnity from the husband to the trustee. The trustee in bankruptcy of the husband claimed the surplus as representing income which would have been due to the husband if there had been no breach of trust. *Held*, as the husband had concurred in the breach of trust he could not require the trustee to make good the income to which he would have been entitled during his life. The husband was therefore not entitled to anything that represented income of the fund replaced by the trustee. The husband's trustee in bankruptcy was in no better position than the husband, and the surplus therefore formed part of the deceased trustee's estate.

Fry v. Fry (1859), 27 Beav. 144   **[107]**

A testator left property on trust for sale. In 1836 the trustees advertised the property for £1000. In 1837 they refused an offer of £900. The property had still not been sold five years later when the opening of a railway caused the property to depreciate in value. When the last trustee died in 1856 the property was still unsold and could not be sold except at a low price. *Held*, the estates of the trustees were liable for the difference between the price for which the property was sold and £900.

Fullwood v. Fullwood (1878), 9 Ch.D. 176   **[108]**

The plaintiff sought an injunction to restrain the defendant from representing that the business carried on by him was the same as that carried on by the defendant. The defendant replied that as the plaintiff had known of the facts for two or three years before taking action, he had lost any claim to an injunction. *Held*, where an injunction was sought to support a legal right, the court was bound to grant it if the legal right was established. Therefore the mere lapse of time within the statutory period would not be a bar to the granting of the injunction. The delay by the plaintiff was therefore no bar to his obtaining an injunction.

Galbraith v. Mitchenall Estates, Ltd., [1964] 2 All E.R. 653   **[109]**

Wishing to provide a caravan home for his family, the plaintiff entered into a simple hire agreement with the defendants, a finance company, whereby he hired a caravan for sixty months at a monthly rental of £12 10s. and under which he made a "first payment" of £550 10s. before the agreement was signed. At the time of concluding the contract the plaintiff mistakenly believed that he was entering into a hire-purchase agreement, but the defendants were in no way responsible for this misunderstanding on his part. The plaintiff failed to pay the monthly rentals and the defendants re-possessed the caravan in accordance with the terms of the contract of hire. Although the retail price of the caravan was originally only £1050, the defendants thus had the caravan then worth about £800 and also the "first payment" of £550 10s. In addition, also in accordance with the terms of the contract, they were entitled to claim thirty-six months' rent. The plaintiff sought, *inter alia*, the recovery of the initial payment on the grounds that its retention was in the nature of a penalty, but the defendants did not counterclaim for thirty-six months' rent. *Held*, although the relevant terms of the agreement were of "undue harshness", as the defendants did not obtain the plaintiff's signature to the contract by fraud, sharp practice or other unconscionable conduct, they were entitled to retain both the caravan and the initial payment. In other words, there was no equity of restitution in respect of the initial payment unless there had been unconscionable conduct at the time at which the contract was concluded. However, a counterclaim by the defendants for the payment of thirty-six months' rent would have failed as the relevant provision of the contract was a penal clause.

Gardom, Re, Le Page v. A.-G., [1914] 1 Ch. 662   **[110]**

A testatrix, who died in 1911, by her will gave property to J. and W. on trust to sell the property and use such portion as was necessary for the maintenance of a temporary house of residence for ladies of limited means, and gave directions regarding the application ot any residue. *Held,* the trust was a valid charitable trust of so much of the estate as might be necessary for the maintenance of the house.

Garrard, Re, Gordon v. Craigie, [1904–7] All E.R. Rep. 237   **[111]**

A testatrix bequeathed £400 " to the vicar and churchwardens for the time being of Kington, to be applied by them in such manner as they in their sole discretion think fit." *Held,* there was a valid charitable gift for ecclesiastical purposes.

Gascoigne v. Gascoigne, [1918] 1 K.B. 223   **[112]**

A husband, who was in debt, took a lease of land. In order to protect himself from his creditors he arranged for the lease to be taken in his wife's name. The wife was aware of the reason for the husband's action. The husband built a bungalow on the land with his own money. Later the husband claimed that the wife held the lease as trustee for him and called on her to assign it to him. The wife claimed that there was a presumption that the husband had intended the lease as a gift, and that she therefore held it absolutely. *Held,* the husband could not be allowed to set up his own fraudulent purpose as rebutting the presumption that the conveyance was intended as a gift to the wife, and the wife was therefore entitled to the property absolutely, notwithstanding that she was a party to the fraud.

George's Will Trusts, Re, Barclay's Bank Limited v. George,   **[113]**
[1948] 2 All E.R. 1004

G., a farmer, in his will left two-thirds of his residue to his son E., and one-third to his son R. The will further provided that if E., within one month of the testator's death notified the trustees of his wish to carry on the farm, the residue was to be valued, that one-third should constitute the share of R. and two-thirds the share of E., and that R. should allow his share to remain invested in the farm for three years. G. later made a gift to E. of the live and dead stock, which was valued at £2060. After G.'s death a summons was taken out to determine whether (under the rule against double portions) the gift to E. was in satisfaction of the legacy. *Held,* the gift to E., which put him into immediate possession of his intended inheritance, was to be deemed to be in satisfaction of the legacy. Although the rule against double portions only applied if the gift and the provision in the will were broadly *ejusdem generis,* this requirement did not apply if the gift was valued at the time it was made. In any case, the gift was sufficiently *ejusdem generis* with the option conferred on E. to carry on the farm to satisfy this requirement.

Gestetner, Re, Barnett v. Blumka, [1953] 1 All E.R. 1150   **[114]**

A settlor conveyed a fund to trustees on trust for a specified class of persons who, however, were not ascertainable at any given time. Under the settlement the trustees were directed to hold the capital "on trust to pay the same for . . . the benefit of such member or members of the specified class as the trustees from time to time determine . . . " There was a remainder over in default of appointment. *Held,* where there was a duty on the donee of a power to appoint among a given number of persons [*i.e.* where there was a "trust" as opposed to a "power"] the objects of the trust must be ascertainable, or the trust will be void for uncertainty; but if the power did not involve such a duty [*i.e.* where there was a "power" as opposed to a "trust"], the fact that the power was exercisable in favour of a definite, though unascertainable, class did not make the power bad so long as it was possible to ascertain whether or not any given person was a member of that class. In the present case there was no duty on the donees of the power to make an appointment, and thus there was a "power" and not a "trust". Therefore, the power was not void for uncertainty.

Gibbard, Re, Public Trustee v. Davis, [1966] 1 All E.R. 273   [115]

A testator, who died in 1934, by his will gave his trustees power to appoint his residuary estate " amongst . . . any of my friends ", with a gift over in default of appointment. On the question of the validity of the power, it was *Held*, that since, for a power of appointment to be valid, it was necessary only to be able to ascertain whether a particular claimant was within the description of objects (and it was not necessary to be able to ascertain who all the objects of the power were); and since the description " any of my old friends " was precise enough for there to be claimants who could clearly satisfy this description, the power was valid.

Gibson v. South American Stores (Gath & Chaves), Ltd.,   [116]
[1949] 2 All E.R. 985 (Court of Appeal)

A company established a trust fund to be used for the benefit of " necessitous and deserving" employees of the company and their families. As the income of the fund was greater than the calls on it, the company wished to wind up the fund and use part of the money to contribute to a new pension scheme and return the rest to the company free of the trusts. *Held*, the trust was of a sufficiently public character to be charitable; but as there was no general charitable intention, the suplus funds were not to be applied *cy-près*, but were to revert to the company.

Gilchester Properties, Ltd. v. Gomm, [1948] 1 All E.R. 493   [117]

During negotiations for the purchase of certain premises the defendants, the vendors, stated in answer to inquiries by the purchasers, the plaintiffs, that the rents payable by the tenants were £449 10s. which was an innocent misrepresentation as they actually amounted to £398 10s. The plaintiffs sought specific performance of the contract and abatement of purchase price. *Held*, their claim would fail as to award specific performance with a deduction in purchase price would be the equivalent of an award of damages in respect of an innocent misrepresentation. The appropriate remedy was rescission.

Gillingham Bus Disaster Fund, Re, Bowman v. Official   [118]
Solicitor, [1958] 2 All E.R. 749 (Court of Appeal)

In 1951, following an accident in which twenty-four sea cadets were killed or injured, the Mayors of Gillingham, Rochester and Chatham wrote to the press inviting subscriptions for a fund to be devoted " among other things, to defraying the funeral expenses . . . , caring for boys who may be disabled, and then to such worthy cause or causes in memory of the boys who lost their lives, as the Mayors may determine ". In order to determine who was entitled to the surplus of the fund it was necessary to decide whether the trust was charitable. *Held*, the purposes for which subscriptions were invited were not exclusively charitable. The trust was therefore not charitable. The charitable objects were not saved by the Charitable Trusts (Validation) Act 1954, since the letter did not constitute an " imperfect trust provision " within s. 1 (1) of that Act. As a private trust it failed for uncertainty of objects. The surplus was therefore held on a resulting trust for the contributors.

Gilmour v. Coats, [1949] 1 All E.R. 848 (House of Lords)   **[119]**

The income of a trust fund was to be applied to the purposes of a Carmelite convent, if those purposes were charitable. The convent consisted of a community of cloistered nuns who devoted themselves to prayer and contemplation and engaged in no work outside the convent. *Held,* the purposes of the convent were not charitable as they were not for the public benefit. The requirement as to public benefit applied equally to religious as to other charities. The benefit of inter-cessory prayer to the public is not susceptible of legal proof and the court can only act on such proof. Further, the element of edification by example is too vague and intangible to satisfy the test of public benefit.

Gray, Re, Todd v. Taylor, [1925] Ch. 362   **[120]**

A testator left money to form a fund for his regiment " for the promotion of sport (including in that term only shooting, fishing, cricket, football and polo)." *Held,* the gift was charitable, as being for the purpose of promoting physical efficiency in the army.

Green, Re, Lindley v. Green, [1950] 2 All E.R. 913   **[121]**

On August 31, 1940, a testator and his first wife executed wills in identical form, under which it was agreed that if the survivor of them had the use of the other's property during his or her life time, he or she would provide in his or her will for carrying out the wishes expressed in the will of the other. By his will of August 31, 1940, the testator gave his residuary estate, including his half share in their house, to his first wife absolutely if she should survive him, but, if she should not survive him, he gave the house in its entirety to a certain hospital and directed that the remainder should be divided into two equal shares, one moiety being considered as his own personal estate and the other moiety as the equivalent to any benefit which he had received from the first wife by reason of her predeceasing him. By clause 6 (b) he disposed of the half share which he regarded as his personal estate, and by clause 6 (c) he disposed of the half share which he regarded as the first wife's moiety. The first wife died on April 28, 1942, and, under the terms of her will, her residue passed to the testator absolutely. On April 25, 1945, the testator re-married, and on December 19, 1946, he made a second will, whereby he gave certain pecuniary legacies, some of which were to beneficiaries to whom he had given pecuniary legacies (though not in every case of an identical amount) by clause 6 (c) of the will of August 31, 1940. Subject to these and other legacies, he gave the whole of his residuary estate to his second wife. The testator died in 1946. *Held,* (i) as the testator's will of August 31, 1940, and his first wife's will of the same date each agreed to make mutual wills and as the testator had approved the first wife's will by accepting property thereunder, the provisions contained in his first will regarding (a) the gift of the house to the hospital and (b) disposition of the first wife's notional half share of the testator's residuary estate took effect as a trust, and, therefore, the executors of the last will held his estate on trust, first to give effect to the gift of the house to the hospital and then to carry into effect the provisions of clause 6 (c) of the first will out of one half of the moiety of the residue, the other moiety passing under the provisions contained in the testator's last will; (ii) as the pecuniary legacies given by the last will were not in every case identical with the pecuniary legacies given to the same legatees under clause 6 (c) of the first will, the beneficiaries were entitled to take both a share in the trust fund under clause 6 (c) and the legacies under the last will.

Gresham's Settlement, Re, Lloyds Bank, Ltd. v. Gresham,   **[122]**
[1956] 2 All E.R. 193

In clause 6 of a settlement made in 1936 a husband directed that " the [trustee] shall pay all or any part of the said income to or apply the same for the main-tenance and personal support or benefit of all or any one or more to the exclusion of the others of the following persons namely (a) the husband and his wife . . . for the time being and his children and remoter issue for the time being in existence . . . and (b) any persons in whose house or apartments or in whose company or under whose care or control or by or with whom the husband may from time to time be employed or residing . . . ". On a summons to determine whether that clause was valid or void for uncertainty, it was conceded that although in terms it was imperative, the clause conferred on the trustee a mere power which it was not bound to exercise. *Held*, (1) the power conferred by clause 6 was a single power to benefit a category of people and was not a series of different powers. (2) Part of that category of people (namely the persons described under (b) above) were defined with insufficient certainty for the trustee to be able to postulate of any living person whether or not he was within the description. " It seems to me that the difficulty comes with these words, ' in whose company he is " residing ", or ' with whom ' he is " residing " '. What does ' residing ' mean for this purpose? Is he to reside for a week, or a month, or a year? Is he permanently to reside? It does not say so; if it had said ' permanently reside ' I could see that might be much easier. Who is it that is envisaged by this settlor as an object of the possible bounty of the trustee? I do not find it possible to say with any certainty. It seems to me, giving the most benevolent meaning to the clause that I can, that there must or may be a number of persons, of whom it could not be postulated that they were (or were not) within the dragnet of this unusually constructed clause." (*per* HARMAN, J.) (3) The power was therefore void. (But see *Re Gulbenkian's Settlement Trusts*, (*No. 1*), *post*.)

Grey v. Inland Revenue Commissioners, [1959] 3 All E.R. 603   [123]

In 1949 H. transferred property to trustees on trust for his grandchildren. In 1955 he transferred 18000 £1 shares to the same trustees on trust for himself. He subsequently orally instructed the trustees to hold the shares on trust for the grandchildren. The trustees later executed deeds of declaration of trust declaring that they held the shares on the trusts specified by H. H. executed the deeds to confirm the oral instruction he had previously given to the trustees. The Inland Revenue charged stamp duty *ad valorem* on the deeds of declaration, on the grounds that as s. 53 (1) (c) of the Law of Property Act 1925 required that " a disposition of an equitable interest . . . must be in writing signed by the person disposing of the same . . ." the oral instruction by H. had been insufficient to make an effective disposition, and that no effective disposition took place until the deeds of declaration of trust were executed. *Ad valorem* stamp duty was accordingly chargeable on these. *Held*, the instructions given by H. were dispositions by him of his equitable interest in the shares within the meaning of s. 53 (1) (c) of the Act and because they were not in writing they were ineffective. The deeds of declaration of trust were thus chargeable *ad valorem* with stamp duty.

Grierson v. National Provincial Bank, [1913] 2 Ch. 18   [124]

F. charged certain leasehold property as security for a loan from the G. and M. Bank, and deposited the lease with the bank. F. later created a legal mortgage of the same property in favour of G., the mortgage being made expressly subject to the bank's charge. G., as second mortgagee, failed to follow the usual practice of giving notice of his mortgage to the first mortgagee, the G. and M. Bank. F. then paid off the G. and M. Bank's mortgage, recovered the lease from the bank, and deposited it with the N. P. Bank as security for a loan. The N. P. Bank had no notice of the prior mortgage to G. G.'s executors sought priority over the N. P. Bank. *Held*, although G. had been careless in failing to notify the M. and G. Bank of his second mortgage, his negligence had not been sufficient to deprive him of the priority which his prior mortgage gave him.

Griffith v. Hughes, [1892] 3 Ch. 105   [125]

A beneficiary under a trust requested a trustee to advance £80 to her out of trust funds, in breach of the terms of the trust (the beneficiary being a married woman under a restraint from anticipation). The trustee advanced the money but claimed that he was entitled to be indemnified out of the beneficiary's interest under s. 6 of the Trustee Act 1888 (now replaced by s. 60 of the Trustee Act 1925). The section states that a trustee is entitled to be indemnified "where a trustee shall have committed a breach of trust at the instigation or request or with the consent in writing of a beneficiary". *Held*, the words "in writing" referred to "consent" alone, and not to "instigation or request". The instigation or request could therefore be oral or written. The fact that the request had been made orally was therefore no bar to the trustee seeking indemnity under the section, and the trustee was entitled to such indemnity.

Grove-Grady, Re, Plowden v. Laurence, [1929] 1 Ch. 557   [126]
(Court of Appeal)

A testatrix, who died in 1925, gave her residuary estate to trustees on trust for the founding of an institution to be called " The Beaumont Animals Benevolent Society ", having as one of its objects the acquisition of land for the provision of refuges for the preservation of " all animals, birds or other creatures not human ". *Held*, " It seems to me impossible to say that the carrying out of such a trust necessarily involves benefit to the public. Beyond perhaps hearing of the existence of the enclosure the public does not come into the matter at all. Consistently with the trust the public could be excluded from entering the area or even looking into it. All the public need know about the matter would be that one or more areas existed in which all animals . . . were allowed to live free from any risk of being molested or killed by man; though liable to be molested and killed by other denizens of the area. For myself I feel quite unable to say that any benefit to the community will necessarily result from applying the trust fund to the purposes indicated in the first object." (*per* RUSSELL, L. J.) The trust was therefore not charitable.

Gulbenkian's Settlement Trusts, Re, Wishaw v. Stephens,   [127]
[1968] 3 All E.R. 785 (House of Lords)

Under a settlement made by G. in 1929 it was directed that the trustees " shall during the life of (N.) at their absolute discretion pay . . . all or any part of the income of the . . . trust fund to or apply the same for the maintenance . . . or benefit of all or any one or more . . . of the following persons, namely, (N.) and any wife and his children or remoter issue for the time being in existence . . . and any person or persons, in whose house or appartments or in whose company or under whose care or control or by, or with whom (G.) may from time to time be employed or residing . . . " In default of appointment the trustees were directed to hold the surplus income on trust for the purposes for which it would be held if N. were dead. *Held*, (1) the clause gave to the trustees a mere or bare power of appointment among a class of objects; (2) provided that there was a valid gift over or trust in default of appointment such a power was valid if it could be said with certainty whether any given individual was or was not a member of that class; (3) where the language of the document concerned was obscure or ambiguous or imperfectly expressed, it was the duty of the court to make sense of the intentions which the settlor or parties had attempted to express, and to give reasonable meaning to that language provided that this could be done without doing complete violence to the language used. (4) Applying this principle, the clause was to be construed as meaning " and any person or persons by whom (G.) may from time to time be employed and any person or persons with whom (G.) from time to time is residing whether in the house or appartment of such person or persons or whether in the company or under the care or control of such person or persons . . . ". (5) Applying the principle in (2) above to the clause so construed, the clause was not void for uncertainty.

Gulbenkian's Settlement Trusts (No. 2), Re, Stephens v. Maun, [128] [1969] 2 All E.R. 1173

Under a settlement made by G. in 1929 (A.) trustees were given directions as to the application of income from settled property. (The directions are set out under *Re Gulbenkian's Settlement (No. 1)* above.) The settlement continued (B.) by giving the income from certain property on trust for N.'s issue after his death and it was provided that if no child of N. should attain 21 the trustees were to hold the income on trust for G. absolutely or, if he were then dead, on trust for such persons as N. should by will appoint. G. died in 1955. N. had no children and was unlikely to have any. The trustees paid income to N. until 1957 when, doubts having arisen (following *Re Gresham's Settlement (ante)*) as to the validity of the trusts, they began to accumulate the income. In 1958 N. challenged the validity of G.'s will and in proceedings in Lisbon a compromise was agreed under which N. renounced, for valuable consideration, on behalf of himself and his wife, all right to income under the settlement (under (A.) above) and his testamentary power of appointment (under (B.) above). In 1961 the trustees took out a summons to determine the validity to the terms of the settlement and in 1968, in *Gulbenkian's Settlement (No. 1)*, the House of Lords held these to be valid. The trustees then sought directions as to whether they had power to exercise their discretion (under (A.) above) retrospectively in respect of the accumulated income (which was by then in excess of £50,000) and, if so, whether and how far the discretion still existed in the light of the agreement made in Lisbon. (It was not disputed that the agreement operated as a release of the testamentary power of appointment under (B.) above, with the result that the capital belonged ultimately to the residuary legatee.) *Held*, (1) since a person could not be compelled to accept a gift, there was no reason why he should not be equally free to refuse an appointment made in his favour. Such a refusal could be made in respect of capital or income. Thus from the date of the agreement made in Lisbon, N. and his wife ceased to be objects of the power of appointment, under (A.) above. Consequently from the date of the Lisbon agreement the trustees could exercise no discretion in their favour. (2) Although it was the duty of trustees to exercise their discretion within a reasonable time after receipt by them of income, a postponement might be justified by special circumstances. The circumstances here justified the postponement, and the discretion was still exercisable.

Gwyon, Re, Public Trustee v. A.-G., [1930] 1 Ch. 255 [129]

The Rev. John Gwyon left property on trust to establish a foundation to provide knickers for boys of a specified age, the sons of parents resident in the district of Farnham. Boys supported by charitable institutions or whose parents were in receipt of parochial relief were to be ineligible. *Held*, the trust was not for the relief of poverty and was not charitable. "A trust which is not charitable cannot be changed into a charitable one by limiting the area in which it is to operate" (*per* EVE, J.). As a private trust, the trust failed and the property passed as on intestacy.

Hagger, Re, Freeman v. Arscott, [1930] 2 Ch. 190 [130]

A husband and wife made a joint will in which it was stated that they had agreed to dispose of their property by the will and that there was to be no alteration or revocation except by agreement. By the will they gave the whole of their property at the death of the first spouse to die, to the survivor for life with remainders over. The wife died in 1904 and the husband received the income from the whole estate until his death in 1928. By a will made in 1921 the husband gave "everything of which he was able to dispose" to be divided between various persons, of whom some were not mentioned in the joint will. One of the persons entitled in remainder under the joint will had died in 1923. Her personal representatives claimed for her estate the portion left to her in the joint will. *Held*, from the death of the wife, the husband held the property, subject to his own life interest, on trust for those entitled in remainder under the joint will. The legatees in remainder under the joint will took a vested interest in the property, subject to the life interest of the husband, from the date of death of the wife. The death of such a legatee after the death of the wife but before the death of the husband did not occasion a lapse. The claim of the personal representatives of the deceased legatee therefore succeeded.

Hain's Settlement, Re, Tooth v. Hain, [1961] 1 All E.R. 848   [131]
(Court of Appeal)

By clause 3 of a settlement made in 1954 trustees were directed to apply the income to the fund for the benefit of all or one or more of " the beneficiaries " as the trustees should think fit. Clause 2 of the settlement defined beneficiaries as meaning such of the following persons as should for the time being be in existence, namely, the children and remoter issue of the settlor and the past present or future employees of the settlor. At the time of the settlement the settlor had had in his employment only domestic servants, of whom there would have been about two dozen, but in 1960 at the date of the proceedings he would have been unable to compile a complete list of all his present and past employees. It was not established that such a list could not have been made at the date of the settlement. On the question was whether clause 2 was valid or was void for uncertainty, *Held*, assuming that clause 3 constituted a trust and not a power, the question was whether at the date of the settlement, which was the relevant date, the class of beneficiaries defined in clause 2 was capable of being ascertained. If it was, the trust would not be rendered invalid by the subsequent disappearance of some members of the class. There was no difficulty of ascertainment save in regard to past employees and as on the evidence it was not proved that they were unascertainable, the trust was valid.

Hallett's Estate, Re, Knatchbull v. Hallett (1880), 13 Ch.D. 696   [132]

By a marriage settlement money was settled for the benefit of Hallett, his wife and his children. The trustees of the settlement allowed the money to come into the hands of Hallett who appropriated it to his own use. As a solicitor Hallett also received money belonging to a client, Mrs. C., and this too he credited to his own account. He subsequently drew money out of the account for his own purposes, but paid in other sums. *Held*, where trust money is mixed with a trustee's own money in one fund, the beneficiaries have a first charge on the whole fund for the trust money. If a trustee draws on the mixed fund for his own purposes he is deemed to draw out first his own money. [This is contrary to the rule in *Clayton's Case* which normally governs the operation of a banking account, and under which money is deemed to be drawn out of an account in the order in which it was paid in.]

Hancock v. Watson, [1900–3] All E.R. Rep. 87   [133]

A testator gave the residue of his personal property to trustees on trust for his wife for life and on her death directed that the property should be divided into five portions. The will stated "To Susan Drake I give two such portions". After allocating the remaining three portions, the will went on "But it is my will and mind that the two-fifth portions allotted to the said Susan Drake shall remain in trust and that she shall be entitled to take only the interest . . . of the shares . . . during her natural life . . ., and from . . . her decease in trust for . . . any children born unto . . . Susan Drake upon their attaining the age of twenty-five . . . if sons, or if . . . daughters upon their attaining the age of twenty-one years, or upon their marriage . . .; but in default of any such issue, then in that case the two-fifths of my residuary estate . . . shall be divided among the children of my brother Charles " payable to the sons at twenty-five or daughters at twenty-one or marriage. Susan Drake died without having had a child. At her death there were children of Charles, daughters, who had all attained twenty-one or married. *Held*, where there is an absolute gift to a legatee in the first instance, and trusts are added on the absolute interest which fail, then the legatee takes absolutely. The gift over on the death of Susan Drake was void for remoteness. Susan Drake therefore took the two-fifths portion absolutely and on her death it formed part of her estate.

Harari's Settlement Trusts, Re, Wordsworth v. Fanshawe,   **[134]**
[1949] 1 All E.R. 430

A settlement made in 1938 stated " The trustees shall hold the said investments " (none of which were trustee investments) " so transferred to them as aforesaid upon trust that they may either allow the same to remain in their present state of investment so long as the trustees may think fit or may at any time or times with the consent of the daughter realise the said investments or any of them or any part thereof respectively and shall with the like consent invest the moneys produced thereby and also all capital moneys which may be or become subject to the trusts upon such investments as to them may seem fit . . . ". *Held*, on the true construction of the settlement, there was no justification for implying any restriction of the words " in or upon such investments as to them may seem fit ", and the trustees had power, under the plain meaning of those words, to invest in any investments which they honestly thought to be desirable, whether or not they were investments authorised by law for the investment of trust funds.

Hardoon v. Belilios, [1901] A.C. 118   **[135]**

A firm of stockbrokers, B. and K., purchased 50 shares in a banking company and placed them in the name of one of their employees, Hardoon. [Thus Hardoon held the shares on an implied trust for B. and K.] The beneficial ownership of the shares became transferred to Belilios. When the banking company went into liquidation, the liquidator made calls on Hardoon for £402. Hardoon brought an action claiming indemnity from Belilios for the amount called for by the liquidator. *Held*, Belilios, being *sui juris* and the beneficial owner of the shares, was bound, in the absence of agreement to the contrary, to indemnify Hardoon, the registered holder, against any calls upon him.

Harpur's Will Trusts, Re, Haller v. A.-G., [1961] 3 All E.R. 588   **[136]**
(Court of Appeal)

A testatrix, who died in 1946, directed her trustees to divide her residuary estate " between such institutions and associations having for their main object the assistance and care of soldiers, sailors and airmen, and other members of H.M. Forces who have been wounded or incapacitated during recent world wars " in such manner and in such proportions as the trustees should deem appropriate. *Held*, since the gift did not so describe the objects of the gift that the property could be used exclusively for charitable purposes, but could nevertheless be used for purposes which were not charitable, the gift was not an " imperfect trust provision ", within s. 1 (1) of the Charitable Trusts (Validation) Act 1954. The gift was thus not validated by the Act (and, not be exclusively charitable, failed).

Harwood, Re, Coleman v. Ianes, [1935] All E.R. Rep. 918   **[137]**

A testatrix bequeathed legacies to the "Wisbech Peace Society, Cambridge", a society, which had existed, but had ceased to exist before the testatrix's death; and to "the Peace Society of Belfast", which evidence showed had never existed. *Held*, where a testator selects a particular charity and takes care to identify it and the named charity ceases to exist before the testator's death, it is difficult for the court to find sufficient evidence of general charitable intent for *cy-près* to apply. Thus the gift to the Wisbech Peace Society was not applied *cy-près* and lapsed. But where a will describes a charitable institution which has never existed, a general charitable intention may be inferred. The bequest to the Peace Society of Belfast was therefore applied *cy-près*.

Head v. Gould, [1898] 2 Ch. 250 [138]

Houlditch and Clapp were trustees of marriage settlements under which property was settled on Mrs. Head for life with remainder to her children. The trustees were empowered to advance a proportion of the share of any of the children for their benefit. There were three children, at the request of one of whom, Miss Head, the trustees advanced money to Mrs. Head, who was in financial difficulties. When the trustees had advanced the whole of Miss Head's share to her mother, they suggested, when Miss Head pressed for further advances, that they should be released from trusteeship and replaced by other trustees who might be willing to risk advancing further money. By exercise of the powers of appointment in the settlements, Houlditch and Clapp were replaced by Gould and Miss Head. Thenceforth Gould acted as solicitor to the trust. ʲThe new trustees sold a house forming part of the trust property and, in breach of trust, passed the proceeds of sale to Mrs. Head. The new trustees were also in breach of trust in surrendering to Mrs. Head certain policies of insurance on her life which she had mortgaged to the previous trustees as securities for a loan by them to her of money from the trust fund. As a result of these transactions the share to which Mrs. Head's son, W. R. Head, was entitled was lost. He sought to make the two former and the two latter trustees liable to make good the loss. *Held*, (i) Houlditch and Clapp were not liable for the breaches of trust by Gould and Miss Head, as in order to make a retiring trustee liable for a breach of trust committed by his successor it must be shown that the breach of trust which was in fact committed was not merely the outcome of or rendered easy by the change in trustee, but was contemplated by the former trustee when the change took place; (ii) Gould and Miss Head were liable for the breaches of trust committed by them; (iii) although Gould had acted as solicitor to the trust, he could not be required to indemnify Miss Head, as she had participated actively in the breaches of trust, and had not participated merely in consequence of the advice of Gould.

Heather, Re, [1906] 2 Ch. 230 [139]

In his will H. bequeathed £3000 to M. F. his adopted daughter, and the residue of his property equally to M. F. and C. B. to whom H. was not *in loco parentis*. H. subsequently gave M. F. a gift of £1000. On H.'s death a summons was issued to determine whether the legacy of £3000 was partially adeemed by the gift of £1000. *Held*, even if the gift of £1000 had been a portion, which on the evidence was not the case, the legacy would not have been adeemed by the gift as the effect of such ademption would be to benefit a stranger at the expense of a child and, "A rule designed to produce equality among children cannot be extended to reduce their shares for the benefit of a stranger" (*per* SWINFEN EADY, J.).

Henry Wood National Memorial Trust, Re, [1967] 1 All E.R. 283 [140]

In 1944 an appeal was launched to raise money to build a concert hall to be named after Sir Henry Wood. On May 6, 1946 the trustees in whom the fund was vested declared that they held it on trust ". . . for improving and extending the knowledge and appreciation of good music . . ." and in particular by building a concert hall. The money raised proved insufficient to build a concert hall and the trustees took out a summons to determine what should be done with the money collected. *Held*, the money had been given for a specific charitable purpose which had failed. The subsequent declaration of trust by the trustees did not affect the rights of the contributors on the failure of the original purpose. The particular charitable purpose having failed *ab initio*, the fund. so far as arising from identifiable sources, and subject to s. 14 of the Charities Act 1960, was held on resulting trusts for the donors. Contributions of over £2 2s. 0d. made before May 6, 1964 by donors who could be identified, and who had not disclaimed their right to have their contributions returned, were declared to be returnable to the donors.

Hilton, Re, Gibbes v. Hale-Hinton, [1909] 2 Ch.D. 548   [141]

A testator bequeathed to trustees the residue of his personal estate on trust to sell and convert into money such parts as did not consist of money, with power to retain as investments any shares of public companies held by the testator at the time of his death, and to invest the proceeds of sale in specified investments. The trustees were directed to hold the investments retained or purchased on trust for the testator's daughter for life with gifts over. The trustees disagreed as to whether certain shares should be retained. *Held*, notwithstanding the fact that the shares in question were within the investment clause in the will, in the absence of unanimity between the trustees the trust for sale prevailed and the investments had to be sold.

Hobourn Aero Components, Ltd.'s Air-raid Distress Fund Trust,   [142]   Re, Ryan v. Forrest, [1946] 1 All E.R. 501 (Court of Appeal)

In 1941 H. Ltd. sent a circular to all its employees asking them to contribute towards a war emergency fund for providing parcels and leave grants for ex-employees in the Forces and also, from August 1940, grants for employees in respect of air-raid damage. By a circular sent out in November 1940, in place of the former voluntary contributions to the fund, employees were asked to contribute 2d. in the £ a week from their wages towards an Air-Raid Distress Fund, the object of which, it was stated, was to help any employee " in dire distress as the result of enemy action ". All the employees, excepting about seven, became subscribers to the fund. Only claims from subscribers to the fund were considered and no means test was applied in the administration of the fund. Help was given to subscribers awkwardly situated as a result of air-raids whether they were in financial distress or not. In 1944, the fund was closed down and the question arose as to what was to be done with the surplus money. On the question whether the fund constituted a charitable trust, *Held*, whilst the relief of distress caused by air-raids might be a charitable purpose under the fourth head of Lord Macnaughton's classification in *Pemsel's Case* (see *Commissioner of Income Tax* v. *Pemsel, ante*). the present fund, being the benefit of the employees of a particular company, was not for the public benefit and thus (poverty not being a necessary qualification for recipients) was not charitable.

Holt v. Heatherfield Trust, Ltd., [1942] 1 All E.R. 404   [143]

On June 14, 1940, P. obtained judgment for a sum of money against the C. Company. On the same day P. assigned the sum due to H. H. received the assignment on June 15. Also on June 15, H. T. Ltd. obtained a garnishee order *nisi* on the sum due from the C. Company to P. The order was served on the C. Company on June 17. H. sent notice to the C. Company of the assignment to him on June 17, and the C. Company received the notice on June 18. *Held*, there had been a valid equitable assignment by P. to H., which lacked only notice to C. to become a valid legal assignment. Consideration was not required for an equitable assignment of a debt or other legal chose in action [although consideration from H. to P. had been present in this case]. The garnishee order could only charge property with which P. could honestly deal at the time when the order was served. As P. had before this time made a valid equitable assignment of the property to H., the garnishee order did not change the debt assigned which had become the property of H. Notice to the debtor under s. 136 of the Law of Property Act 1925 takes effect when it is received by or on behalf of the debtor.

Holt's Settlement, Re, Wilson v. Holt, [1968] 1 All E.R. 470   [144]

By a settlement made in 1959 the income from a fund was held on trust for W. for life with remainder for her children who should attain the age of twenty-one years and, if more than one, in equal shares. The approval of the court was sought under the Variation of Trusts Act 1958 for an arrangement under which W. should surrender her life interest in one half of the income of the trust fund (which had greatly increased in value since the date of the settlement), that the income of that half should be accumulated, and that the vesting of the interests of children in that half fund should be deferred until they reached the age of thirty years. The arrangement took the form of a proposed revocation of existing trusts and the establishment of new trusts, many of which would be similar to the former trusts; and it was proposed that advantage should be taken in the arrangement of the provisions of the Perpetuities and Accumulations Act 1964, which, by s. 15 (5) applied only, so far as material to the case, to instruments taking effect after the commencement of the Act. *Held*, (1) where the court made an order under s. 1 of the Variation of Trusts Act 1958, approving an arrangement, it was the arrangement, made binding on infants and unborn persons by the court's approval, that varied the trusts, not the order of the court itself. (2) Although the arrangement, when approved, would revoke all prior trusts and establish new trusts, the new trusts would be in many respects similar to the old trusts, and accordingly the arrangement in the present case would be a " variation " of the former trusts for the purposes of s. 1 of the Act of 1958. (3) The arrangement coupled with the court's order constituted an instrument for the purposes of s. 15 (5) of the Perpetuities and Accumulations Act 1964, with the consequence that provisions deriving their validity from the Act of 1964 might properly be included in the arrangement. (4) As regards unborn persons on whose behalf approval was sought, the court should be prepared to take the sort of risk that an adult would be prepared to take and, on the merits, the proposed arrangement would be approved.

Hooper, Re, Parker v. Ward, [1932] 1 Ch. 38   [145]

A testator bequeathed property to trustees on trust to provide "so far as they legally can do so and . . . for as long as may be practicable" for the care and upkeep of certain graves in a church yard and a tablet and window in a church. *Held*, the phrase "so far as they legally can do so" being indistinguishable from the phrase "so long as the law for the time being permits", the trust for the upkeep of the graves was valid for a period of 21 years. The trust for the upkeep of the tablet and window [being part of the fabric of the church] was a charitable gift, and thus the rule against inalienability did not apply to it.

Hopkins' Will Trusts, Re, Naish v. Francis Bacon Society Incorporated, [1964] 3 All E.R. 46   [146]

By her will, a testatrix gave one third of her residuary estate to " the Francis Bacon Society Incorporated . . . to be earmarked and applied towards finding the Bacon-Shakespeare manuscripts ". One of the main objects of the society was " to encourage the general study of the evidence in favour of Francis Bacon's authorship of the plays commonly ascribed to Shakespeare ". The society was registered as a charity under the Charities Act 1960. The court found that the degree of improbability of discovering manuscripts of the plays was not so great as to justify rejecting the trust as wholly impracticable or futile. On the question whether the expressed purpose of the gift was in law a valid charitable purpose, *Held*, (1) the trusts on which the gift was to be held were, on the true construction of the bequest, to use the money to search for manuscripts of plays commonly ascribed to Shakespeare believed by the testatrix and the society to have been written by Bacon. (2) Approaching the question whether these were valid charitable trusts on the basis that the court had to decide each particular case as best it could, on the evidence available as to public benefit, the purposes of search or research for original manuscripts of England's greatest dramatist was within the law's conception of charitable purpose either as being for education or as being for other purposes beneficial to the community within the classification in *Pemsel's* case (see *Commissioner of Inland Revenue* v. *Pemsel, ante*), for it was a gift for the improving of the country's literary heritage. (*Per curiam*: in order that a gift for research should be charitable the research must either (i) be of educational value to the researcher; or, (ii) be so directed as to lead to something which will pass into the store of educational material; or, (iii) be so directed as to improve the sum of communicable knowledge in an area which education (including in this last context the formation of literary taste and appreciation) may cover.)

Hopkinson, Re, Lloyds Bank, Ltd. v. Baker, [147]
[1949] 1 All E.R. v. 346

By clause 5 of his will, a testator gave property to four prominent members of the Labour Party " as trustees of the educational fund hereinafter mentioned upon trust that they shall stand possessed of the same as an educational fund and shall apply the same both capital and income at their absolute discretion for the advancement of adult education with particular reference to the following purpose (but in no way limiting their general discretion in applying the fund for adult education) that is to say, the education of men and women of all classes (on the lines of the Labour Party's memorandum headed A Note on Education in the Labour Party, a copy whereof is annexed to this my will and signed by me) to a higher conception of social, political and economic ideas and values and of the personal obligations of duty and service which are necessary for the realisation of an improved and enlightened social civilisation ". The court found as a fact that the object of the memorandum annexed to the will was to advance the cause of the Labour Party by improving its methods of propaganda and increasing its electoral efficiency. *Held*, the direction to the trustees to have particular reference to the memorandum dominated the whole trust forming its overriding and essential purpose and was not merely intended to serve as a guide in the administration of the fund, and, therefore, the trust was one for the attainment of political objects, and not charitable.

Horlock, Re, Calham v. Smith, [1895] 1 Ch. 516 [148]

H. covenanted with C. that his executors should pay C. £300 within three months after his death. In his will H. left C. £400, but fixed no limit of time within which the legacy was to be paid. *Held*, the legacy was not to be regarded as being in satisfaction of the amount due under the covenant. C. was entitled to receive both.

Houston v. Burns, [1918–19] All E.R. Rep. 817 [149]

A testatrix directed trustees to apply the residue of her estate "for such public, benevolent, or charitable purposes" in connection with a particular parish as they should think proper. *Held*, the words "such public, benevolent or charitable purposes" must be construed to mean "public purposes or benevolent purposes or charitable purposes". The gift was not exclusively charitable and was therefore a private, and not a charitable gift. As a private trust, it failed for lack of certainty of objects.

Howe v. Earl of Dartmôuth (1802), 7 Ves. 137 [150]

A testator left all his real and personal property to his wife for life and after her death to various persons in succession. Part of the personal estate consisted of bank stock and annuities. The trustees sold these and purchased authorised trustee investments. *Held*, the trustees had acted properly in converting the bank stock (which, being subject to fluctuations in trade, was an unauthorised security) and the annuities (which were of a wasting nature) into authorised investments. [Note: Under the rule in *How* v. *Dartmouth* when a testator leaves residuary personalty on trust for persons in succession, then unless the will shows a contrary intention the trustees or executors must sell and convert into authorised trustee investments any items of the residue which consist of (a) wasting, hazardous or unauthorised investments, and (b) "reversionary interests" (*i.e.* interests not yet in possession)].

Hummeltenberg, Re, Beatty v. London Spiritualistic   [151]
Alliance, Ltd., [1923] All E.R. Rep. 49

A testator bequeathed a legacy to the treasurer of the London Spiritualistic Alliance for the purpose of establishing a college for the training of suitable persons as mediums "preference being given to healing mediums and those for diagnosis of disease . . ." *Held*, "no matter under which of the four classes [of Lord Mac-naghten's classification of charitable gifts (*Commissioners of Income Tax* v. *Pemsel*)] a gift may *prima facie* fall, it is still . . . necessary (in order to establish that it is charitable in the legal sense) to show (1) that the gift will or may be operative for the public benefit, and (2) that the trust is one the administration of which the court itself could if necessary undertake and control . . ." (*per* Russell, J.). The opinion of the donor of a gift or the creator of a trust that the gift or trust is for the public benefit did not make it so, the matter being one for the court to determine. The gift was not for the public benefit and could not be administered by the court and was thus not charitable. The gift therefore failed as it infringed the perpetuity rule.

Incorporated Council of Law Reporting for England and   [152]
Wales v. A.-G., [1971] 3 All E.R. 1029 (Court of Appeal)

The primary object of the Council, as stated in its memorandum of association, was "The preparation and publication . . . at a moderate price, and under gratuitous professional control, of Reports of Judicial Decisions of the Superior and Appellate Courts in England." The memorandum however contained no statement saying what the purpose of the preparation and publication of the reports was. The reports published by the Council were used for the purpose of the courts in drawing the attention of judges to relevant case law and for the purpose of members of the legal profession in practice and others engaged in a study of law. Although the Council was carrying on a business, profits, if any, could not be distributed to its members but had to be applied in the further pursuit of its objects. The Charity Commissioners refused to register the council as a charity under s. 4 of the Charities Act 1900. *Held*, (1) while the court could not construe the objects of the Council by reference to evidence outside the terms of the memorandum, once it was established what the objects were then in order to determine whether they were charitable or not, the court was entitled to look at the circumstances in which the institution came into existence and the sphere in which it operated. (2) The Council was established for exclusively charitable purposes, and was accordingly entitled to be registered as a charity for the following reasons. (a) The publication and dissemination of reports of judicial decisions was a purpose beneficial to the community in that it made a significant contribution to the sound development, administration and knowledge of the law; furthermore the object of the Council fell within the spirit and intendment of the preamble to the Statute of Elizabeth. (b) Alternatively, the preparation of law reports could be regarded as being for the advancement of education since their purpose was to record in an accurate manner the development and application of judge-made law and thereby disseminate knowledge of that law in a way which was essential to a study of it. (c) The fact that the reports were used by members of the legal profession for earning fees did not have the effect that the Council's purposes were not charitable; if the publication of reliable reports of judicial decisions was for a charitable purpose it was an inevitable and necessary step in the achievement of that purpose that members of the legal profession should be supplied with the tools of their trade. (d) The fact that in publishing the law reports the Council was carrying on a business did not prevent its purposes from being charitable since the profits, if any, could not be distributed to the members of the Council but could only be applied in the further pursuit of the Council's objects.

Inwards v. Baker, [1965] 1 All E.R. 446 (Court of Appeal)   [153]

In 1931 a father suggested to his son, who wanted a piece of land on which to build a bungalow, that the son should build the bungalow on a piece of his, the father's, land. The son gave up the idea of purchasing other land and built the bungalow on the father's land. The father made no contractual arrangement or promise as to the terms on which the son should occupy the land or for how long he should remain in occupation, but the son believed that he would be allowed to remain there for his life time or for so long as he wished. The father died in 1951. Under his will, made in 1922, the land vested in trustees for the benefit of persons other than the son. In 1963 the trustees sought possession of the bungalow. *Held*, where a person spends money on the land of another in the expectation, induced or encouraged by the owner of the land, that he will be allowed to remain in occupation, equity will protect his occupation of the land in such manner as the court will determine. The son was permitted to remain in occupation of the bungalow for so long as he desired.

Inland Revenue Commissioners v. Baddeley, [1955]   [154]
   1 All E.R. 525 (House of Lords)

Property was conveyed to trustees who were directed to permit it to be used by the leaders of a Methodist mission for the religious, social and physical well-being of such residents of West Ham and Leyton who, in the opinion of the leaders of the mission, were or likely to become members of the Methodist church and who were of insufficient means to otherwise enjoy the facilities to be provided. *Held*, the trust was not charitable as it was expressed in terms which would permit the property to be used for purposes which were non-charitable. "... its ambit is far too wide to include only purposes which the law regards as charitable" (*per* VISCOUNT SIMONDS).

Inland Revenue Commissioners v. Broadway Cottages Trust,   [155]
   [1954] 3 All E.R. 120 (Court of Appeal)

Property was given to trustees on trust to apply the income for the benefit of all or any of a class of beneficiaries, which included, *inter alia*, the settlor's wife, certain of his relatives, and the Broadway Cottages Trust, an institution established for charitable purposes only. It was not possible at any given moment to ascertain all the persons who might come within the class of beneficiaries, but it was possible to determine with certainty whether a particular person was a member of the class. The trustees paid income to the Broadway Cottages Trust, and exemption from income tax was claimed by the Trust in respect of this. *Held*, a trust for the benefit of such members of a class as the trustees should select was void for uncertainty unless the whole range of beneficiaries was capable of ascertainment. It was not sufficient for trustees to be able to determine whether an individual was or was not within the class. If under a trust which was void for this reason, income were paid to a charity which was a member of the class, the income was not income of the charitable institution for the purpose of exemption from income tax, but must be regarded as having been income of the settlor under a resulting trust paid to the charitable institution by his authority. [But see *McPhail* v. *Doulton, post.*]

Inland Revenue Commissioners v. City of Glasgow Police   [156]
   Athletic Association, [1953] 1 All E.R. 747 (House of Lords)

In 1938 various clubs connected with the Glasgow city police merged in an association of which the objects were " to encourage and promote all forms of athletic sports and general pastimes ''. The chief constable was president of the association, and all resolutions and decisions passed at meetings of the association were subject to his approval. Membership was confined to officers and ex-officers of the city police, and, until 1947, was compulsory for a police officer. Members paid a small subscription, which was deducted from their pay. *Held,* although the association had official importance and a public aspect, its provision of recreation for members was an essential non-charitable purpose which was not subsidiary or incidental to the furtherance of a public purpose, and, therefore, the association was not a body established for charitable purposes only within the Finance Act 1921, s. 30 (3) and it was not entitled to exemption from income tax under s. 30 (1) (c) of that Act.

Inland Revenue Commissioners v. Educational Grants Association, Ltd., [1967] 3 W.L.R. 41 (Court of Appeal)   [157]

A director of M. B., Ltd. promoted the defendant company, which was established for the advancement of education, *inter alia* by making grants towards the cost of education of individuals. The council of management were all connected with M. B., Ltd. The income of the Association consisted in the main of money provided by M. B., Ltd. M. B., Ltd. was not mentioned in the memorandum of association of the company, but in the relevant years between 76 and 85 % of the income was applied for the children of persons connected with M.B., Ltd. The Association claimed exemption from income tax for four years on the ground that it was applied for charitable purposes only within s. 447 (1) (b) of the Income Tax Act 1952. The Commissioners admitted that the Association was established for charitable purposes only within s. 447 (1) (b) of the Act, and accepted the Association's claim to exemption from income tax in respect of income applied to individuals other than persons connected with M. B., Ltd., but rejected the claim to exemption in respect of income applied to persons connected with M. B., Ltd. *Held,* the application of 85% of the income for the private benefit of children connected with M. B., Ltd. was not an application for charitable purposes, and thus the Association's claim to exemption from income tax failed.

Jared v. Clements, [1903] 1 Ch. 428   [158]

X. created an equitable mortgage of leasehold property in favour of J. X. later sold the property to C. Before completion the existence of the equitable mortgage accidentally came to the knowledge of C. X.'s solicitor asured C. that the mortgage had been paid off and gave C. a document purporting to be a receipt for the mortgage money signed by J. The property was assigned to C. The receipt later turned out to be forged, the mortgage not having been paid off. J. claimed priority over C. *Held,* C. took the property subject to the equitable interest held by J. Where a purchaser chooses to accept property in reliance upon the assurance of the vendor that an equitable interest has been discharged, he does so at his own risk.

Jefferys v. Jefferys (1841), Cr. and Ph. 138   [159]

A father by deed conveyed certain freeholds and covenanted to surrender certain copyholds to trustees on trust for his daughters. The daughters gave no consideration to the father in respect of the covenant. The father failed to surrender the copyholds to the trustees in accordance with the covenant and devised the copyholds, together with the freeholds, to his widow. After the father's death the daughters sought to have the trusts of the deed carried into effect and to compel the widow to surrender the copyholds, to which she had been admitted, to the trustees. *Held,* the trustees held the freeholds, as these had been conveyed to them by the deed, but as the trust of the copyholds was incompletely constituted and the daughters were merely volunteers, they had no equity to compel the widow to part with the legal interest which she had properly acquired.

Jenkins' Will Trusts, Re, Public Trustee v. British Union   [160] for the Abolition of Vivisection, [1966] 1 All E.R. 926

A testatrix left her residuary estate to "the British Union for the Abolition of Vivisection . . . or any other institution with a similar aim should the former not exist at the time of my death provided by then an Act . . . has been passed prohibiting by law such . . . cruelty to animals . . . Otherwise I desire my estate to be divided into seven equal parts and distributed among the following animal institutions (1) To the British Union for the Abolition of Vivisection . . . or any other institution with a similar aim should the former not exist at the time of my death" to promote the cause of anti-vivisection. Gifts to six other institutions concerned with animal welfare followed. *Held*, (i) the British Union for the Abolition of Vivisection did not take absolutely; (ii) the gift of one seventh to the Union on trust failed; (iii) the promotion of an Act prohibiting vivisection was not charitable because it was a political object and because the object to be achieved was not charitable (*National Anti-Vivisection Society* v. *Inland Revenue Commissioners*); (iv) the fact that a gift for a non-charitable purpose was found among other gifts for charitable purposes could not be taken to mean that the testatrix intended the non-charitable gift to take effect as a charitable gift, even though the purpose of the non-charitable gift was akin to that of the charitable gifts. (v) as the gift was not charitable the court could not give effect to it by means of a scheme; (vi) the gift of one seventh was therefore undisposed of and passed as on the intestacy of the testatrix.

Johnson v. Ball (1851), 6 De G. & Sm. 85   [161]

A testator bequeathed the proceeds of an assurance policy on his life to B. and M. "to hold the same upon the uses appointed by letter signed by them and myself". No such letter existed at the date of the will, but the testator had previously asked B. and M. to accept the bequest on trust for Mrs. J. and her children, and B. and M. had agreed to this. A year and a half later the testator dictated a letter to the executors of his will informing them that in his will he had left his life assurance policy to B. and M. ". . . for certain purposes, which they have agreed to carry out". This letter was signed by the testator and attested by one of the testator's daughters. At the same time the testator dictated a memorandum setting out in detail the trusts on which B. and M. were to hold the policy. This memorandum was signed by the testator, and was unattested. *Held*, the language of the will appeared to point to some letter already signed by the testator and the trustees. No such letter existed. If the will intended to refer to a letter to be signed subsequent to the will, such a disposition would be invalid as a testator could not by his will prospectively create for himself a power to dispose of his property by an instrument not duly executed as a will or codicil. There had thus been no proper communication of the trusts to B. and M., and B. and M. therefore held the property on trust for the residuary legatees.

Jones v. Lock (1865), 1 Ch.App. 25. (Lord Chancellor's Court)   [162]

A father put a cheque for £900 into the hand of his nine-month-old son, saying "I give this to baby; it is for himself, and I am going to put it away for him . . ." He then took the cheque from the child, saying to the nurse: "Now, Lizzie, I am going to put this away for my own son." He put the cheque in his safe. A few days later he said to his solicitor: "I shall come to your office on Monday to alter my will, that I may take care of my son". He died the same day. Did the cheque belong to the child or to the residuary legatees under the father's will? *Held*, there had been no gift to the child as the father had not meant to deprive himself of all property in the note [*i.e.* there had been no delivery to the child]. Nor had any trust been created as the father had not intended to declare himself a trustee of the money for the child. The cheque was therefore part of the residuary estate.

Jones v. Maynard, [1951] 1 All E.R. 802   **[163]**

A husband and wife operated a joint bank account into which they both paid their earnings, and out of which they drew for their requirements. The husband, who paid in more than the wife, from time to time withdrew money to pay for investments purchased in his own name. In 1946 the wife left the husband and he closed the account and drew out the balance. After the husband had obtained a decree of divorce against the wife, she brought an action against him claiming half the final balance in the account and half the value of the investments. The husband contended that the balance and the investments should be divided proportionately to the payments in by the parties. *Held*, applying the principle "equality is equity", the wife was entitled to one half of the final balance and to one half of the value of the investments existing at the date when the account was closed. (See also *Re Bishop*.)

Kay's Settlement, Re, Broadbent v. Macnab, [1939]   **[164]**
1 All E.R. 245

A spinster covenanted voluntarily to settle after-acquired property on trust, *inter alia*, for any children she should have. She later married and had three children. She subsequently became entitled under a will to certain property. The trustees of the settlement asked her to settle this property in accordance with the covenant. *Held*, the children, being volunteers [the settlement not having been an ante-nuptial settlement], had no right to enforce the covenant, and therefore the trustees were directed not to take any proceedings to enforce the covenant. (See also *Re Cook's Settlement Trusts, ante*).

Keech v. Sandford (1726), Sel. Cas. Chan. 61   **[165]**

A trustee held a lease of Romford Market on trust for an infant. The trustee attempted to renew the lease in his capacity as trustee. The lessor only agreed to renew the lease on condition that the trustee was to hold the lease beneficially. The trustee agreed and the lease was renewed on these terms. *Held*, despite the unwillingness of the lessor to grant a renewal of the lease to the trustee in his capacity as trustee, the trustee held the renewed lease on a constructive trust for the infant.

Keen, Re, Evershed v. Griffiths, [1937] 1 All E.R. 452   **[166]**

On March 31, 1932 a testator made a will in which he gave £10,000 to H. and E. on trust for such persons or charities as he might notify to them in his lifetime. On the same date the testator handed to E. a sealed envelope containing the name of the intended beneficiary but without disclosing its contents to E., and directing him not to open it until after his death. On August 11, 1932 the testator made a fresh will which revoked the will of March 31, but which contained a clause (clause 5) in identical terms to that set out above. When the new will was executed the testator gave no fresh directions to E. E. regarded himself as being bound by the previous direction. After the testator's death the envelope was opened and found to contain a paper stating "£10,000 to G". *Held*, clause 5 of the will dated August 11, 1932 referred to dispositions which the testator might notify subsequent to the date of the will. The sealed envelope was delivered before the date of that will and was thus not a communication consistent with the terms of the will. Therefore no communication had taken place. Further, on the true construction of the will, it reserved the power to the testator to dispose of property by a future unattested disposition contrary to the Wills Act 1837. The trust therefore failed and the legacy fell into residue.

King, Re, Kerr v. Bradley, [1923] 1 Ch. 243   [167]

A testatrix directed that the residue of her estate should be applied in providing a stained-glass window in memory of herself and certain of her relatives in the church at Irchester. The residue amounted to some £1094. The estimated maximum cost of the window was £800. *Held,* (1) since the bequest was for the benefit of the church, and since the testatrix' motive (to perpetuate the memory of herself and her relatives) was immaterial, the bequest was charitable. (2) The surplus was to be applied *cy-près.*

King's Settlement, Re, [1931] 2 Ch. 294   [168]

A father who wished to create a secret trust in favour of himself, his wife and his daughter conveyed land to his son and his son's wife. The conveyance, which was stated to be made in consideration of his love and affection for them, made no reference to the trust. On the recommendation of the father's solicitor, a declaration of trust was executed by the son and his wife. The son and his wife later created an equitable mortgage in favour of B., who made the proper searches, but without obtaining notice of the trust. When this transaction came to light the father, his wife and daughter claimed priority for their equitable interest under the trust against the equitable mortagee, B. *Held,* "*prima facie* the beneficiaries' equity, being earlier in date, ought to prevail. But when I find that their title is based on a document wholly misleading and resulting in third parties being wholly misled as to the character in which the defendants" (the son and daughter) ". . . take the property, I should be going against all equitable principles if I were to hold that the beneficiaries' equity prevailed over that of other persons acting in complete innocence . . ." (*per* Farwell, J.). The equitable mortgagee therefore took priority over the beneficiaries under the trust.

Knott v. Cottee (1852), 16 Beax. 77   [169]

A testator directed trustees to invest in specified securities. In 1845 the trustees invested in securities not authorised by the testator. A year later these were sold at a loss. *Held,* the trustees were liable for the loss, *i.e.* the difference between the sum invested and the sum realised on sale.

Knox, Re, Fleming v. Carmichael, [1936] 3 All E.R. 623   [170]

A testatrix left the residue of her estate to "the Berwick-upon-Tweed Infirmary, the Newcastle-upon-Tyne Infirmary, the Newcastle-upon-Tyne Nursing Home and Dr. Barnardo's Homes, London, in equal shares". No such institution as the Newcastle-upon-Tyne Nursing Home had ever existed. *Held,* (i) the gift to the Newcastle-upon-Tyne Nursing Home was not necessarily charitable. The institution "might or might not be a charity so far as its name is concerned"; (ii) "In cases where there is a gift to some body or institution which has never existed, the question whether there is a charitable intention or not, is always a matter of construction of the will"; (iii) in construing the will "it is very important . . . to consider the actual collocation in which the named institution is found"; (iv) the three other institutions named were *strict* charities within the strict meaning of the term; (v) the context of the gift was thus sufficient to show an intention of charity. The gift therefore did not lapse, but was applied *cy-près,* one half going to the Northumberland County Nursing Association and one half to the Cathedral Nursing Society. [In the case of a trust which is "impossible" (as defined by the Charities Act 1960, s. 13 (1)) *ab initio,* for the gift to be applied *cy-près* it must be shown that the donor manifested a paramount intention of charity.]

Lacey, *Ex parte* (1802), 6 Ves. 625   [171]

A trustee in bankruptcy purchased part of the bankrupt's estate at a sale by auction. He had also purchased from creditors the debts due to them by the bankrupt. *Held*, a trustee must not make a profit as a result of his position as trustee. If he does so he holds the profit on trust for the *cestuis que trust*.

Lawes v. Bennett (1785), 1 Cox, Ch. Cas. 167 [172]

In 1758, Witterwonge leased a farm to Douglas for seven years, and agreed at the same time that if Douglas should give written notice before September 29, 1765 of his intention to purchase the farm for £3000, Witterwonge would sell it to him for this amount. Witterwonge died in 1763 having in his will left all his realty to Bennett and all his personalty to Bennett and Lawes equally. In 1762 Douglas assigned the lease and the option to purchase to Waller. On February 2, 1765, Waller exercised the option and the farm was conveyed to him, the purchase money being paid to Bennett. Lawes then claimed that since the exercise of the option related back to the date of the original agreement in 1758, conversion operated as from that date: the land should thus be considered as personalty since 1758, and should pass to Bennett and Lawes equally as the persons entitled to the testator's personalty. Lawes therefore claimed half the purchase money received by Bennett. *Held*, Lawes's contention was correct and Bennett should pay over half the purchase money to him.

Lawton, Re, Gartside v. Attorney-General, [1936] [173]
3 All E.R. 378

A testatrix by her will bequeathed money to the trustees of a certain Methodist chapel for the purchase of a field for use as a recreation ground by children attending the chapel Sunday School. The trustees of the chapel disclaimed the legacy. *Held*, as it was not of the essence of the bequest that the trustees of the chapel should be the trustees of the charity, the bequest did not lapse, but ought to be applied *cy-près*.

Leahy v. A.-G. for New South Wales, [1959] 2 All E.R. 300 [174]
(Privy Council)

By clause 3 of his will, a testator who died in 1954 left certain property "upon trust for such order of nuns of the Catholic Church . . . as my executors . . . shall select. . ." By clause 5 of his will the testator left the residue of his property "upon trust to use the income as well as the capital . . . in the provision of amenities in such convents as my said executors . . . shall select . . ." Questions arose as to the validity of clauses 3 and 5. It was not disputed that the phrase "such order of nuns" might include contemplative orders, which were not charitable in the legal sense. *Held*, regarding clause 5, this clause was validated by s. 37 D (1) of the Conveyancing Act 1919–1954 of New South Wales. ("No trust shall be held to be invalid by reason that some non-charitable and invalid purpose as well as some charitable purpose is . . . included in any of the purposes . . . of the trust . . .".) Although the testator had not expressly indicated alternative purposes, the one charitable and the other non-charitable, but had used a compendious expression apt to include both charitable and non-charitable purposes, the section applied none-the-less. Regarding clause 3, since the bequest showed an intention to create a trust not merely for the benefit of existing members of the order selected but also for the benefit of the order as a continuing society, the gift infringed the rule against inalienability [the rule against "perpetual trusts"]. If the order selected were non-charitable, the gift would fail for this reason. However, s. 37 D (1) validated the trust, but the court ordered (in accordance with s. 37 D (2) of the Act) that the power of selection given to the trustees should not extend to contemplative orders of nuns.

Learoyd v. Whiteley (1887), 12 App. Cas. 727 (House of Lords) [175]

The trustees of a settlement who were authorised to invest trust money in real securities, invested £3000 of trust money and £500 from another source in a 5%

mortgage of a brickworks near Pontefract. Before lending the money the trustees asked a local valuer of experience to advise on the value of the brickworks. He reported that it provided good security for the loan, but the report did not state that the valuation was based on the brickworks as a going concern. The business failed in August, 1884, and was sold for £3300. *Held,* "the law requires of a trustee no higher degree of diligence in the execution of his office than a man of ordinary prudence would exercise in the management of his own private affairs. Yet he is not allowed the same discretion in investing the moneys of the trust as if he were a person *sui juris* dealing with his own estate . . . it is the duty of a trustee to confine himself to the class of investments which are permitted by the trust and likewise to avoid all investments of that class which are attended with hazard. The courts . . . have indicated . . . principles for the guidance of trustees in lending money upon the security of real estate . . ." (*per* LORD WATSON). The trustees, although acting *bona fide,* had not acted with ordinary prudence, and were liable to make good the money with interest at 4% from the date of the last payment.

Lechmere v. Lady Lechmere (1735), Cas. temp. Talb. 80 [176]

In 1719, Lord Lechmere on his marriage to Lady E. covenanted to lay out £30,000 within one year of the marriage in the purchase, with the consent of trustees, of freehold lands in fee simple in possession in the south part of Great Britain. The land so purchased was covenanted to be settled on Lord Lechmere for life, with a jointure in remainder to his widow, with remainder to the first and other sons of the marriage in fee tail male, with remainder to Lord Lechmere in fee simple. At the time of the marriage Lord Lechmere already held some lands in fee simple. After the marriage, but not within the year, and without the consent of the trustees, Lord Lechmere purchased and contracted to purchase certain lands in fee simple in possession. He also purchased some lands for life interests and fee simples in remainder. None of these lands were settled in accordance with the covenant. Lord Lechmere died intestate in 1727, leaving a widow but no issue. The heir-at-law maintained that a sum of £30,000 out of the personalty should be laid out in accordance with the covenant with the result that it would pass to him under the ultimate remainder. The next-of-kin argued that the heir at law, not being a party to the covenant. could not enforce its performance, but that if he could the lands purchased by Lord Lechmere (and which descended to the heir at law under the intestacy) should be taken to have been purchased towards performance of the covenant and their value deducted from the £30,000 which the next-of-kin claimed should be laid out in accordance with the covenant. *Held,* (i) the heir-at-law was entitled to specific performance of the covenant; (ii) the freehold lands in fee simple in possession purchased and contracted to be purchased by Lord Lechmere after the marriage were to be taken to have been purchased towards performance of the covenant, and their value deducted from the £30,000. But land held by Lord Lechmere before his marriage, and the lands for life estates and in remainder purchased by him after his marriage were not to be taken towards performance of the covenant.

Lepton's Will Trusts, Re, Lepton's Charity, Ambler v. [177]
Thomas, [1971] 1 All E.R. 799

A testator, who died in 1716, by his will devised certain land to trustees on trust to pay the rents and profits to the " . . . Protestant Dissenting Minister . . . the yearly Summe of Three pounds . . . the Overplus . . . unto the poor Aged and Necessitouse people . . . of Pudsy ". The trust property had greatly increased in value, the income in 1967 being about £792 compared with £5 in 1716. Two questions arose for the determination of the court: (i) whether, on the true construction of the will, the minister should be paid the fixed sum of £3, or three-fifths of the annual income; (ii) whether the *cy-près* doctrine could be applied to the whole of the trusts on the ground that the original purposes of the gift had ceased to provide a suitable and effective method of using the property, so that a scheme could be ordered whereby an agreed figure of £100 payable annually to the minister could be substituted for the £3 contained in the will. *Held,* (1) the first question was one of the proper construction of the will; the construction was susceptible of only one meaning, i.e. that the minister should be paid the yearly sum of £3. (2) Where income was divided into a fixed annual sum for one charity and the residue for the other charity, there was an obvious inter-relation between the trusts, in that changes in the amount of income and the value of money might completely distort the relative benefits taken under the respective trusts. For this reason the original purposes had therefore ceased to provide a suitable and effective method of using the property, and the property would be applied *cy-près* by a scheme substituting the figure of £100 for £3.

Letterstedt v. Broers (1884), 9 App. Cas. 371 (Privy Council)   [178]

The Board of Executors of Cape Town were the sole surviving executors and trustees of a will. One of the beneficiaries alleged misconduct in the administration of the trust and claimed that the Board were unfit to continue as trustee and should be replaced by a new trustee. *Held,* the courts of equity have jurisdiction to remove a trustee and substitute a new one in his place. The principal consideration of the court in exercising this jurisdiction is the welfare of the beneficiaries. The Board had not been guilty of misconduct but in view of the hostility that had arisen it was necessary for the welfare of the beneficiaries that the Board should be replaced by other trustees.

Lewis, Re, [1954] 3 All E.R. 257   [179]

By his will a testator provided: "I leave to ten blind girls Tottenham residents if possible the sum of £100 each". *Held,* although the will did not require that the legatees should be poor as well as blind, the gift was charitable, because the words "aged, impotent and poor" in the Charities Act 1601, ought to be read disjunctively so far as the word "impotent" was concerned and, therefore, a condition of their being poor was not essential to enable a gift to blind girls to be charitable.

Lister & Co. v. Stubbs (1890), 45 Ch.D. 1 (Court of Appeal)   [180]

L. & Co. employed S. as their foreman. In the course of his work S. bought certain materials on behalf of L. & Co. for use in its manufacturing business. S. obtained a secret commission totalling over £5,540 from firms from which he ordered materials. S. invested part of this money in land and in certain other investments. L. & Co. (1) brought an action against S. for the recovery of the money he had received and (2) claimed to be entitled to trace the money into the land and other investments which S. had bought. *Held,* (on 2), that since the relationship between L. & Co. and S. was that of debtor and creditor (and not that of trustee and beneficiary) L. & Co. were not entitled to trace the money which S. had received into the land and other investments he had purchased.

Llewellyn's Settlement, Re, Official Solicitor v. Evans,   [181]
[1921] 2 Ch 281

Under a marriage settlement property was vested in trustees on trust for a wife for life, with remainder to her husband for life, if he survived her, with remainder on trust for such children of the marriage as the wife should by deed or will appoint. There was no gift over on default. The wife survived the husband and died, leaving children, without having exercised the power. *Held,* the marriage settlement was to be construed as implying a gift over on default of appointment to the children of the marriage. (Thus a "trust power" and not a "pure power" existed.) Therefore, in default of appointment, the property was to be divided equally between the children.

Low v. Bouverie, [1891] 3 Ch. 82   **[182]**

H. H. P. Bouverie was a trustee of certain funds. Admiral Bouverie was a beneficiary under the trust and held a life interest in the funds. Admiral Bouverie asked Low to lend him £600, and offered as security his life interest in the funds. He stated that he had not charged his life interest as security for any previous loans and referred Low to H. H. P. Bouverie. Low wrote to H. H. P. Bouverie asking whether Admiral Bouverie had assigned his interest in the funds. In reply H. H. P. Bouverie referred to several charges which Admiral Bouverie had created but failed to inform Low of several others. Low then lent Admiral Bouverie £600, accepting a charge over Admiral Bouverie's interest as security. Admiral Bouverie later left the country without repaying the debt. Low found that the security was worthless owing to earlier charges which Admiral Bouverie had created taking priority over his charge. Low sued H. H. P. Bouverie. *Held,* (a) it is not a duty of a trustee to give a beneficiary information as to the way in which the beneficiary has dealt with his interest, for it is not his duty to assist the beneficiary in squandering or anticipating his fortune; (b) it is not a trustee's duty to give such information to a person proposing to take an assignment of the beneficiary's interest, as such a person cannot have a right to information which the beneficiary is not himself entitled to demand.

Lucas, Re, Sheard v. Mellor, [1948] 2 All E.R. 22 (Court of Appeal)   **[183]**

By her will, a testatrix who died in 1943 bequeathed a legacy to " the Crippled Children's Home, Lindley Moor, Huddersfield", and a share of her residuary estate to " the Crippled Children's Home " without repeating the address, but clearly intending to refer to the same object. The home which had existed at the address and has been called " The Huddersfield Home for Crippled Children ", had been closed on the expiration of the lease in 1939, but in 1941, as funds still remained, a scheme, maintaining the primary purpose of the charity, was approved by the Charity Commissioners, under the title of " The Huddersfield Charity for Crippled Children ". The testatrix was unaware at the time of making her will that the home had been closed and that a scheme was in operation. *Held,* on their true construction, the bequests were by way of addition to the endowment of the charity and not merely for the upkeep of the particular premises of the home, and were effective gifts to the Huddersfield Charity for Crippled Children.

Lumley v. Wagner (1852), 1 De G.M. & G. 604   **[184]**

The defendant contracted to sing at the plaintiff's theatre for a certain period and promised that she would not sing elsewhere during that time without his written consent. *Held,* an injunction would be granted to restrain the defendant from singing for a third party in breach of this agreement.

Lyle v. Rosher, [1958] 3 All E.R. 597 (House of Lords)   **[185]**

W. and his father had a joint power of appointment under a settlement. When W. became a member of Lloyds he had to deposit a sum of money at Lloyds. In order to satisfy this requirement W. and his father exercised their power of appointment in favour of Lloyds, the money transferred to Lloyds being stated to be held by Lloyds to pay certain claims if they arose, and subject thereto on trust for W. In 1953 W. purported to charge the money deposited with Lloyds in favour of L., Ltd. Written notice of the charge was given to Lloyds. When W. became bankrupt in 1954 L. claimed that their charge took priority over any interest of the trustees of the settlement. *Held,* the exercise of the power of appointment had not had the effect of conferring any equitable interest on W. W. was thus not capable of charging or assigning the fund deposited at Lloyds. The case therefore did not come within the rule in *Dearle* v. *Hall* and the trustees of the settlement were entitled to the trust fund (subject to the interest of Lloyds) in priority to L., Ltd.

Lysaght, Re, Hill v. Royal College of Surgeons of England,   [186]
[1965] 2 All E.R. 888

A testatrix by her will, after reciting that it had long been her wish to found medical studentships within the gift of the Royal College of Surgeons, gave £5000 to the College on trust to apply the income in establishing studentships, and provided that the students must not be of the Jewish or Roman Catholic faith. The College declined to accept the gift on the terms stated in the will, but stated that it was willing to accept with the paragraph excluding Jews or Roman Catholics deleted. A summons was taken out to determine the effect of the gift. *Held*, (i) the requirement of religious discrimination did not make the gift void for uncertainty; nor was it void as being contrary to public policy. Thus the gift was charitable; but (ii) as it was of the essence of the trust that the trustees selected by the donor and no one else should act, and since those trustees were unwilling to undertake the office, the trust failed; however, (iii) on the true construction of the will, the basic intention of the testatrix was to found medical studentship administered by the College, and the remaining provisions, including that as to religious discrimination, concerned the machinery of the trust and were not essential parts of her intention; (iv) since the impracticability of giving effect to that inessential part of her intention could not be allowed to defeat a paramount charitable intention, [the *cy-près* doctrine applied]; and (v) the court ordered by way of a scheme that the £5000 be paid to the college, to be held on the trusts declared in the will omitting the words "and not of the Jewish or Roman Catholic faith".

Macdonald v. Macdonald, [1957] 2 All E.R. 690   [187]

A husband and wife lived, together with the wife's mother, in a cottage of which the mother was tenant for life and the wife was remainderman. In 1935 the cottage was sold and the three moved into a house in Edgware. The house cost £715, to which the mother and wife contributed £215 out of the proceeds of sale of the cottage. The husband raised the rest of the money by mortgaging the house which, without the agreement of the mother and wife, had been conveyed to the husband alone. The mother died intestate later in 1935 leaving the wife entitled to her estate. The husband paid the mortgage repayments until he joined the forces in 1939. Between 1939 and 1948 the interest due was paid by the wife. In 1948 the wife divorced the husband. Between 1948 and 1950 the mortgage repayments were paid by a lodger as part payment for his accommodation. In 1950 the husband resumed the mortgage repayments and continued to make the repayments until his death in 1954. The question arose as to who was entitled to the house. *Held*, the house had been purchased as a joint family enterprise. The husband and wife and the wife's mother had each had a substantial beneficial interest in the house. As it was not possible to make a precise calculation of their interests, they should be regarded as having been entitled in equal shares. Thus the wife was entitled to a two-thirds share (the mother's share and her own share) and the husband to a one-third share.

Maddison v. Alderson (1883), 8 App. Cas. 467 (House of Lords)   [188]

Thomas Alderson induced the appellant to serve him for many years without wages as his housekeeper by making an oral promise to leave her a life estate in his land. Alderson did in fact make a will which purported to carry out his promise but it was of no effect as it was not properly attested. The appellant sought a decree of specific performance in respect of the intestate's oral promise. *Held*, her plea would be rejected as her acts in serving the intestate until his death were not unequivocally, and in their own nature, referable to some such agreement as that alleged and therefore would not constitute such part performance as to take the case beyond the provisions of s. 4 of the Statute of Frauds (now s. 40 (1) of the Law of Property Act 1925). The fact that the Statute had not been complied with rendered the contract unenforceable but not void.

Marchant v. Morton, Down and Co., [1901] 2 K.B. 829   [189]

One of two members of a partnership, W., signed a document assigning to the defendants money owed to the partnership by C. The defendants gave notice to C. of the assignment. The other partner, A., later executed a deed in the name of the partnership purporting to assign the same debt to the plaintiff, who gave notice to C. W. had not told A. that he had assigned the debt to the defendants. *Held,* W. had made a valid equitable assignment of the debt to the plaintiff, and the plaintiff, having given notice to the debtor, took priority over the subsequent assignee. [*I.e.,* the rule in *Dearle* v. *Hall* applied to equitable assignments of legal choses in action.]

Mariette, Re, Marriette v. Aldenham School, [1915] 2 Ch. 284   [190]

A testator bequeathed money on trust for the purpose of building fives courts, providing books as a prize for classics and for providing a prize for athletics. The parties agreed that the school was a charity within the statute of Charitable Uses 1607. *Held,* whilst "it is quite possible that a gift to charity may be of such a character as not to be in itself a charitable gift", (*per* EVE, J.) the gifts in question were valid charitable bequests. The bequest for a prize for classics was clearly educational and hence charitable. The bequests for building fives courts and for a prize for athletics were within the objects of the charity, it being necessary for the games to be organised at the school. and the bequests were thus charitable.

Master's Settlement, Re, Master v. Master, [1911] 1 Ch. 321   [191]

By a marriage settlement dated 1878, money was settled on trust for a wife for life, and after her death, on trust for the husband for life or until he should become bankrupt, with remainder on trust for such children of the marriage as the survivor of the spouses should by deed or will appoint, with a gift over on default of appointment to all the children equally. The wife died in 1905 and in 1906 the husband, who had gone to Australia many years before, was adjudicated bankrupt. There were three children of the marriage. The trustees did not know of any appointment having been made. On the question as to how the trustees should deal with the income from the fund during the life-time of the husband and pending the exercise of the power. *Held.* that since the interests of the children in the settled fund were vested interests subject to being divested by the exercise of the power, the income from the trust fund was dis-tributable in equal shares amongst the children unless and until the power of appointment was exercised.

McArdle, Re, McArdle v. McArdle, [1951] 1 All E.R. 905
(Court of Appeal)   [192]

A testator, who died in 1935, left his residuary estate on trust for his widow for life with remainder to his five children. Part of the testator's estate con-sisted of a bungalow at Wimborne which was occupied in 1943 by M., one of the testator's sons, and Mrs. M., his wife. During 1943 they made certain repairs and improvements to the bungalow. These cost £488, and were paid for by Mrs. M. In 1945 the testator's five children signed a document in these terms: " To Mrs. M. . . . In consideration of your carrying out certain alterations and improvements to the property . . . at present occupied by you, we the bene-ficiaries under the will of [the testator] hereby agree that the executors . . . shall repay to you from the said estate when so distributed the sum of £488 in settle-ment of the amount on such improvements." The testator's widow died in 1948. In 1950 Mrs. M. claimed payment of the £488 from the executors. The testator's children (other than M.) objected to the sum being paid. *Held,* (1) the document executed in 1945 constituted an agreement. However, since all the work had been completed before the execution of the document, the consideration from Mrs. M. was past consideration and accordingly the agreement for payment of the £488 was not enforceable as a contract. (2) Since the document purported to be a contract for valuable consideration that the executors should, at a future date, (*i.e.* when the estate was distributed) pay the £488, the document could not be construed as constituting an immediate assignment by the beneficiaries of an equitable interest to Mrs. M. The claim therefore failed.

McGeorge, Re, Ratcliff v. McGeorge, [1963] 1 All E.R. 519   **[193]**

A testator, by his will made in 1960, devised land to his daughter and bequeathed a pecuniary legacy to his son. By clause 4 he declared (i) that " the . . . devise and pecuniary legacy shall not take effect until after the death of my . . . wife ", and (ii) that, if his daughter should die in the lifetime of the survivor of himself and his wife leaving issue, then the issue on attaining twenty-one " shall take by substitution . . . the aforesaid devise in favour of . . . " his daughter. The testator bequeathed his residuary estate on trust for his wife for life and after her death to divide the capital between his son and daughter in equal shares. His son and daughter survived him, she being married and having three children living. *Held,* (1) the declaration that the devise should not take effect deferred its vesting in possession (but not its vesting in interest) until the death of the testator's widow. (2) The devise was a future specific devise within s. 175 of the Law of Property Act 1925, and accordingly carried the intermediate income of the land devised (notwithstanding the residuary gift in the testator's will) but, as the devise was subject to defeasance during the lifetime of the testator's widow, the income should be accumulated during the shorter of the two periods, viz., the widow's lifetime or twenty-one years from the testator's death. (3) The testator's daughter was not entitled to payment of the income by virtue of s. 31 (1) of the Trustee Act 1925 because her interest in the income was a vested interest, and because the will showed a contrary intention (within s. 69 (2)) which excluded s. 31.

McPhail v. Doulton, [1970] 2 All E.R. 228 (House of Lords)   **[194]**
(See *Baden's Deed Trusts, Re Baden v. Smith (No. 1), ante.*

Meads Trust Deed, Re, Briginshaw v. National Society of   **[195]** Operative Printers and Assistants, [1961] 2 All E.R. 836

In 1920 the defendant Society, a trade union, decided to set up a home as a war memorial. Land was purchased out of contributions made for the purpose. The land was conveyed to trustees in a trust deed which declared the trusts on which the land was to be held. Clause 2 of the deed expressed the intention that the home should be (a) a sanatorium for consumptive patients who were members of the Society, (b) a convalescent home for members of the Society, and (c) a home for aged members of the Society who were no longer able to support themselves by working at their trade and the wives of such members. The convalescent home and the home for aged retired members and their wives had been established but it was found unnecessary to erect a sanatorium. The persons accommodated in the home for the aged were selected exclusively from the poor deserving members of the society, but no means test was required for admission to the convalescent home, which was supported chiefly by the society. On the question whether the trusts of the trust deed were charitable. *Held,* (1) the trust, not being exclusively for the relief of poverty, was not a charitable trust, because members of a trade union, however numerous, like employees of a large company employing most, but not all, of the persons engaged in a particular industry, were not a section of the public for the purpose of the law relating to charities, and, moreover, the element of self-help loomed large. (2) Clause 2 of the trust deed was an " imperfect trust provision " within s. 1 (1) of the Charitable Trusts (Validation) Act 1954, and was validated by s. 1 (2) because there was nothing in the terms of the trust deed to prevent the trustees e.g. from closing the convalescent home and applying the trust property to the provision of homes for aged retired members, who could not support themselves, and their wives, or from confining the potential beneficiaries of the trust to poor persons (both of which purposes were charitable purposes); accordingly, as from July 30, 1954, the trust had been validated and the property had been held by the trustees for the benefit of those members of the Society only who were from time to time poor persons and, in the case of the home for the aged, retired members and their wives.

Milroy v. Lord (1862), 4 De G.F. and J. 264   [196]
(Court of Appeal in Chancery)

M. purported to assign to the defendant fifty shares in the Louisiana Bank on trust for the plaintiff. The shares were transferable only by entry in the books of the bank. The defendant held a power of attorney authorising him to transfer M.'s shares, but he did not exercise this power and no transfer of the shares was ever made. The share certificates were held by the defendant and at M.'s death, the defendant passed the certificates to M.'s executor O. *Held*, "in order to render a voluntary settlement valid . . . the settlor must have done everything . . . necessary to be done in order to transfer the property to the persons for whom he intends to provide . . . and it will be equally effectual if he transfers the property to a trustee for the purposes of the settlement or declares that he himself holds it in trust for those purposes; and if the property be personal, the trust may . . . be declared either in writing or by parol; but in order to render the settlement binding, one or other of these modes must . . . be resorted to, for there is no equity in this court to perfect an imperfect gift" (*per* Turner, L. J.). Therefore, as the shares had not been effectually transferred to the defendant, no trust had been created.

Ministry of Health v. Simpson, [1950] 2 All E.R. 1137   [197]
(House of Lords)

This was an appeal from the Court of Appeal in the case *Re Diplock*. The facts were as stated in that case. The House of Lords considered only the claim *in personam* against the recipients from the personal representatives, and confirmed the judgments of the Court of Appeal on this claim.

Moate v. Moate, [1948] 2 All E.R. 486   [198]

In 1930 H. purchased a house which was conveyed into the name of his fiancée, W. The house was subject to a mortgage. H. and W. were later married and H. thereafter paid the mortgage instalments. The final payment was made in 1946, the receipt endorsed on the mortgage stating that repayment had been made by W. In 1947 W. commenced proceedings against H. for divorce on the ground of cruelty. H. took out a summons under the Married Women's Property Act 1882, to determine the beneficial ownership of the house. *Held*, a presumption of advancement arose in the case of a purchase by an intending husband in the name of an intending wife, provided the marriage took place. As H. had failed to rebut this presumption, W. was beneficially entitled to the house. The mortgage repayments were to be regarded as supplementary gifts and the presumption of advancement applied to these as to the original purchase.

Moon's Will Trusts, Re, Foale v. Gillians, [1948] 1 All E.R. 300   [199]

By his will, made in 1927, a testator, who died in 1928, directed that after the death of his wife, his trustees should out of the residue pay certain legacies including "£3000 to the trustees of the Gloucester Street Wesleyan Methodist Church at Davenport on trust to invest the same . . . and to apply the income thereof to mission work in the district . . . particularly John Street and Moon Street". The widow died in 1944. The district in which the street was situated had been badly damaged by bombing during the war. The church was demolished in 1941 and had not been rebuilt, and most of the houses in John Street and Moon Street were uninhabited. There was a proposal on foot that the Admiralty should take over the district under a scheme for the extension of the Davenport Dockyard, and that proposal, if carried out, would render impracticable the rebuilding of the church and the performance of mission work in the area. *Held*, (i) the term "mission work" was to be construed as meaning "Christian mission work". The gift was therefore charitable; (ii) the moment at which to determine whether a charitable purpose lapsed for impracticability was the moment when the charity trustees became absolutely entitled, *i.e.* at the moment of the testator's death, and not at the moment when it became payable (*i.e.* on the death of the widow). [Since the trust was not impracticable at the testator's death, *i.e.*, it was not "impossible *ab initio*", there was no need to produce evidence of a general charitable intention and the property could be applied *cy-près*.] The court ordered a scheme.

Morice v. Bishop of Durham (1804), 9 Ves. 399; (1805), [200] 10 Ves. 522

A testatrix bequeathed her personal property to the Bishop of Durham upon trust to pay her debts and legacies, and to dispose of the residue to "such objects of benevolence and liberality as the Bishop of Durham in his own discretion shall most approve of". The next-of-kin of the testatrix claimed that the trust failed owing to the absence of certainty as to the objects of the trust, and to the fact that objects were no̱t charitable. They claimed that the Bishop of Durham therefore held the property on a resulting trust for them. *Held*, the trust, if charitable, would not fail for lack of certainty of object. "Where a charitable purpose is expressed, however general, the bequest shall not fail on account of the uncertainty of the object; but the particular mode of application will be directed by the King in some cases, in others by this court". But in order to be charitable a gift must be framed in such a way as to be exclusively charitable. "I am not aware of any case, in which the bequest has been held to be charitable, where the testator has not either used that word, to denote his general purpose or specified some particular purpose, which this court has determined to be charitable in its nature" (*per* GRANT, M. R.). The words "objects of benevolence and liberality" were thus not charitable. The Bishop of Durham held the property on trust for the next-of-kin among whom he was directed to distribute it.

Morse v. Royal (1806), 12 Ves. 355 [201]

Vanheylin and Green were co-trustees of property for a beneficiary Morse. In 1785 Morse persuaded Vanheylin to buy his equitable interest in the trust property. Five years later the value of the property had increased and in 1790 Morse (the plaintiff) sought an order that the contract of sale to Vanheylin (the defendant) be set aside, or that Vanheylin should give him the amount by which the property had increased in value since the sale. *Held*, as Vanheylin had not acted fraudulently and as Morse had acquiesced in the sale for five years, Morse had lost the right to have the contract set aside. [Note: This case is an illustration of the maxim "Delay defeats equity".]

Moss v. Cooper (1861), 1 J. & H. 352 [202]

A testator gave his residuary estate to G., S. and O. At the time the will was made, a memorandum was prepared in the handwriting of G. to the effect that the testator had suggested that, after the residuary legatees had retained £25 each for their own use, the residue might be divided in a particular way for the benefit of certain charities. G. communicated this to S. and O. S. later told the testator he would abide by his wishes. O. made no such promise. G. died before the testator. *Held*, on a gift to two persons on the faith of a promise made by one of them before or at the time of making the will, the trust is binding on both of them. Where the will is made first, and the promise by one person made subsequently, then the person who has made the promise is bound by the trust, but the other person takes free of it. There was evidence that G. was authorised to communicate the testator's intention to S. and O., and that G. was believed by S. and O. to be so authorised. S. and O. were therefore bound by the secret trust and could not take for their own benefit.

Munton, Re, [1927] Ch. 262 [203]

A testatrix left money to trustees on trust for E. W. Munton for life, with remainder to his children in equal shares. The money was invested in War Stock. One of the trustees, Tucker, suggested that the money should be reinvested in other stock. The other trustees agreed and gave Tucker authority by a power of attorney to carry out the transaction. Tucker instructed brokers to sell the stock and reinvest half the proceeds and to give him a cheque for the balance. Tucker misappropriated the money he had received. Munton sued all the trustees for breach of trust. *Held*, as the other trustees had no reason to suspect Tucker of fraud, they were not liable for wilful default under s. 30 (1) of the Trustee Act 1925.

National Anti-Vivisection Society v. Inland Revenue [204]
Commissioners, [1947] 2 All E.R. 217 (House of Lords)

The Society claimed exemption from income tax on investment income on the ground that they were a body of persons established for charitable purposes only within the meaning of the Income Tax Act 1918. *Held*, the society was not charitable because any assumed public benefit in the advancement of morals would be far outweighed by the detriment to medical science and research and consequently to public health; and because the main object of the society was political in the promotion of legislation.

National Provincial Bank v. Ainsworth, [1965] 2 All E.R. 472 [205]
(House of Lords)

A husband deserted his wife, leaving her in occupation of the matrimonial home. The wife obtained a decree of judicial separation and permanent alimony on the basis that she was provided with rent-free accommodation. The husband later conveyed the house to a company into which his business incorporated. The company was registered as proprietor of the house at H. M. Land Registry. The company mortgaged the house to a bank, and the mortgage was duly registered. On the failure of company to repay the money advanced by the bank, the bank sought possession of the house. At the time the mortgage was created the bank was unaware that the husband had deserted the wife, and had made no enquiries as to the wife's occupation of the house. *Held*, (i) the rights of a deserted wife were personal rights and did not constitute an interest which would run with land. Thus a deserted wife could not resist a claim by a purchaser from her husband of the matrimonial home, whether the purchase took place before or after the desertion; (ii) the right of a deserted wife could not from its nature be an "overriding" interest under s. 70 of the Land Registration Act 1925. (See Matrimonial Homes Act 1967, *post*.)

Neville Estates, Ltd. v. Madden, [1961] 3 All E.R. 769 [206]

The Catford Synagogue launched an appeal to raise money to buy a house. Money was collected and a house bought. The house was conveyed to trustees by a deed which recited that the purchase moneys were the property of members of the synagogue. The lower part was used as a synagogue and the upper as the minister's residence. Later, following another appeal, other land was bought and conveyed to trustees on the same terms. On part of the land a squash court was converted into a synagogue and a communal hall was built near it. The synagogue subsequently contracted to sell part of the land to the plaintiff for £10,000. After the contract had been concluded the synagogue received other offers of up to £14,300. The Charity Commissioners informed the synagogue that they refused consent to a sale to the plaintiff for less than £14,300. The plaintiff sought specific performance of the contract for a price of £10,000, contending that the consent of the Charity Commissioners was not required because the land was not held on charitable trusts. *Held*, (i) the purchase moneys paid for the two lots of land had not belonged beneficially to the members of the synagogue, as the donors had intended the fund and land purchased with it to be held on trust for the synagogue as a quasi-corporate entity: thus the trustees held the fund and the land on trust for the purposes of the synagogue; (ii) the communal hall fulfilled a purpose which was ancillary to the religious purpose; (iii) although an unincorporated association supported by its members to provide benefits for themselves would not generally be regarded as a charity, that principle did not apply fully to trusts for religious purposes; (iv) thus the trust was charitable and the consent of the Commissioners to the sale was required.

Nisbet and Potts' Contract, Re, [1906] 1 Ch. 386 [207]
(Court of Appeal)

In 1872, K. entered into a restrictive covenant with a neighbour providing that no buildings other than private houses should be erected on K.'s land. H. obtained title to K.'s land by adverse possession and in 1878 sold the land to N. In 1903, N. agreed to sell the land to P. P. agreed not to require any evidence of N.'s title to the land beyond his conveyance from H. This conveyance did not disclose the existence of the covenant, but if P. had made enquiry as to title for the full statutory period (then 40 years) he would have discovered the existence of the covenant. P. wished to build shops on the land. The question arose whether the covenant could be enforced against him. *Held*, a restrictive covenant can be enforced against any subsequent owner of the land except a *bona fide* purchaser for value of the legal estate without notice. Such a covenant is enforceable against a squatter, both before and after he has acquired a statutory title by adverse possession. If a purchaser from a person who has acquired such a statutory title chooses to accept evidence of title for a shorter period than the statutory period he is fixed with constructive notice of all equitable interests which he would have discovered if he had made enquiries for the full period. P. was therefore bound by the covenant.

Norman, Re, Andrew v. Vine, [1947] 1 All E.R. 400 [208]

A testatrix left property " to the editors of the missionary periodical called ' Echoes of Service ' to be applied by them or him for such objects as they may think fit ". The evidence showed that the editors were in reality trustees for the missionary activities of a religious body known as the Brethren; and, further, that for many years they had distributed gifts sent to them for the charitable objects of the Brethren. *Held*, the gift was a valid gift to the editors on trust for the charitable objects of the Brethren.

North Devon and West Somerset Relief Fund Trusts, Re, Hylton v. [209] Wright, [1953] 2 All E.R. 1032

Following many deaths and great damage to property caused by floods due to torrential rain in north Devon and west Somerset, a relief fund was opened by this appeal: " We invite not only the people of the West Country, but everyone who has known and loved Lynmouth, and the quiet villages of North Devon and West Somerset, which have suffered so grievously in this disaster, to contribute to a fund for the relief of all who have suffered . . . Many holiday makers . . . have suffered grievously. These need help every bit as much as our own people and for that reason we do ask the whole country to support this fund . . . ." A large sum was collected, and it was expected that a considerable surplus would remain after all proper claims under the appeal had been met. On the questions (1) whether the fund was charitable, and (2) how any surplus should be disposed of; *Held*, (1) " . . . this appeal . . . bears the stamp of having as its authors people who had not time, if indeed the desirability ever crossed their minds, of consulting their legal advisers. In the case of a document issued in such circumstances it does not appear to me to be proper that the court should be astute to fix on any particular word or words and give to it too wide or, in some circumstances, too narrow a meaning . . . In my judgment, looking at the document as a whole, I extract from it an intention upon the part of the authors to apply money which may be subscribed at their invitation to relieve hardship and suffering which has been experienced both by what are called ' the local people ' and others who were within that area at the time of the disaster . . . I am unable to dissect this document in such a way as to discover in it, either by looseness of phrasing and therefore by inference, or by express words, any intention to benefit this part of the community in any way which the law would not regard as charitable " (*per* Winn-Parry, J.). (2) The trust was therefore disclosed a charitable intention and any surplus could therefore be applied *cy-près*.

Northern Counties of England Fire Insurance Co. v. Whipp   [210]
(1884), Ch.D. 482

C., the manager of a company, executed a legal mortgage of his own land to the company and handed over the title deeds to them. The title deeds were placed in a safe, to which there were duplicate keys, one of which was held by C. C. later removed the title deeds and executed a second mortgage to W., depositing the title deeds with her. W. was unaware that the land had already been mortgaged to the company. *Held*, " (i) the Court will postpone the prior legal estate to a subsequent equitable estate: (a), where the owner of the legal estate has assisted in or connived at the fraud which had led to the creation of a subsequent equitable estate, without notice of the prior legal estate; of which assistance or connivance, the omission to use ordinary care in the inquiry after or keeping title deeds may be, and in some cases has been, held to be sufficient evidence, where such conduct cannot otherwise be explained; (b), where the owner of the legal estate has constituted the mortgager his agent with authority to raise money, and the estate thus created has by the fraud or misconduct of the agent been represented as being the first estate. But (ii) . . . the Court will not postpone the prior legal estate to the subsequent equitable estate on the ground of any mere carelessness or want of prudence on the part of the legal owner " (*per* Fry, L. J.). The conduct of the company, although careless, was not evidence of fraud. The mortgage to the company therefore took priority over the mortgage to W.

Nottage, Re, [1895–9] All E.R. Rep. 1203 (Court of Appeal)   [211]

A testator bequeathed money to trustees on trust to purchase annually a cup to be given to the most successful racing yacht of the season, declaring that his object in giving the cup was " to encourage the sport of yacht racing ". *Held*, as a gift for the encouragement of sport was not charitable the gift was void for perpetuity.

Oatway, Re, Hertslet v. Oatway, [1903] 2 Ch. 356   [212]

O., a trustee under a will, paid certain trust money into his private bank account, which already contained some of O.'s own money. O. later purchased shares in the Oceana Company for £2137, which he paid for by a cheque drawn on his private account. After paying for the shares O. paid further sums into the account, but his subsequent drawings for his own purposes exhausted the whole amount standing to his credit. The shares were later sold for £2474. O. died insolvent. The beneficiaries under the will claimed that the proceeds of the sale of the shares should be treated as trust money. The personal representative of O. claimed that as, when O. had bought the shares, there had been sufficient of his own money in his account to pay for the shares, O. should be deemed to have used his own money to buy the shares; with the result that the shares belonged to O.'s estate. *Held*, " when the private money of the trustee and that which he held in a fiduciary capacity have been mixed in the same banking account, from which various payments have from time to time been made, then, in order to determine to whom any remaining balance or any investment that may have been paid for out of the account ought to be deemed to belong, the trustee must be debited with all the sums that have been withdrawn and applied to his own use so as to be no longer recoverable, and the trust money in like manner debited with any sums taken out and duly invested in the names of the proper trustees. The order of priority in which the various withdrawals and investments may have been respectively made is wholly immaterial" (*per* JOYCE, J.). Thus the £2474 was trust money.

Ogilvie, Re, Ogilvie v. Ogilvie, [1918] 1 Ch. 492   **[213]**

A testatrix, who died domiciled in England, left property in Paraguay to trustees on trust for sale for charitable purposes, and property in England to her heirs. By Paraguayan law the gift to charity was valid only as to one-fifth, the other four-fifths passing to the testatrix's heirs. *Held*, the heirs must elect to take under the will (and retain the English property, but give their four-fifths share in the proceeds of sale to the trustees) or against the will (and retain the four-fifths share in the proceeds of sale, but compensate the trustees to the extent of this share).

Oldham, Re, Hadwen v. Myles, [1924] All E.R. Rep. 288   **[214]**

In 1907 a husband and wife made mutual wills in the same form in pursuance of an agreement to make them in this way. Each gave his or her property to the other absolutely with the same alternative provisions in the case of lapse. There was no evidence of any further agreement in the matter. The husband died in 1914 and his widow received his property under his will. The widow subsequently married again, and made a fresh will which departed entirely from her 1907 will, giving a life interest in a large portion of her estate to her second husband and the remainder of her estate almost entirely to her own relatives. She died in 1922. The plaintiff, who was entitled to a portion of the residue under the mutual wills, sought a declaration that the executors of the wife's second will held the estate on the trusts set out in the wife's mutual will of 1907. *Held*, an implied trust will not be presumed from the simultaneous execution of virtually identical wills, but must be proved by independent evidence of an agreement not merely to make identical wills but to dispose of the property in a particular way. There was no evidence of such an agreement and thus there was no implied trust which prevented the wife from disposing of her property as she pleased.

Oppenheim v. Tobacco Securities Trust Co., Ltd., [1951]   **[215]**
1 All E.R. 31 (House of Lords)

The Tobacco Securities Trust Co., Ltd., held certain investments on trust to apply the income "in providing for the . . . education of children of employees or former employees" of British American Tobacco Co., Ltd. *Held*, a class of persons determined by applying a test of relationship with a given person or body is not a section of the public for the purpose of satisfying the requirement that for a gift to be charitable it must be for the "public benefit". The trust was thus not charitable, and so failed for perpetuity. (See also *Inland Revenue Commissioners* v. *Educational Grants Association, Ltd.*)

Ottaway v. Norman, [1971] 3 All E.R. 1325   **[216]**

A testator, T., owned a bungalow where he lived with his house-keeper, H. T. and H. had lived together as man and wife for many years. W., T.'s son by his former (deceased) wife visited T. and H. often. On one of W.'s visits T. told him in H.'s presence that it was his intention that H. should have the bungalow for the rest of her life but that she should leave it to W. on her death. H. agreed to this plan. In March 1960 T. made his will by which he devised the bungalow to H. in fee simple. Between the date of the will and his death in 1963 T. discussed future plans for the bungalow with H. and W. on a number of occasions. These discussions always proceeded on the assumption that the bungalow would pass to W. on H.'s death. Immediately after T.'s death H. made a will whereby she devised and bequeathed all her real and personal property to W. and his wife. In 1966 H. made a new will whereby she appointed N., who had since T.'s death become a close friend, to be her executor but made no alteration to the dispositions under the previous will. In 1967, following a minor disagreement with W., H. made what proved to be her last will in which she left the bungalow to N. and his wife, and her residuary estate to W. and N. in equal shares. Following H.'s death in January 1968, W. and his wife O. claimed a declaration that the bungalow was held by N., and H.'s executor, on trust for them absolutely. *Held*, there was clear evidence that it was T.'s intention that H. should be obliged to dispose of the bungalow at her death in favour of W., that the testator had communicated that intention to H., and that she had accepted it. Accordingly N., as H.'s executor, was bound by a secret trust and held the bungalow on trust for W. and O. absolutely.

Oughtred v. Inland Revenue Commissioners, [1959] [217]
3 All E.R. 623 (House of Lords)

Trustees held certain shares on trust for a mother for life, with remainder to her son absolutely. On June 18, 1956 the mother and son agreed orally that the son should transfer his interest to his mother in exchange for certain other shares owned by the mother. The son authorised the trustees to transfer the shares to the mother "to the intent that her life interest should be enlarged into absolute ownership" in a deed of release dated June 26 between the son, the mother and the trustees. On the same date the trustees transferred the shares by deed to the mother. The Commissioners claimed that the transfer was "a conveyance or transfer on sale of any property" under the Stamp Act 1891, and so attracted *ad valorem* stamp duty on the value of the consideration. *Held*, as a result of the transaction the mother had acquired the son's interest as effectively as if he had conveyed it to her direct. Every transfer by which an agreement for sale was implemented was liable to stamp duty on the value of the consideration. The deed of release constituted such a transfer and the transaction thus attracted *ad valorem* stamp duty.

Overton v. Banister (1844), 3 Hare 503 [218]

An infant, who was entitled to receive a sum of money from trustees on attaining full age, obtained the sum from the trustees by fraudulently misrepresenting herself to be of full age. *Held*, the infant could not compel the trustees to pay the sum over again on attaining full age.

Owen, Re, Slater v. Owen, [1912] 1 Ch. 519 [219]

A testator left residuary property on trust for sale and conversion, with discretion to postpone sale and conversion, and directed that the proceeds of sale should be invested in authorised securities and held on trust for his wife for life with remainder to his sons. The will contained no direction as to whether or not the tenant for life was to be paid the income *in specie* pending conversion. The property consisted largely of unauthorised securities, some of which paid more than 4% interest and some less. *Held*, the wife was entitled to receive interest at 4% *p.a.* on the aggregate value of all the unauthorised securities at the testator's death.

Oxford Group v. Inland Revenue Commissioners, [1949] [220]
2 All E.R. 537 (Court of Appeal)

The memorandum of association of the Oxford Group set out the following objects of the company:—

"3 (A) The advancement of the Christian religion, and, in particular, . . . in accordance with the principles of the Oxford Group Movement . . .

(B) The maintenance, support, development and assistance of the Oxford group in every way . . .
(C) To establish . . . any charitable or benevolent associations . . ., and to subscribe . . . money for charitable or benevolent purposes in any way connected with the purposes of the association . . ."
The company sought exemption from income tax on the ground that it was a body of persons established for charitable purposes only. *Held*, (i) the words in 3 (B) extended beyond purely religious activities and authorised the expenditure of funds on matters which were not charitable, and, therefore, the company was not formed for charitable purposes only; (ii) the objects set out in 3 (C) were not merely ancillary to the main objects in (A) and (B), but themselves conferred powers on the company which were so wide that they could not be regarded as charitable.

Paradise Motor Co. Ltd., Re, [1968] 2 All E.R. 625 (Court of Appeal)   **[221]**

In 1948, W. executed a transfer of 350 shares owned by him in a private company to J., his stepson. What appeared to be, but what was not, J.'s signature appeared on the transfer. J.'s name was entered in the company's register of members. In 1954, W. having fallen out with J., wished to take back 300 of the shares and for this purpose procured a purported transfer to himself of 300 shares which appeared to bear J.'s signature. The register of members was altered accordingly. In 1964 the company was wound up and there was a surplus of £12,000 for distribution. The liquidator informed J. that he was registered as the holder of 50 shares in the company. J., who until then had known nothing of the shares, nor of the purported transfers of 1948 and 1954 said he did not claim to be a shareholder of the company. In 1966 he confirmed, when speaking to a half-brother, that he laid no claim to the shares. Later, he changed his mind, and claimed to be entitled to 350 shares in the company and to share in the liquidation. The company's articles of association provided that " the transfer of a share shall be in writing signed by both the transferor and the transferee ". Before falling out with J., W. had treated him in the same way as he treated his own three sons. *Held*, (1) the relationship between W. and J. was such as to give rise to a presumption of advancement in favour of J., and W. was therefore to be presumed to have intended a gift of the 350 shares to J. (See *Bennet* v. *Bennet, ante.*) (2) For the purpose of complying with the company's articles of association, the fact that J. had not signed the transfer was an unessential matter. W. was therefore to be treated as having done everything necessary on his part to complete the gift, and thus the gift of the shares to J. had been effective. (See *Re Rose post.*) (3) J.'s statement to his half-brother in 1966 had showed that he was in no circumstances accepting entitlement to any shares and constituted a disclaimer by him of the gift. (4) Such disclaimer operated by way of avoidance and not of disposition, and therefore did not need to be evidenced in writing signed by the donee under s. 53 of the Law of Property Act 1925. (5) That a disclaimer of a gift made *inter vivos* could not be withdrawn. (W. was therefore entitled to the proportion of the £12,000 attributable to 350 shares.)

Pardoe, Re, McLaughlin v. A.-G., [1906] 2 Ch. 184   **[222]**

A testatrix, who died in 1903, bequeathed (1) £200 to the vicar and church-wardens of the parish of Cirencester, the income to be distributed annually at Christmas as to the sum of 1s. to the ringers of the church who should ring a peal of bells on the anniversary of the restoration of the monarchy in commemoration of that event: (2) £700 to the vicar and churchwardens of the parish of Bitterly, the income to be applied (among other things) in the erection and maintenance of headstones to the graves of pensioners in the almshouses at Bitterly Church: (3) the residue to trustees on trust to pay and distribute the same amongst " such public charities and institutions or for such charitable purposes for the public advantage " as the trustees should think fit. *Held*, regarding (1) " . . . the object of the gift was that the restoration of the monarchy should be brought back to the memories of those who listened to the ringing of the bells, and the testatrix speaks of it as a happy restoration, about which, of course, no Englishman can express a doubt at the present moment. The notion of the testator evidently is that it shall bring back happy thoughts; and, seeing that this is to be brought about by listening to a peal of bells rung in a church tower, I think that those happy thoughts necessarily connote a feeling of gratitude to the Giver of all good gifts. I think I can see that in the testatrix's mind, as expressed in her words. If that is so I do not think there is any doubt that it is a good charitable gift ". (2) " The object here is to make the grave neat; to show what it is; nothing more . . . I venture to say . . . that the headstone has not fallen into such disuse that it may not be regarded . . . as a proper way of marking a grave . . . and adding to the decency and repair of the churchyard." Regarding (3) " But the great point, to my mind, is that she says ' or for such charitable purposes '. It seems to me impossible to construe that language as comprising anything which was not charitable. It seems to me that if these trustees were to select, assuming that it is possible to select, a public institution which is not charitable, then they would be doing that which the will does not allow, and that charity must really govern their selection. It is all coloured with the notion of charity." (*Per* KEKEWICH, J.) All three bequests were therefore charitable.

Parry, Re, Brown v. Parry, [1946] 2 All E.R. 412   [223]

A testator left residuary property on trust for sale and conversion, with discretion to postpone sale and conversion, for persons in succession. The will contained no direction as to whether or not the tenant for life was to be paid the income *in specie* pending conversion. The property included securities invested in a manner not authorised by the investment clause in the will. *Held*, the tenant for life was entitled to receive interest at 4% *p.a.* of the value of the unauthorised securities at the testator's death. Where no power is given by a testator to postpone conversion, the proper date for a valuation is one year after the testator's death.

Partington, Re, Partington v. Allen (1887), 57 L.T. 654   [224]

A testator left money to trustees (a solicitor and the testator's widow) on trust for the widow for life with remainders over. The testator directed that the money should be invested on the security of freehold or leasehold property. The solicitor, whom the testator had directed should be entitled to professional charges, undertook the investment of the money and employed valuers to value certain properties on the security of which it was proposed to advance trust money. In instructing the valuers the solicitor failed to inform them that, under the rule then current, it was not desired to lend more than one-half the value. Further, the solicitor failed to instruct the valuers to ascertain whether the particulars submitted by the mortgagors were correct, and failed to draw the attention of the valuers to circumstances which might have affected the value. The valuers expressed the opinion that a sum of more than one half might be advanced on the properties, and such a sum was advanced. The mortgagors later went bankrupt. On the sale of the properties a loss resulted to the trust fund. *Held*, (i) the trustees were jointly and severally liable for the loss, on the grounds that the investment was unauthorised, and that they had been negligent in giving instructions to the valuers and in acting on the valuations received; (ii) as the solicitor had been acting as solicitor to the trust, and as the breach of trust had been committed on his advice, the widow was entitled to be indemnified by the solicitor.

Pauling's Settlement Trusts, Re, Younghusband v. Coutts & Co. [225]
(No. 1), [1963] 3 All E.R. 1

Under a settlement made in 1919, income from a trust fund was held on trust for a mother for life with remainder to her children or remoter issue. There were three sons of the marriage, F., G. and A.; and one daughter. By clause 11 of the settlement, C. & Co., a bank, who were the trustees, were empowered with the written consent of the mother to raise any part " not exceeding in the whole one half . . . share of any child . . . and to pay the same to him or her for his or her absolute use or pay or apply the same for his or her advancement or otherwise for his or her benefit in such manner as the trustees shall think fit ". All advances hereinafter mentioned were made by the bank under this clause with the consent of the mother. After the war of 1939–45, the family lived above their means, and the father was always in need of money. In 1948 the father was seeking a means of obtaining a house in the Isle of Man, and counsel advised that advances could be made to F. and G., who could then if they wished settle the property purchased on the mother for life and on themselves after her death. F. and G. were then over twenty-one years of age. The bank advanced £8450, (" advance A "), the price of the house, to F. and G. on a written request from the mother and with the written authority of F. and G., who elected not to be separately advised. Contrary to the legal advice previously given but with the knowledge of the bank and without the consent of F. and G., the house purchased was conveyed to the father and the mother and was not settled. It was subsequently mortgaged by the father for £5000 and ultimately was sold for less than that sum, so that the sons lost the whole of the £8450. On the advice of the bank's solicitor a sum of £1000 was advanced (" advance B "), in respect of F.'s and G.'s shares, with their assent, for the purchase of furniture. This was credited to the mother's account with the bank. At that time the bank did not know that the house would not be settled. Subsequently £2600 was advanced (" advance C ") to F. and G. and applied in paying off a loan which the bank as trustees of another settlement had advanced to the mother, the two sons being assigned insurance policies on the mother's life, these policies having a surrender value of £650. The sons had separate advice, but the transaction as carried out was not as originally advised, the difference being to the son's disadvantage. In 1949, at the father's instance, the bank advanced to F. and Co. £200 (" advance D "), which was paid to the mother's account; this was done with the written consent of the sons, stating that they appreciated that the money was being used for improvements to the property in the Isle of Man belonging to the mother. The sons had no separate advice. At that time G. was 23; E. was 28 but mentally ill (though the bank did not know this) and was living with his grandmother. Subsequently sums amounting to £3260 (" advance E ") were advanced by the bank in respect of the daughter's share, nominally for furnishing a house which had been bought for the family in Chelsea, but in fact the money was spent on the property in the Isle of Man or was applied to reduce the mother's overdraft, the bank not seeing any bills for the expenditure. The daughter, who was under 21, requested that the advances should be made, well knowing that only £300 was being used for furniture. She conceded that the £300 was not recoverable by her. Later, a total of £6500 (" advance F ") was advanced by the bank to the youngest son, A, and was paid into his mother's account. A. was then just 21. He consented to this step, but had no proper separate advice. In 1958 the four children brought an action against the bank for breach of trust, each suing to recover only advances purported to have been made to him or her or for his or her benefit. In addition to pleading by way of defence the consent of beneficiaries, the bank pleaded the Limitation Act 1939, and the defences of laches and acquiescence, and claimed relief under s. 61 of the Trustee Act 1925. Held, (1) the bank's liability was to be determined according to the following principles. (a) The power under clause 11 to raise a part of the share of a child and to pay it to the child " for his or her own absolute use " could only be exercised for the benefit of the child to be advanced, *viz.*, if there were a good reason for the advance and if it would be beneficial to the child. (b) When making an advance for a particular stated purpose, the bank could properly pay it to the child advanced if the bank reasonably thought that the child could be trusted to carry out the prescribed purpose, but the bank could not properly leave the child entirely free, legally and morally, to apply the sum for that purpose or to spend it in any way that he or she chose, without any responsibility on their part to enquire as to its application. (c) If trust money were advanced for an express purpose, the child advanced was under a duty to carry out that purpose and could not properly apply it to another purpose, and, if any misapplication came to the bank's notice, they could not safely make further advances for a particular purpose without making sure that the money was applied for that purpose. (d) A trustee who carried out a transaction in breach of trust with the beneficiary's apparent consent might yet be liable if the trustee knew or ought to have known that the beneficiary was acting under the undue influence of another or might be presumed to have so acted. (e) For the purpose of (d) above the presumption of undue influence of a parent over his child endures for a time, which may be defined as a " short " time, after the child has attained twenty-one, the duration being in each case a question of fact. (f) Where a bank undertook to act as a paid trustee, and placed itself in a position where its duty as trustee conflicted with its interest as banker, the court should be very slow to grant relief under s. 61 of the Trustee Act 1925. (2) The bank were in breach of trust in making all the advances. Relief under s. 61 of the Trustee Act 1961 was granted in respect of (C.) above. The consent of the beneficiaries afforded a defence in the case of (D.). The bank was liable in the case of (A.), (B.), (C.), (E.), and (F.) above. (3) The Limitation Act 1939, did not afford a defence because the plaintiffs' interest was a future interest within the proviso to s. 19 (2) and did not fall into possession when an invalid advance was made; accordingly the plaintiffs' rights were preserved by the proviso to s. 19 (2). (4) In view of the express statutory provision of a period of limitation for the plaintiffs' claim there was no room for the equitable doctrine of laches; and having regard to the many matters to be explored before instituting an action the four years that had elapsed between the plaintiffs' discovery of what their rights were and the issue of the writ did not establish a defence of acquiescence on their part.

Pauling's Settlement, Re, Younghusband v. Coutts & Co. (No. 2), [226] [1963] 1 All E.R. 857

The plaintiffs brought an action against a bank, Coutts & Co. alleging that the bank, as trustees, had improperly paid out capital by way of advancement to beneficiaries and claiming that the amount be made good to the trust fund of the settlement. At the trial it was ordered, among other matters, that two or more persons should be appointed trustees of the settlement under s. 41 of the Trustee Act 1925, in place of the bank. An appeal and cross-appeal in the action were pending. The bank objected to the appointment of new trustees at that stage on the grounds, among others, that the bank's right by way of impounding the interest of the life tenant in the trust fund or the income of the trust fund would be imperilled if new trustees were appointed forthwith and if the fund were handed over to them; further that if the trust fund were transferred to new trustees, the bank would be deprived of the security of the trust fund for costs that might be awarded on the appeal, and that, although deprived of the trust fund, the bank would remain liable for possible future estate duty in respect of advances. *Held*, (1) no valid objection to the appointment of new trustees arose out of the bank's right to impound the life tenant's interest or to be recouped out of income of the trust fund, because (a) the equitable right of a trustee, who has committed a breach of trust at the instigation of a beneficiary, that the beneficiary's interest should be impounded or that the trustee should be recouped by the beneficiary, did not depend on the trustee's being in actual possession of the trust fund, but was by way of indemnity to the trustee; (b) a trustee's right of indemnity under s. 62 of the Trustee Act 1925, by way of the impounding of the interest of a beneficiary who instigated a breach of trust (or consented in writing thereto) extended, on the true construction of s. 62, in favour of a former trustee who committed the breach of trust. (2) An order for the appointment of new trustees would not, however, be made for the time being, having regard particularly to the two following grounds of objection: (a) the bank as trustees were entitled to have security for the substantial costs that might be payable to the bank as result of the decision of the appeal, and to vest the trust fund in new trustees would deprive the bank of that security, and (b) until the appeal was determined, it was not possible to predicate with certainty that, if new trustees were constituted, the bank could not thereafter be under liability, as trustees at or after the time when advances were made to the sons of the life tenant, in respect of estate duty at her death on the sums advanced, such liability being possible by reason of the Finance Acts 1894, 1940, and 1950.

Peel's Settlement, Re, Biddulph v. Peel, [1911] 2 Ch. 165   [227]

By his will, P., the donee of a special power of appointment, appointed certain property equally among his children who should be living at his death. P. later appointed a one-seventh share each to his children F. P. and E. P. When P. died he was survived by seven children. *Held*, under the rule against double portions, the appointments in the will to F. P. and E. P. were adeemed by the subsequent *inter vivos* appointments to them and they were therefore not entitled to any further share under the will.

Penn v. Lord Baltimore (1750), 1 Ves. Sen. 444   [228]

Following a dispute between the provinces of Pennsylvania and Maryland, articles were entered into in England between Penn and Lord Baltimore concerning the boundaries of the two provinces. The articles provided for the appointment of commissioners to determine a boundary line. *Held*, for a court of equity to have jurisdiction, it is not necessary for the *res*, the property in dispute, to be within reach of the courts' authority, but it is necessary for the person against whom an order is to be made to be within the jurisdiction (*per* LORD HARDWICKE) "for the strict primary decree in this court, as a court of equity, is in *personam*". The defendant was in England and the court ordered specific performance.

Perrins v. Bellamy, [1899] 1 Ch. 797 (Court of Appeal)   [229]

Trustees of a settlement, erroneously assuming that they had a power of sale, sold leaseholds comprised in the settlement and thereby diminished the income of the plaintiff, who, as tenant for life, was entitled to the rents and profits *in specie*. The tenant for life sought to make the trustees liable for the diminution of income. *Held*, as the trustees had acted honestly and reasonably, they were entitled under s. 3 of the Judicial Trustee Act 1896 (now s. 61, Trustee Act 1925) to be relieved from personal liability in respect of the breach of trust.

Pettingall v. Pettingall (1842), 11 L.J. Ch. 176   [230]

A testator made the following bequest: " Having a favourite black mare, I hereby bequeath, that at my death, £50 *p.a.* be paid for her in some park in England or Wales; her shoes to be taken off, and she never to be ridden or put in harness; and that my executor consider himself in honour bound to fulfil my wish .... At her death all payment to cease." *Held*, that so much of the £50 as was required to keep the mare comfortably was to be applied by the executor for that purpose, and that the executor was entitled to any surplus. The executor was to give information, when required, about the mare. If the mare was not properly attended to, any of the parties interested in the residue might apply to the court.

Phillips' Trusts, Re, [1903] 1 Ch. 183   [231]

Miss M. was entitled, under the will of a testator, J. P., who died in 1850, to a share of a trust fund in reversion on the death of her mother. In 1882 in contemplation of her marriage Miss M. settled her existing and any after-acquired property upon certain trusts. This settlement was prepared by a solicitor, G. L. P., who was one of the trustees of J. P.'s will; the other trustees of the will being J. G. and H. M. T. In 1887, J. G. and G. L. P. being dead, two other persons were appointed trustees in their place. In 1894 Mrs. M. (*née* Miss M.) assigned her reversionary interest under the will to the Law Life Assurance Society. Prior to the assignment the Society had enquired from the trustees of the will as to whether they had received notice of any dealings by Mrs. M. with her reversionary interest. The Society was not informed of the settlement of 1882, none of the then existing trustees ever having received notice of it. The Society gave notice to the trustees of the assignment to them by Mrs. M. Mrs. M. survived her mother and died in 1901 leaving one daughter who was now the sole beneficiary under the settlement of 1882. The Society claimed priority over the beneficiary under the settlement. *Held*, as notice of the settlement had been given to only one of several trustees of the settlement, and as that trustee had not communicated that notice to any of the others in office at the time of the settlement, the notice was ineffective in relation to transactions effected after the death or retirement of the trustee who had received the notice. The Society, having given notice, therefore took priority.

Phillipson v. Gatty (1850), 7 Hare 516   [232]

Trustees sold an authorised investment and purchased an unauthorised investment. *Held*, the trustees must replace the authorised investment and were liable for the difference between the price obtained on the sale of the authorised investment, and the cost of purchasing the same investment again.

Phipps v. Lovegrove (1873), L.R. 16 Eq. 80   [233]

On her marriage in 1834 L. M. conveyed property to three trustees on trust for herself for life, with remainder to the children of the marriage, or if there were none, if she should die in her husband's lifetime, as she should appoint. Before the marriage the husband had incurred a debt to A. D. In 1843 the wife appointed that if there should be no child of the marriage, and if she should die in the husband's lifetime, the trustees of the settlement should make a payment out of the trust fund sufficient to pay the husband's debt to A. D. Notice of the appointment to A. D. was given to the two surviving trustees of the settlement of 1834. In 1848 three new trustees were appointed, one of whom later died. The surviving trustees E. P. and H. H. sold out part of the trust fund. Part of the proceeds was used to purchase leasehold property in Camberwell and part was paid to L. M. In 1863 E. P. died. In 1870 L. M. died without having had any child. The husband survived. In May 1870 the sole surviving trustee H. H. received notice from R. L. of a charge made by L. M. in 1864 of the leasehold property in R. L.'s favour. In October 1870 H. H. received notice of the appointment of 1843. H. H. sought the direction of the court as to distribution of the trust property. A. D. claimed that if there was insufficient to satisfy the husband's debt to her, H. H. and E. P.'s estate should be ordered to make good the deficiency. *Held*, A. D. took priority over R. L. (See *Re Wasdale*.) A. D. was entitled to the funds which remained in part satisfaction of the debt owed. H. H. and E. P.'s estate were not liable to make good the money which had been advanced to L. M., as A. D. had failed to give fresh notice to the fresh trustees appointed in 1848.

Pilcher v. Rawlins (1872), 11 Eq. 53   **[234]**
(Court of Appeal in Chancery)

In 1851 P. and his co-trustees lent money, which they held on trust, to R. on the security of the mortgage of certain property. The documents of title to the property were delivered to P. In 1856, by which time he had become the sole surviving trustee, P. reconveyed the property to R., in consideration of a payment to him by R. The deed of reconveyance discharged the mortgage on the property, and P. and R., who were both solicitors, made out an abstract of title which showed R. as the fee simple owner and omitted any reference to the mortgage and reconveyance. R. then created a legal mortgage of the property to S. and L. The money advanced by S. and L. on the security of the mortgage was shared by P. and R. The beneficiaries under the trust, on discovering the fraud, claimed priority over S. and L. *Held*, S. and L. as *bona fide* purchasers of the legal estate for value, without notice of the equitable interests of the beneficiaries, took free of those interests.

Pilkington v. Inland Revenue Commissioners, [1962] 3 All E.R. 662 **[235]**
(House of Lords)

By his will made in 1934, a testator who died in 1935, gave his residuary estate to trustees on protective trusts for all his nephews and nieces living at his death in equal shares for life (with a direction that their consent to any exercise by the trustees of any applicable power of advancement should not cause a forfeiture of their interests under the protective trusts), and after the death of a nephew or niece, for his or her children or remoter issue as he or she should appoint and in default of appointment for his or her children at 21. The will contained no provision replacing or excluding the power of advancement conferred by s. 32 of the Trustee Act 1925. One of the testator's nephews had an infant daughter. The trustees wished to exercise the statutory power of advancement in her favour in order to avoid estate duty. They proposed to advance up to one half of her expectant share and with the money advanced create a fresh trust under which the income was to be applied for the child's maintenance until she was 21. From then until she was 30 the income was to be paid to her, and when she was 30 the capital was to be hers absolutely. If she should die under 30, the capital was to be held on trust for her children who should attain 21. The trustees took out a summons to determine whether they could lawfully exercise the power of appointment in this way. *Held*, (1) s. 32 did not restrict the width of the manner or the purpose of an advancement. In particular, provided the advancement was for the benefit of the person in whose favour it was made, it was no objection that other persons benefited incidentally as a result of the advancement, nor that the money advanced was settled on fresh trusts. (2) But the exercise of a statutory power of advancement which took form of creating a fresh settlement was analogous to the exercise of a special power of appointment and, as such, was subject to the perpetuity rule governing the exercise of special powers of appointment. The grant of what was to be treated for the purpose of perpetuities as a special power of appointment was contained in the testator's will, the new settlement being created by the operation of a fiduciary power which " belonged " to the old settlement established by the will. This being so, the new settlement proposed by the trustee infringed the perpetuity rule (since, under the perpetuity rule at common law, property appointed under a special power must be bound to vest, if it vests at all, within a perpetuity period determined from the time when the grant came into operation, *i.e.* the testator's death. The provision in favour of the daughter's children which was to take effect in the event of the daughter dying under 30 was not bound to vest within the perpetuity period determined at the testator's death.) Thus the exercise of the power of advancement proposed by the trustees could not lawfully be made.

Pilkington's Will Trusts, Re, [1959] 2 All E.R. 623   **[236]**

Trustees of a trust fund established by a testator's will, wished to exercise a statutory power of advancement in favour of a beneficiary for the purpose of avoiding death duties. *Held*, they were entitled to do so.

Pinion, Re, Westminster Bank, Ltd. v. Pinion, [1964] 1 All E.R. 890 **[237]**
(Court of Appeal)

A testator by his will and codicils gave his freehold studio and his pictures, one of which he attributed to Lely and some of which were painted by himself, his antique furniture and some silver, china and miniatures, etc. to be offered to the National Trust to be kept intact in the studio and maintained as a collection, and, if the Trust declined the gift, he authorised his executors to appoint trustees to carry it out. He gave his residuary estate as an endowment to maintain the collection. The National Trust declined the gift. There was expert evidence that the collection was of low quality, that the one picture stated by the testator to be the work of Lely was not by that master, that the studio was squalid and that the testator's pictures were bad, but that among the furniture were a dozen or so genuine English and continental pieces of the seventeenth and eighteenth centuries which perhaps might be acceptable as a gift to a minor provincial museum. The experts were of opinion that the collection as a whole had no educational value. *Held*, (1) where the educational value of a gift made for a purpose which it was sought to uphold as a valid charitable purpose, that is, as being for the advancement of education was in question, expert evidence, on the quality of the gift was admissible to assist the court in judging the educational value of the gift. In the present case the few pieces of furniture and articles of minor merit were insufficient to give educational value to the gift as a whole, since they would be stifled by worthless articles, if the whole collection were exhibited, and a selective exhibition of the articles of merit would not comply with the terms of the gift, which provided that the collection should be kept intact. The gift was not for the advancement of education, was not charitable and so failed.

Pitcairn, Re, Brandreth v. Colvin, [1896] 2 Ch. 199   **[238]**

A testator left his property to trustees on trust for his mother for life with remainder to other persons. He gave the trustees a discretionary power to sell any part of the property if they considered it expedient. The testator's property included of a reversionary interest (an interest in remainder on the death of his mother), which the trustees did not sell during the mother's life. *Held*, the discretionary power of sale given to the trustees was a sufficient indication of intention to exclude the rule in *Howe* v. *Dartmouth*, and the personal representative of the mother was not entitled on her death to claim what would have accrued to the mother if the conversion had been made.

Pledge v. White, [1896] A.C. 187 (House of Lords)   **[239]**

Banks was the owner of seven houses and he mortgaged these houses to different persons. He subsequently created a second mortgage on the houses by assigning his equity of redemption to Pledge. Later the (first) mortgages all became vested in White. Pledge then sought to redeem the mortgage of one house. White argued that he must at the same time redeem the mortgages on the other six houses (*i.e.* White claimed the right to consolidate). *Held*, White was entitled to consolidate. "It has long been settled that the right of consolidation may be exercised by the transferee of the mortgages as well as by the original mortgagee, and may be exercised in respect of equitable mortgages as well as by a mortgagee holding the legal estate absolute at law; and on the other hand that it may be asserted against the assignee of an equity of redemption from the mortgagor as well as against the mortgagor himself" (*per* LORD DAVEY).

Plumtre's Marriage Settlement, Re, Underhill v. Plumptre,   [240]
[1910] 1 Ch. 609

In 1878 a husband and wife on their marriage covenanted with the trustees of their marriage settlement to settle any property subsequently acquired by the wife on the usual trusts for the wife and the husband successively for life, then for the issue of the marriage, with an ultimate trust in favour of the next-of-kin. In 1884 the husband purchased some stock in the wife's name. The wife later sold this and purchased other stock with the proceeds. When she died in 1909 the stock amounted to £1125. The wife died intestate and without issue. The husband obtained administration of the estate. *Held*, (i) the covenant to settle a property subsequently acquired by the wife extended to the gift of property by the husband to the wife; (ii) the next-of-kin, being volunteers, and not being parties to the covenant, could not enforce the covenant against the husband (as the wife's administrator); (iii) the trustees of the settlement could not sue for breach of the covenant as the claim was statute-barred.

Plunkett v. Lewis (1844), 3 Hare 316   [241]

A fund, which was held on trust for a father with remainder to his son and daughter, was sold and the proceeds received (in breach of trust) by the father. Subsequently, on the marriage of the daughter, the father settled property for her benefit of a larger value than the amount which she would have received under the trust. *Held*, the settlement of property by the father was (not withstanding the daughter's ignorance of the father's breach of trust) to be presumed to be in satisfaction of the claim by the daughter against the father in respect of her interest in the trust fund.

Pooley v. Quilter (1858), 2 De G. & J. 327   [242]

P., a creditor of H., a bankrupt, sold his claim against H. to W. P. later discovered that W. had purchased as trustee for Q., the assignee in bankruptcy of H. P. sought to have the sale to W. set aside. *Held*, the sale must be set aside and Q. must refund to the bankrupt's estate dividends received by him. The rules as to a purchase by a trustee from his *cestui que* trust applied with still greater force to a purchase, for his own benefit, by an assignee of a bankrupt's estate from a creditor of the estate.

Porter, Re, Porter v. Porter, [1925] 1 Ch. 746   [243]

A testator left £10,000 to the trustees of a masonic temple erected by him in memory of his son, and directed that the money was to be invested and the income applied to the maintenance of the masonic temple, and the balance (if any) to be applied in favour of any masonic charities which the trustees might select. The temple was used for masonic ceremonies and meetings of a social and business nature. *Held*, (1) the decisions in the " tomb cases " that a trust for the upkeep of a tomb might constitute a valid trust of imperfect obligation were inapplicable to an institution of this character. (See *Re Chardon, Re Dalziel, Re Endacott, Re Hooper, Re Pardoe, Re Tylers' F. T.*). (2) Since the gift in favour of the temple was void (being a trust of imperfect obligation) and since the Court was not entitled to determine what amount of income would have been needed to maintain the temple, the whole legacy was void for uncertainty.

Power's Settlement Trusts, Re, [1951] 2 All E.R. 513   [244]
(Court of Appeal)

Under clause 16 of a settlement the power of appointing new trustees was vested in P., who was also tenant for life. P. purported to appoint himself to be an additional trustee. It was not disputed that the power referred to in clause 16 was the statutory power contained in s. 36 (6) of the Trustee Act 1925. *Held*, the person authorised by s. 36 (6) of the Trustee Act 1925, to appoint an additional trustee may not appoint himself to be an additional trustee.

Protheroe v. Protheroe, [1968] 1 W.L.R. 519 (Court of Appeal) **[245]**

In 1954 H. acquired the leasehold of the matrimonial home. H. held the lease on trust for himself and his wife, W. In 1964, following separation from W., H. purchased the freehold by borrowing money on mortgage. After the property had been sold, W. claimed to be entitled equally with H. to the proceeds of sale. *Held,* as H. was trustee of both W's and his own interest in the lease when H. acquired the freehold (under the rule in *Keech* v. *Sandford, post*) the freehold became trust property in which W. had an equal interest with H., subject to the expenses incurred by H. in purchasing the freehold.

Pugh's Will Trusts, Re, Marten v. Pugh, [1967] 3 All E.R. 337 **[246]**

By this will a testator appointed M. trustee of his will, and devised and bequeathed the residue of his state to M. absolutely, directing him " to dispose of the same in accordance with any letters or memoranda I may leave with this my will and otherwise in such manner as he may in his absolute discretion think fit ". The testator left no letters or memoranda with his will. *Held,* the direction imposed on M. a fiduciary obligation in the nature of a trust. As no letters or memoranda had been found, the residuary estate was held on trust for undefined objects. That trust was void for uncertainty and accordingly the estate was held on trust for the testator's next-of-kin.

Pullan v. Koe, [1911–13] All E.R. Rep. 334 **[247]**

A marriage settlement of 1859 contained a covenant by the husband and the wife for the settlement of after-acquired property of the wife beyond a certain value. The wife subsequently received a present of a sum of money of more than the stipulated amount, which was paid into the husband's bank account in breach of the covenant part of it being invested in certain bonds. The bonds remained at the bank until the husband's death in 1909, and then passed into the possession of his executors. The trustees of the marriage settlement claimed delivery up of the bonds. There were several children of the marriage. *Held,* the money was bound by the covenant from the time it was received by the wife, and was subject to the trust of the settlement. The trust was enforceable by persons within the marriage consideration (the children) unless it had passed to a *bona fide* purchaser. The trustees were therefore entitled to recover the bonds from the husband's executor.

Ralli's Will Trusts, Re, [1963] 3 All E.R. 940 **[248]**

In 1892 T. made a will leaving his residue on trust for his wife for life and then to his children absolutely. T. died in March 1899, leaving a widow and two daughters, H. and I. In 1924 H. covenanted in her marriage settlement to settlement to settle all her "existing and after-acquired property" on certain trusts which, in the event, failed, and ultimately on trust for the children of I. The settlement declared that all the property comprised within the terms of the covenant to settle existing and after-acquired property should " become subject in equity to the settlement hereby covenanted to be made ". I.'s husband was appointed one of the trustees of the settlement. In 1946 I's husband was also appointed a trustee of T's will. In 1956, H. died and in 1961 T.'s widow died. I.'s husband was the sole surviving trustee of both T.'s will and H.'s settlement. Did I.'s husband hold H.'s share of T.'s residue on trust for H.'s estate under the trusts of T.'s will, or on the trusts of H.'s settlement? *Held,* that, by virtue of the declaration in H.'s settlement, H., and since her death, her personal representatives, held her share of T.'s residue on the trusts of H.'s settlement. Further, the same result was reached by virtue of the fact that since the legal title to the property in question (i.e. H.'s half share of the residue under T.'s will) had become vested in I.'s husband (as sole surviving trustee of T.'s will), this completely constituted the trust set up in H.'s settlement. I's husband therefore held the property as trustee under H.'s settlement on the trusts of that settlement.

Rattenberry, Re, Ray v. Grant, [1906] 1 Ch. 667   [249]

In 1899 Mrs. R. borrowed £150 from her sister, C., at 5% *p.a.* In her will, made in 1903, Mrs. R. appointed C. as her executor and gave her a legacy of £400. The will did not contain any direction to pay debts. When Mrs. R. died in 1904 the debt to C. had not been repaid. *Held*, the legacy was given in satisfaction of the debt.

Recher's Will Trust, Re, National Westminster Bank, Ltd. v.   [250] National Anti-Vivisection Society, Ltd., [1971] 3 All E.R. 401

In her will, made in 1957, a testatrix gave certain property to " The Anti-Vivisection Society, 76 Victoria Street, London, S.W.1." She died in 1962. Until the end of 1956, a non-charitable unincorporated society, known as " The London and Provincial Anti-Vivisection Society " had carried on its activities at 76 Victoria Street, but on 1st January, 1957, it was amalgamated with a larger non-charitable unincorporated society, " The National Anti-Vivisection Society ", and its premises at 76 Victoria Street were closed down. On amalgamation the larger society changed its named to " The National Anti-Vivisection Society (incorporating the London and Provincial Anti-Vivisection Society) "; in 1963 the Society was incorporated as " The National Anti-Vivisection Society Ltd." The company was not charitable. On the question whether the gift was valid, it was *held*, (1) the gift must be construed as gift to the London and Provincial Anti-Vivisection Society, and could not be construed as a gift to the larger combined society. (2) If the London and Provincial Society had continued its separate existence until the testatrix's death, the gift could have taken effect as a legacy to the members of the society beneficially, not so as to entitle each member to receive a share, but as an accretion to the funds which constituted the subject-matter of the contract by which the members had bound themselves *inter se*. (3) The gift ought not to be construed as a gift on trust for the purposes of the London and Provincial Society. (Such a construction would, in any case, result in the gift being void [as being a trust of imperfect obligation].) (4) The gift could not be construed as a gift to the members of a different association as an accretion to its funds. (5) In view of (1) and (4), and since the London and Provincial Society had been dissolved and the contract between its members terminated before the date of the will, the gift failed.

Rice v. Rice (1853), 2 Drew 73   [251]

A vendor conveyed land to a purchaser without receiving the purchase money. The deed of conveyance contained a receipt for the money by the vendor, who delivered the title deeds to the purchaser. The purchaser created an equitable mortgage by deposit of the title deeds with a mortgagee. He then absconded with the money advanced to him without paying the vendor or the mortgagee. The question arose as to which should take priority, the vendor's equitable lien for the unpaid purchase money or the equitable mortgage. *Held*, " as between persons having only equitable interests, if their equities are in *all other respects* equal, priority of time gives the better equity; or, *qui prior est tempore potior est jure* " (*per* KINDERSLEY, V.-C.). Although the vendor's lien was prior in time, owing to the negligence of the vendor in giving a receipt when the money had not been paid, the equities were not equal. The mortgagee's equitable interest took priority over the vendor's.

Richards v. Delbridge (1874), 18 Eq. 11 [252]

A grandfather attempted to assign a lease of business premises to his grandson R., an infant, by endorsing on the lease and signing this memorandum: "This deed and all thereto belonging I give to R. from this time forth, with all the stock-in-trade". He gave the lease to R.'s mother on R.'s behalf. The grandfather later died. His will made no reference to the business premises. Did the lease belong to the grandson or the residuary legatees? *Held*, there had been no gift to the grandson as the assignment, not being under seal, was ineffectual to transfer the lease. Nor had any trust been created as the grandfather had not declared himself as trustee of the lease for the grandson. The court would not construe an ineffectual transfer as a declaration of trust.

Richardson's Will Trusts, Re, Public Trustee v. Llewellyn [253]
Evans' Trustee, [1958] 1 All E.R. 538

A testator gave £2000 to trustees to hold the income on protective trusts under s. 33 of the Trustee Act 1925, for the benefit of his grandson until he reached the age of 35, when he was to receive the capital absolutely. In the event of any occurrence sufficient to determine the protective trusts under s. 33 of the 1925 Act the trustees were to hold the income on protective trusts for the grandson for the rest of his life, and on his death the capital was to go to the grandson's children. In November, 1954 the grandson's wife obtained a decree absolute of divorce against him. In June, 1955 a court order was made charging the grandson's interest under the will with a payment of £50 *p.a.* as maintenance to the wife. In October, 1955 the grandson became 35. In August, 1956 he went bankrupt. *Held*, the charge created by the order of the court was an occurrence sufficient to determine the grandson's interest and therefore the trustees held the money on protective trusts for the grandson for the rest of his life. Thus the trustee in bankruptcy had no claim to the money.

Rimmer v. Rimmer, [1952] 2 All E.R. 863 (Court of Appeal) [254]

In 1935 a house was purchased for £460 and conveyed into the name of a husband, the wife paying £29 and the husband providing the balance of £431 by means of a mortgage on the house. The husband paid his wife a weekly house-keeping allowance and out of this the wife made payments on behalf of the husband to the building society in repayment of the mortgage. The wife made payments amounting to £280 to the building society out of her own earnings, with the result that the mortgage was paid off. In 1951 the husband deserted his wife and in 1952 he sold the house for £2117. The wife applied under s. 17 of the Married Women's Property Act 1882 for a share of the sum realized. The case concerned the amount to be awarded her. *Held*, in all the circumstances it was equitable that the sum realized should be divided between the husband and wife equally.

Robinson, Re, Wright v. Tugwell, [1923] 2 Ch. 332 [255]

A testatrix who died in 1889 bequeathed £1500 towards an endowment for a proposed evangelical church at Bournemouth, provided certain conditions were carried out. One of these was that a black gown should be worn in the pulpit. A church was built but a black gown not worn as required. The incumbent sought a scheme dispensing with the condition and transferring the £1500 (which had been carried over to a separate account) to the Ecclesiastical Commissioners. *Held*, (i) as the observance of the condition had been shown to be impracticable, unless it was dispensed with the fund would remain set aside for all time thus defeating the main intention of the testatrix; (ii) the condition requiring the wearing of a black gown was subsidiary to the main intention of the testatrix; (iii) the fund should be applied *cy près* and the court sanctioned the scheme proposed.

Rochefoucauld v. Boustead, [1897] 1 Ch. 196 (Court of Appeal)   [256]

The Comtesse de la Rochefoucauld owned certain coffee estates in Ceylon. These she mortgaged to a Dutch company. In 1873 the Dutch company sold the estates to Boustead. The conveyance appeared to be absolute. Boustead subsequently sold the estates. The proceeds of the sale were considerably more than the price Boustead had paid for the estates. The Comtesse de la Rochefoucauld, the plaintiff, claimed that although the conveyance to Boustead appeared to be absolute, in fact the estates had been conveyed to Boustead as trustee on trust for the Comtesse, subject to the repayment to Boustead of the amount which he had paid for the estates and of the expenses he had incurred in managing them (*i.e.*, that having reimbursed himself out of the proceeds of the sale, Boustead was trustee of the surplus for the Comtesse). The Comtesse was able to support her contention by oral evidence alone. Boustead argued that under s. 7 of the Statute of Frauds 1677, the creation of a trust must be proved in writing. *Held*, "the Statute of Frauds does not prevent the proof of a fraud; and that it is a fraud on the part of a person to whom land is conveyed as a trustee, and who knows that it was so conveyed, to deny the trust and claim the land himself. Consequently, notwithstanding the statute, it is competent for a person claiming land conveyed to another to prove by parol evidence that it was so conveyed upon trust for the claimant" (*per* LINDLEY, L. J.). Oral evidence was therefore admissible to prove the creation of a trust, and on the evidence submitted it was held that a trust had been created.

Rochford v. Hackman (1852), 9 Hare 475   [257]

A testator bequeathed property to trustees on trust to pay the income to his wife for life, with remainder on trust to pay a quarter of the income to his eldest son for life, with remainder to that son's children. The remaining three-quarters was to be held on similar trusts for the testator's three other sons and their children. The testator then directed "that in case my said wife, or any of my said four sons, shall in any manner sell, assign, transfer, incumber . . . his or their share . . . in the said dividends . . ., then . . . the said several bequests . . . shall cease, determine . . ., as if the same had not been mentioned in . . . my will, and as if my said wife or either of my said sons were dead". After the eldest son had become entitled to a life interest under the will, he became bankrupt. *Held*, property given for life cannot be given in any way other than absolutely; "any mere attempt to restrict the power of alienation . . . is void, as being inconsistent with the interest given". But "although a life interest may be expressed to be given, it may well be *determined* by an apt limitation over" (*per* TURNER, V.-C.). The direction in the will operated to determine the eldest son's life interest on his insolvency. The assignee in the insolvency was therefore not entitled to claim the eldest son's interest under the trust, which passed to his two children.

Roscoe (James) (Bolton), Ltd. v. Winder, [1915] 1 Ch. 62   [258]

A company sold its business to W. It was agreed that W. should get in certain debts owing to the company and pay these over to the company. W. collected the debts concerned, which totalled £623, and of this he paid £455 into his private account at a bank. He later drew out all the money standing to his credit except £25, and used it, not to pay the company, but for his own purposes. Subsequently he paid in money of his own, and drew on the account, again for his own purposes, with the result that at his death there was a credit balance of £358. The company claimed to have a charge on the £358 for the £623 owing to them. *Held*, W. was a trustee for the company for the £455 which he had paid into his account. But where a trustee pays money into a general account, and then withdraws money from the account, and subsequently pays money of his own into the account, there is no presumption, in the absense of evidence to the contrary, that the subsequent payment in is made with the intention of replacing trust money which had been drawn out. Thus the company's charge extended only to the intermediate balance of £25.

Rose, Re, Midland Bank Executor and Trustee Company Limited v. Rose, [1948] 2 All E.R. 971   [259]

This case had two main aspects and these will be treated separately. By his will made in 1943 E. R. left Margaret R. and Michael R. each 500 preference shares in E. P. R., Ltd. In 1945 E. R. gave D., Ltd., an option to purchase his preference shares in E. P. R., Ltd. E. R. died in 1946 and in 1947 D., Ltd., exercised the option and purchased the shares. *Held*, the purchase of the shares by D., Ltd., adeemed the gift of shares to Margaret R. and Michael R.

By another clause in his will, E. R. left 5000 preference shares in S., Ltd., to H. In 1944 E. R. executed a transfer of the shares to H. The transfer was not registered by the company until March 1946, two months after E. R.'s death. Did the gift of shares to H. take effect under the will? *Held*, as E. R. had done everything in his power to divest himself of the shares in S., Ltd., to H, the gift passed *inter vivos* and not by will.

Rose, Re, Rose v. Inland Revenue Commissioners, [1952] 1 All E.R. 1217 (Court of Appeal)   [260]

On March 30. 1943 R. executed a transfer of 10,000 shares in a company to his wife. On the same date he executed a second transfer of a further 10,000 shares to his wife on trust for certain beneficiaries. The transfers were in the form required by the company's articles of association. The transfers were registered in the books of the company on June 30, 1943. R. died on February 16, 1947. In order to escape estate duty the transfers had to have taken place before April 10, 1943. The Crown claimed that duty was payable on the grounds that the transfers were not complete until June 30, 1943, the date of registration by the company. *Held*, as R. had done all in his power to transfer the shares to his wife, the gifts were completed [in the case of the transfer on trust, the trust was " completely constituted "] on March 30, 1943. Accordingly no estate duty was payable on R.'s death. [Between the date of the execution of the transfer and registration R. was in the position of a trustee of the legal title in the shares for the transferee].

Royal College of Surgeons of England v. National Provincial Bank, Ltd., [1952] 1 All E.R. 984 (House of Lords)   [261]

A testatrix, who died in 1943, by her will gave her residuary real and personal estate on trust for conversion and directed that the resulting " endowment fund " should be held on " the following charitable trusts " which were, *inter alia*, " to pay the residue of the income of the endowment fund in each year to the treasurer . . . of the Middlesex Hospital for the maintenance and benefit of the Bland-Sutton Institute of Pathology now carried on in connection with the said hospital . . . Provided always that should the . . . Middlesex Hospital become nationalised or by any means pass into public ownership . . . then . . . the [trustees] shall thereupon pay and transfer the endowment fund . . . to the Royal College of Surgeons . . . ". The Middlesex Hospital was founded in or about 1745. A medical school was founded in 1835, but the school did not form part of the hospital until 1896. The Bland-Sutton Institute was a department of the medical school. On July 5, 1946, under the National Health Service Act 1946, the hospital was designated a teaching hospital, and, by virtue of s. 6 of the Act, the property and liabilities of the hospital were transferred to and vested in the Minister of Health, but the medical school became a separate legal entity with a governing body constituted under s. 15 of the Act. The Royal College of Surgeons claimed that, by reason of the changes brought about by the Act, the gift over took effect. *Held*, (1) notwithstanding that the medical school of the Middlesex Hospital had not been nationalised, the institution known as and referred to in the will as "the Middlesex Hospital " had become nationalised within the meaning of the will, and therefore, the defeasance clause took effect. (2) On the true construction of the royal charter, granted in 1800, by which the

Royal College of Surgeons was incorporated, the objects of the college were "the due promotion and encouragement of the study and practice of the art and science of surgery" and were directed to the relief of human suffering or to the advancement of education or science and not to the promotion of the interests of individuals, although incidentally individuals carrying on their profession as surgeons did derive certain benefits from the college. (3) For the present purpose there was no distinction between a charity incorporated by royal charter and one incorporated by any other means; and, therefore, the college was a charity, and the gift over to it was not void for perpetuity.

Royal Exchange Assurance v. Hope, [1927] All E.R. Rep. 67   [262]
    (Court of Appeal)

By an insurance policy an assurance company, the plaintiffs, agreed to pay the assured, his executors, administrators or assigns the sum of £1000 if he died before July 31, 1926. The assured assigned the benefit of the policy to the defendant and subsequently arranged to extend the period of insurance to October 31, 1926. The benefit of this extension was never assigned and the assured died on October 1, 1926. *Held*, the extension of the policy was not a new contract of insurance but a variation of the original policy, the benefit of which had been vested in the defendant who was therefore entitled to recover £1000 by virtue of the assignment. The defendant was also entitled to the money as the assured would be regarded as having contracted for the extension of the policy for the benefit of and as trustee for the defendant.

Royce, Re, [1940] 2 All E.R. 291   [263]

A testator by his will gave £1000 to the vicar and churchwardens of a church "for the benefit of the choir". *Held*, there was a valid charitable gift, as being for the advancement of religion through musical services.

Rumball, Re, Sherlock v. Allan, [1955] 3 All E.R. 71   [264]

A testator bequeathed property to " the Bishop for the time being of the Diocese of the Windward Islands to be used by him as he thinks fit in his diocese ". *Held*, the bequest was a gift to the bishop on valid charitable trusts, because, being a gift to a holder of an office of a charitable character *virtute officii*, it was a gift on trusts exclusively appropriate to the nature of the office by which he was described, and the words, " to be used by him as he thinks fit in his diocese ", merely gave the bishop an absolute discretion as to the application of the fund within the limits of trusts exclusively appropriate to the nature of his office and confined to the use of the fund in his diocese.

Ryan v. Mutual Tontine Westminster Chambers Association,   [265]
    [1893] 1 Ch. 116 (Court of Appeal)

By the terms of a lease of a residential flat the landlords covenanted to provide a porter, who was to be constantly in attendance, or, during his temporary absence, a trustworthy assistant. The landlords appointed one Benton to be porter but, while he spent much of his time acting as chef at a neighbouring club, boys and charwomen performed his duties as porter. *Held*, the landlords were in breach of their covenant but the court would not grant an injunction to restrain the continuance of the breach or order the covenant to be specifically enforced.

Rymer, Re, Rymer v. Stanfield, [1895] 1 Ch. 19   [266]

A testator bequeathed a legacy "to the rector for the time being of St. Thomas' Seminary for the education of priests in the diocese of Westminster for the purpose of such seminary". At the date of the will the seminary was being carried on at Hammersmith. Shortly before the testator's death the seminary ceased to exist, and the students who were being educated there were transferred to another seminary near Birmingham. *Held*, the bequest was for a particular institution, and that institution having ceased to exist before the testator's death, the legacy lapsed and fell into residue.

Sackville-West v. Viscount Holmesdale (1870), L.R. 4 H.L. 543   [267]
(House of Lords)

In a codicil to her will Lady Amherst directed that certain property should be settled "in a course of entail to correspond as far as may be practicable" with the succession of a newly created peerage. The succession to the peerage laid down in letters patent was to the Countess de la Warr for life with remainder to her second son in tail, with remainder to her third son in tail. *Held*, the codicil to the will created an executory trust, that is, it made the intervention of the trustees necessary to give effect to the intention expressed in it. In deciding the intention of a testator the court was not bound by the technical meaning of the words used by the testator, but might depart from his words if this were necessary to carry out his intention. Since (i) the intention of the testatrix was that the property should endow the title and (ii) a settlement of the property in the same terms as the limitations of the newly created peerage would enable the Countess de la Warr's second son to bar the fee tail and convert it, during his mother's life, into a base fee and, on his mother's death, into a fee simple, thus making the property alienable by him, the property should be settled on the Countess de la Warr for life, with remainder to her second son in tail, with remainder to the second son's son in tail, with remainder, to the third son for life with remainder to the third son's son in fee tail. [By this means the second son would not be able to alienate the property, which would pass with the title to the second son's son before it became possible for the holder to alienate it.]

Sahal's Will Trusts, Re, Alliance Assurance Co. Ltd. v. A.-G.,   [268]
[1958] 3 All E.R. 428

A testator by clause 8 (i) of his will gave a dwelling-house to a local authority on trust "to use and maintain the same as a children's home" and expressed the desire that the home should be conducted along domestic and not along institutional lines "and without discrimination whatsoever on grounds of race religion colour or creed". By clause 8 (iii) the testator bequeathed to the local authority £2000 on trust to apply the income "for the benefit of such one or more of the children for the time being resident in the said house as they shall in their absolute discretion think fit". Clause 8 (iv) provided that "if at any time the said corporation shall discontinue the use of the said dwelling-house as a children's home as aforesaid the said dwelling-house shall be held upon trust to use and maintain the same as a hostel for young soldiers sailors airmen or merchant seamen or for poor aged and infirm people of the neighbourhood" and that the said £2000 and the income therefrom "shall thereafter be applied in purchase of extra comforts for the residents in such hostel". On questions as to the validity of the gifts contained in clause 8, *Held*, (1) the gift in clause 8 (i) for the founding of a children's home was charitable and valid. (2) The gift in clause 8 (iii) of the £2000 was not charitable and failed, since it contravened the rule against inalienability. (3) The gift of the house by clause 8 (iv) for use as a hostel, etc., was a valid charitable gift and created a trust that was alternative to the trust created by clause 8 (i). The local authority was therefore entitled to accept the house for the purposes indicated in clause 8 (iv) without first having used it for the purposes prescribed by clause 8 (i). (4) The gift of the £2,000 fund in clause 8 (iv) failed, because it was alternative to clause 8 (iii) which contravened the rule against inalienability.

Sanders' Will Trusts, Re, Public Trustee v. McLaren, [1954]   [269]
1 All E.R. 667

A testator directed that his trustee should apply certain property "in any manner in which he . . . considers to be in furtherance of my general charitable intention with regard to the disposal thereof, namely, to provide . . . dwellings for the working classes and their families resident in the area of Pembroke Dock, Pembrokeshire, Wales . . ." *Held*, (i) the gift for "the working classes" was not a gift for the relief of poverty and was therefore not a charitable gift; (ii) notwithstanding the testator's reference to his "general charitable intention", no such intention was to be inferred, as the phrase as used by the testator was referable only to the particular non-charitable purpose of erecting houses for the working classes.

Satterthwaite's Will Trusts, Re, Midland Bank Executor &   [270] Trustee Co., Ltd., v. Royal Veterinary College, [1966] 1 All E.R. 919 (Court of Appeal)

A testatrix, who made her will in December 1952 and died in 1962, directed that her residuary estate should be divided in approximately equal proportions among nine organisations, all of whose names appeared to show that they were concerned with animal welfare. One was unidentifiable; six were charities; another was the Animal Defence and Anti-Vivisection Society, which for long was considered to be a charity and another was the "London Animal Hospital". This last share was claimed by a veterinary surgeon, who had carried on his calling under that style from 1943 until July 1952, when, following the Veterinary Surgeons Act 1948, the name was withdrawn from the Register. There was no evidence to show that the testatrix had had any knowledge of the veterinary surgeon's establishment or that she knew that it was conducted for profit. *Held*, (1) the veterinary surgeon was not entitled to the bequest to the "London Animal Hospital" because (a) although accurate use of a name created a strong presumption that a testatrix meant the beneficiary that she named, it appeared that the testatrix meant to benefit a purpose and not an individual. In any case, the presumption did not arise since, when the will was written, the trade name had ceased to be used. Alternatively, (b) the bequest to the London Animal Hospital was gift by a descriptive title and indicated an intention to benefit a charitable purpose and not the proprietor of a business, and the veterinary surgeon's claim would have failed even if the gift had been an isolated gift and if he had continued to carry on his occupation under that style throughout; moreover the veterinary surgeon had not been trading under the style at the date of the will. (2) The nine bequests, by reason of the descriptions of the beneficiaries, showed a general charitable intention on the part of the testatrix through the medium of kindness to animals, notwithstanding that the Anti-Vivisection Society had been held in law not to be a charity [see *National Anti-Vivisection Society* v. *Inland Revenue Commissioners, ante*] (that being a fact unknown to the average testator). Accordingly the one-ninth share should be applied *cy-près*.

Saunders v. Vautier (1841), 4 Beav. 115   [271]

A testator left property on trust to accumulate the income until a sole beneficiary should reach the age of 25, and then transfer to him the principal and accumulated income. When the beneficiary was 21 he claimed to have the fund transferred to him. *Held*, the beneficiary was entitled to have the fund transferred to him. [The "rule in *Saunders* v. *Vautier*" is that where all the beneficiaries are *sui juris* and between them absolutely entitled they may by unanimous direction put an end to the trust, and direct the trustees to hand over the trust property as they direct.]

Saxone Shoe Co., Ltd.'s Trust Deed, Re, Re Abbott's Will   [272] Trusts, Abbott v. Pearson, [1962] 2 All E.R. 904

In a deed of trust executed by a company with the object of establishing a fund for the benefit of its employees, it was provided that "the fund and the income thereof . . . shall in the discretion of the directors be applicable" towards specified purposes including the provision of pensions for employees or former employees and the provision of benefits for employees or dependents. *Held*, (i) the trust was initially void because (a) the phrase "shall be applicable" in the context of the deed meant "shall be applied", so that the deed constituted an imperative trust to apply the income for the purposes specified, and did not merely create a power [*i.e.* a "power collateral", c.f. *Re Sayer Trust, MacGregor v. Sayer*] to apply the income to the purposes specified; (b) in order for such an imperative trust to be created it was necessary to be satisfied that a complete list of the beneficiaries could probably be compiled and this requirement was not met in the present case. (ii) the trust was not validated by the Charitable Trusts (Validation) Act 1954, because it was in substance a private discretionary trust (*viz.*, a trust for the application of income and capital for the benefit of a class of persons in any way that was thought fit) as distinct from a trust for purposes which, though wider than charitable, included purposes that were charitable in law.

Sayer Trust, Re, MacGregor v. Sayer, [1956] 3 All E.R. 600   [273]

S., the governing director of a firm of confectioners, settled money on trusts for employees and ex-employees of the firm. Under the terms of the trust deed, (1) the committee of management of the trust fund were empowered at their discretion to make payments to employees, ex-employees, and their dependent relatives, (2) the fund was to be wound up on the happening of certain events and the committee might then use the fund to buy annuities for any existing beneficiaries, (3) the committee was to use the surplus for the benefit of employees or ex-employees at their discretion. A summons was taken out to determine whether the provisions were valid or void for uncertainty. It was common ground that as regards (1) and (2) the committee would be exercising a power collateral (*i.e.*, a power not coupled with a duty). *Held*, as regards (1) and (2), since, for a valid power collateral to subsist it was not necessary to be able to ascertain the whole class of beneficiaries, provided it was possible to postulate whether a given person was within the class, and since there was sufficient certainty in the deed to satisfy this requirement, the power was valid. As regards (3) the committee would hold the surplus on trust to distribute it as directed. Such a trust was valid only if it was possible to ascertain the members of the class of beneficiaries with sufficient certainty. As this was not possible the trust was invalid and the ultimate surplus was held on a resulting trust for the settlor.

Scarisbrick, Re, [1951] 1 All E.R. 822 (Court of Appeal)   [274]

A testator left property on trust "for such relations of my said son and daughters as in the opinion of the survivor of my said son and daughters shall be in needy circumstances . . ." *Held*, the gift was for the relief of poverty and as such might be charitable even though confined to relations of the donor, this being an exception to the rule that a charitable trust must be for the "public benefit". This exception was not restricted to perpetual or continuing trusts, but covered a trust for immediate distribution. The trust was therefore charitable.

Schalit v. Joseph Nadler, Ltd., [1933] All E.R. Rep. 708   [275]

J. N., Ltd., of which company J. N. was a director and the sole shareholder, wished to acquire the lease of certain premises in Shaftsbury Avenue. The landlord objected to granting the lease to a limited company and so J. N. acquired the lease in his own name and at the same time executed a declaration of trust declaring that he held the premises on trust for the company. J. N. subsequently granted a sub-lease of part of the premises to S. When S. fell into arrears with rent, a warrant of distress was issued on behalf of the company, to whom it was stated that the rent was due. *Held*, J. N., Ltd., were not entitled to distrain. A *cestuis que trust* is not entitled to distrain for rent in respect of trust property merely because he is the beneficial owner of the property. Section 141 (2) of the Law of Property Act 1925, does not affect this position.

Scottish Burial Reform and Cremation Society v. Glasgow   [276]
Corporation, [1967] 3 All E.R. 215 (House of Lords)

A non-profit making limited company had as its main object the encouragement, and provision, of facilities for cremation. The company charged for
its services. On the question whether it was a charity, *Held*, that the disposal
of human remains by inexpensive and sanitary methods was beneficial to the
community and within the spirit of the preamble of the statute 43 Eliz. 1, c. 4.
The fact that the company charged for its services did not preclude it from being
charitable. The company was thus a charity.

Seeley v. Jago (1717), 1 P. Wms. 389   [277]

A testator devised £1000 to be laid out in the purchase of land to be settled on
A, B. and C. equally. A. died leaving an infant heir. B. and C. and A.'s heir asked
the trustees to pay them the money instead of buying land. *Held*, B. and C., being
absolutely entitled in possession, were entitled to have their two-thirds in money,
but the infant's one-third share of the money was to be laid out in the purchase of
land.

Shaw, Re, Public Trustee v. Day, [1957] 1 All E.R. 745   [278]

By his will a testator directed his trustee to hold his residuary trust funds and
the annual income thereof for a period of twenty-one years from his death, on
trust (i) to ascertain by inquiry how much time could be saved by persons who
speak and write the English language, by the substitution for the present English
alphabet of a proposed British alphabet containing at least forty letters; (ii) to
transliterate one of the testator's plays into the proposed British alphabet; to
advertise and publish the transliteration with the original lettering opposite
the transliteration, page by page; and to present copies thereof to public libraries,
so as to persuade the government or the public to adopt the proposed alphabet.
Held, the trusts in connection with the proposed new alphabet were void for the
following reasons: (1) The trusts were for purposes that in law were not charitable
because (a) increase of knowledge is not a charitable purpose unless combined
with an element of teaching or education, and, although the research and propaganda enjoined by the testator might tend to increase public knowledge in a
certain respect, *viz.*, the saving of time and money by the use of the proposed
alphabet, yet they were not for the advancement of education; (b) the trusts
were not within the category of charitable trusts for other purposes beneficial to
the community, because the object of the research and propaganda enjoined by
the testator was to convince the public that the new alphabet would be beneficial
and, analogously to the cases of trusts for political purposes advocating a change
in the law of the land, the court was not in a position to judge whether the adoption of the new alphabet in fact would be beneficial. (2) As private trusts they
failed as being trusts of imperfect obligation. The court was not at liberty to
give validity to the trusts by treating them as conferring on the trustees a power to
carry out the testator's directions.

Shaw v. Cates, [1909] 1 Ch. 389   [279]

In 1897 trustees advanced £4400 out of trust funds to F. on the security of two
houses at Folkestone. The valuer employed by the trustees was the mortgagor's
rent collector. The property depreciated in value and in 1906 interest ceased to be
paid. The beneficiaries claimed that the trustees did not have a valuation made by
an independent valuer, that the valuation was unsatisfactory, that the investment
was hazardous and so not a proper security, and that the security was inadequate
for the sum advanced. *Held*, it had not been proved that the property was of such a
nature as to be wholly improper for the investment of trust money. The valuation
obtained by the trustees was not such a valuation as was contemplated by s. 8 of the

Trustee Act 1893. The trustees had not acted prudently and were not entitled to be relieved of liability under s. 3 of the Judicial Trustees Act 1896. [Now s. 61 of the Trustee Act 1925.] The largest sum for which the property could be considered good security in 1897 was £3400 and the trustees were liable to make good the difference between this sum and the £4400 actually advanced, with interest.

Shaw's Will Trusts, Re, National Provincial Bank, Ltd. v.   [280] National City Bank, Ltd., [1952] 1 All E.R. 49

A textatrix left property to trustees on trust to apply the income towards the appreciation of the fine arts and (*inter alia*): "The teaching promotion and encouragement in Ireland of self-control elocution oratory deportment the arts of personal contact of social intercourse and the other arts of public private professional and business life". *Held*, the trust was of an educational nature and beneficial to the community and therefore constituted a valid charitable trust.

Shephard v. Cartwright, [1954] 3 All E.R. 649 (House of Lords)   [281]

A father promoted several private companies and had the shares for which he had subscribed allotted to his three children. In a series of subsequent transactions, for which the children at the request of their father signed the requisite documents without understanding what they were doing, the shares were sold and the children received cash compensation. He later obtained the children's signatures to documents, the contents of which they were ignorant, authorizing him to draw money from the accounts to which it had been credited. By 1936 the father had withdrawn all the money. Some of it he used for the benefit of the children but a large part remained unaccounted for at his death in 1949. *Held*, the registration of the shares in the names of the children raised a presumption of advancement. In supporting or rebutting such a presumption, the acts and declarations of the parties before or at the time of the transaction are admissible for or against them. Subsequent acts and declarations are admissible only against them. When the shares were allotted to the children there was no evidence to rebut the presumption of advancement. The father's subsequent transactions were not admissible to rebut the presumption. The registration of the shares in the children's names thus constituted an advancement.

Simson, Re, Fowler v. Tinley, [1946] 2 All E.R. 220   [282]

A testatrix, who died in 1943, by her will gave her residuary estate " to the Vicar of St. Luke's Church, Ramsgate, to be used for his work in the parish ". *Held*, " the proper way to construe this gift is as a gift ... to the vicar of St. Luke's Church, Ramsgate, to be used for his work in the sense of work proper, that is to say, in the fulfilment of his functions as Vicar ... " " ... a gift to a vicar for his work in the parish ... merely means that it is to be used for the purposes of such part of his work (that is to say, his functions connected with the cure of souls in the particular district) as lies within the particular parish ". (*Per* Romer, J.). Since such work was charitable, the gift was charitable.

Sinclair v. Brougham, [1914–15] All E.R. Rep. 622   [283] (House of Lords)

The Birkbeck Building Society, having borrowing power, established and developed, in addition to the legitimate business of a building society, a banking business, which was admitted to be *ultra vires*. In connection with this banking business customers deposited sums of money in the usual way. In 1911 the Society was wound up. The assets were claimed by outside creditors, by the shareholders and by the depositors. The assets were not sufficient to pay all three groups. It was not disputed that the outside creditors were entitled to be paid first, but the shareholders and the depositors each claimed priority over the other. *Held*, (1) the doctrine of *ultra vires* excluded any claim *in personam* based on the circumstance that the society had been improperly enriched at the expense of the depositors with the bank, and so the depositors could not recover their money unless, adopting the dealings by the society with the money and claiming *in rem*, they could trace their money into the hands of the society as actually existing assets. (2) At common law money could be followed not only where a fiduciary relationship existed, but in any case where the property in the money had not passed and the money could be earmarked in the hands of the recipient or traced into assets acquired with it, and that was true where money had been paid under an *ultra vires* contract under which no property could pass. (3) In equity, when money had been paid to a person who had wrongfully obtained it, the court would declare that there was a charge on the fund in the bank with which the money had been mixed, and that doctrine applied in the case of money acquired under a transaction which was *ultra vires* the recipient. (4) Accordingly, in the present case the depositors had the right to follow the money so far as it was invalidly converted into the, possibly depreciated, assets in which it had been invested, whether those assets were mere debts due to the society or ordinary securities. (5) No action for money paid under a mistake of fact or for money had and received would lie to enable the depositors to recover their money. (6) Subject to the payment expenses, the liquidator, in distributing the remaining assets of the society between the depositors and the unadvanced shareholders, should proceed on the principle of distributing them *pari passu* in proportion to the amounts properly credited to them respectively in the books of the society in respect of their advances at the date of the commencement of the winding-up.

Slatter's Will Trusts, Re, Turner v. Turner, [1964]   [284]
  2 All E.R. 469

By her will, dated June 8, 1955, a testatrix devised her residuary estate upon trust for the Malahide Red Cross Hospital in Australia. The hospital had been opened by the New South Wales Division of the Australian Red Cross Society, for the treatment of tuberculosis in the area. On June 30, 1955, the hospital was closed down by the Division as there was no longer any need for its work. The testatrix died in 1960. She had learned the year before that the hospital had been closed. It was conceded that there was no general charitable intention in the will. *Held*, assuming that the gift was for the work of the hospital (and not for the hospital as a specific institution, in which case the gift would certainly lapse), since (a) where a charity closes down because the need for it had gone, or for lack of funds, and no funds were dedicated to its work before it closed, and none were so dedicated after, the charity ceases to exist with the closure, and (b) since there was no general charitable intention in the will, the gift was not to be applied *cy-près*, but lapsed and, being residue, passed as on intestacy.

Slevin, Re, [1891] 2 Ch. 236 (Court of Appeal)   [285]

A testator bequeathed a number of legacies, using the introductory words "I bequeath the following charitable legacies". Among these was one to an orphanage voluntarily maintained by a lady at her own expense which was in existence at the testator's death, but was discontinued shortly afterwards, and before receiving the legacy. *Held*, a gift to an institution which was in existence at a testator's death but which subsequently ceases to exist before receiving the legacy, belongs to the institution and on its dissolution passes with the rest of its property to the Crown, which may allow the legacy to be applied *cy-près*. The legacy therefore became the property of the orphanage and when the orphanage ceased to exist passed to the Crown.

Smith, Re, Public Trustee v. Aspinall, [1928] All E.R. Rep. 520   [286]

A testator gave one-quarter of the residue of his estate to trustees on trust, at their absolute discretion, to pay the income or capital for the maintenance of Mrs. Aspinall, or the income for the maintenance of all or any of Mrs. Aspinall's children. In 1923 (when she was too old to have further children) Mrs. Aspinall joined with her two surviving children and the personal representatives of her deceased child (there being no other children), in executing a mortgage of the interest which Mrs. Aspinall and the three children took under the will. The mortgage took the form of an assignment of the interest to the Legal and General Assurance Company. The trustees took out a summons to determine whether they were bound to pay the whole of the income to the Company until the discharge of the mortgage or whether they were at liberty at their discretion to pay income or capital for the maintenance of Mrs. Apsinall. *Held*, Mrs. Aspinall, the two surviving children and the personal representatives of the deceased child, as the sole objects of the discretionary trust were entitled to dispose of the whole income. The trustees were therefore directed to pay the income to the Company during the lifetime of Mrs. Aspinall or until the mortgage was discharged.

Smith, Re, Public Trustee v. Smith, [1932] 1 Ch. 153   [287]
(Court of Appeal)

A testator, who died in 1930, gave his residuary estate " unto my country England for—own use and benefit absolutely ". *Held*, since " a gift or trust for the inhabitants of a particular place is a good charitable gift or trust " (*per* ROMER, L.J.) the gift was a valid gift for charitable purposes.

Smith v. Jones, [1954] 2 All E.R. 823   [288]

The plaintiff held the lease of a farm, which he occupied. His landlord sold the land to the defendant. After the sale a disagreement arose between the plaintiff and the defendant as to which of them was responsible for carrying out repairs. The plaintiff brought the action to obtain rectification of his tenancy agreement so as to make the defendant responsible for repairs. The defendant argued that even if rectification could have been obtained against the original lessor, he, as *bona fide* purchaser for value without notice (*i.e.*, without notice of the existence of a possible right to seek rectification), was not bound by this equity of rectification. *Held*, no claim for rectification would have lain against the original lessor and thus the question did not arise as to whether the defendant was bound by it. On this latter point, however, it was stated that the defendant could not be deemed to have had constructive notice of the existence of the possible claim to rectification, and therefore, as *bona fide* purchaser for value without notice, he took free of it.

Snowden, Re, Shackleton v. Methodist Missionary Society,   [289]
[1969] 3 All E.R. 208

A testator, who died in 1964, by clause 3 of his will, dated June 12, 1954, bequeathed all the shares which he might have in three named companies to his trustees on trust to hold one half of the shares for D. and the other half for M. and A. By clause 6 he bequeathed pecuniary legacies totalling £6,200 to ten named charities. By clause 7 he bequeathed pecuniary legacies totalling £4,000 to seven named individuals. By clause 8, he gave his residuary estate to the charities named in clause 6, in the same proportions as the legacies given in the clause. D., M. and A. were the testator's nearest relatives and he had always taken a great interest in them, both when they were children and later when they were grown up. D. was his godson. At the time of the will, the shares in the three companies represented a large part of his estate. Between the date of the will in 1954 and his death in 1964, the testator sold all the shares. Thus on his death, under his will, D., M. and A. received nothing, and the proceeds of sale passed, under clause 8, to the charities named in clause 6.

Six of the charities expressed the wish to give up either in whole or part, the share of residue to which they were entitled under clause 8, in favour of D., M. and A. *Held*, (1) The court and the Attorney-General have power to give authority to charity trustees to make *ex gratia* payments out of funds held on charitable trusts. The power cannot be exercised lightly or on slender grounds, but only in cases where it can be fairly said that, if the charity were an individual, it would be morally wrong to refuse to make the payment. (2) In view of the fact that it was highly likely that the testator did not intend the charities to benefit under his will to the extent they had benefited, and that he had overlooked the effect which the sale of the shares had on his testamentary dispositions and that, if he had realized the effect of the sale, he would have left the three persons pecuniary legacies in order to compensate them for their loss, the court authorised the six charities which had expressed a wish to make some payment to pay, if they so decided, not more than 50% of their respective shares of residue to D., M. and A.

Somerset, Re, Somerset v. Earl Poulett, [1894] 1 Ch. 231   **[290]**
  (Court of Appeal)

Under a marriage settlement of 1875 property was settled on a husband and wife successively with remainder to their children. The trustees were to retain the property or, with the consent of the husband and wife, or the survivor, to sell and reinvest in specified securities, including mortgages of freehold or leasehold properties. In 1876 the husband wished to have the trust property sold and re-invested in a mortgage of an estate at Hawkestone owned by Lord Hill. The solicitors acting for the trustees instructed a firm of valuers to value the estate. The valuers stated that they considered that the estate represented a sufficient security for an advance of £35,000. In 1878, with the consent of the husband and wife, the trustees advanced £34,612 to Lord Hill on the security of mortgages of the Hawke-stone estate. Interest was paid on the mortgages until 1890, but interest due in 1891 was not paid. The husband (whose wife had died in 1889) and children brought an action against the trustees for a declaration that the mortgage loan was a breach of trust, on the grounds that the Hawkestone estate was an insufficient and unauthorised security, and seeking to make the trustees make good the loss. The trustees conceded that they were liable to make good the loss to the estate as far as the infant children were concerned, but contended that they were entitled under s. 6 of the Trustee Act 1888 [now replaced by s. 62, Trustee Act 1925] to be indemnified by the husband out of his life interest. *Held*, (i) although the husband had instigated, requested and consented to the investment, it did not appear that he had intended to be a party to any breach of trust, and had in effect left it to the trustees to determine whether the security was sufficient for the money advanced. The trustees were therefore not entitled under s. 6 of the Trustee Act 1888 to be indemnified by the husband out of his life interest against their liability for the loss to the trust; (ii) the effect of s. 8 of the Trustee Act 1888 [now replaced by s. 19, Limitation Act 1939] is that time begins to run in favour of a trustee from the time when the breach was committed, whether the beneficiary knew of it or not. The action by the husband to compel the trustees to make good the loss was therefore statute barred. Thus the husband was entitled during his life to receive the income of only so much of the trust fund as was not lost, and the trustees were entitled to retain for their own use the interest on the money paid by them to make good to the trust fund the amount of the loss.

Speight, Re, Speight v. Gaunt (1883), 22 Ch.D. 727   **[291]**
  (Court of Appeal)

A trustee employed a broker for the purpose of investing trust money. At the request of the broker the trustee made out a cheque for the necessary amount payable to the broker. The broker appropriated the money to his own use and a month later became bankrupt. The beneficiaries claimed that the trustee was personally liable to make good the loss. *Held*, the trustee having acted in the ordinary course of business was not liable to make good the loss. " In the first place, I think we ought to consider what is the liability of a trustee who undertakes an office which requires him to make an investment on behalf of his *cestui que trust*. It seems to me that on general principles a trustee ought to conduct the business of the trust in the same manner that an ordinary prudent man of business would conduct his own, and that beyond that there is no liability or obligation on the trustee. In other words, a trustee is not bound because he is a trustee to conduct business in other than the ordinary and usual way in which similar business is conducted by mankind in transactions of their own. It never could be reasonable to make a trustee adopt further and better precautions than an ordinary prudent man of business would adopt, or to conduct the business in any other way. If it were otherwise, no one would be a trustee at all" (*per* JESSEL, M. R.).

Spensley's Will Trusts, Re, Barclays Bank, Ltd. v. Staughton,   **[292]**
    [1954] 1 All E.R. 178 (Court of Appeal)

A testator, who died in 1938, by his will devised land and buildings at Westoning to the National Trust for Places of Historic Interest or Natural Beauty on trust for F.'s life, with remainder to S. for life, and on the death of both for the use of the High Commissioner for Australia as a country residence in a similar way to that in which Chequers was used by the Prime Minister of England. The will further provided: " Should the government of the Commonwealth of Australia refuse this bequest at the time of my death or renounce it at any future date then for such other uses preferably for some purpose in connection with Australia as the said National Trust . . . may decide ". In July 1938, the National Trust disclaimed the gift under the will. In September 1938, the High Commissioner for Australia disclaimed all his interest and that of the government of Australia under the will. *Held*, (1) The primary trust, being " simply a trust to provide certain amenities for a person for the time being holding in this country a particular office under the Australian government " (*per* JENKINS L.J.) did not fall within the fourth head of charity in the classification in Pemsel's Case (See *Commissioner of Income Tax* v. *Pemsel, ante*) and was not charitable. (2) The alternative trust was invalid for two reasons (a) although a gift to a holder of an office of a charitable character *virtute officii*, with the addition of words conferring wide powers of disposition, was charitable, a gift to such a person on trust for purposes which were not exclusively charitable was not charitable: the secondary trust was thus not made charitable merely because the trustee had charitable status; (b) (i) the primary trust, if accepted, could be renounced at any time in the future; (ii) the primary trust could thus last for any length of time; (iii) the primary trust might thus endure for longer than, and the alternative trust thus vest outside, the perpetuity period; (iv) the alternative trust was therefore void as infringing the rule against perpetuities.

Stead, Re, Witham v. Andrew, [1900] 1 Ch. 237   **[293]**

A testatrix, who died in 1898, by her will gave her residuary estate to M., W. and A., the executors and trustees of her will, on trust for W. and A. After the death of the testatrix, W. alleged that, prior to the execution of the will, the testatrix had informed her that she proposed to leave her residuary estate to W. and A., but that this was subject to a trust not declared on the face of the will that £2000 should be given from the residuary estate to C., and that any balance should be given to such of the charities mentioned in the will as W. and A. should think proper. W. further alleged that the testatrix executed her will on the faith of a promise by W. to carry out the trust. A. claimed that no communication had been made to her in the life time of the testatrix regarding the alleged intention of the testatrix that the property should be held on trust. *Held*, (1) where property is given in a will to two persons as joint tenants on the faith of a promise made to the testator before the execution of the will by one of them to hold the property subject to a secret trust, the trust binds both of them. (2) The evidence of W. was rejected and that of A. accepted. A. therefore took one moiety of the residuary estate beneficially. (3) Although W.'s evidence as to the existence of a secret trust had been rejected, she was nevertheless bound by her own admissions, and therefore held the other moiety of the residuary estate on the trusts she had alleged.

Steed's Will Trusts, Re, Sandford v. Stevenson, [1960]   [294]
1 All E.R. 487 (Court of Appeal)

A testator devised a farm to trustees upon trust for sale upon protective trusts as defined by s. 33 of the Trustee Act, 1925 for the benefit of the plaintiff for life, and after her death for such persons as she might appoint, with a proviso that the plaintiff should have the use and enjoyment of the capital value of the property if she needed it. The trustees proposed to sell the farm in exercise of their powers but the plaintiff opposed the sale and applied to court under s. 1 of the Variation of Trusts Act 1958 for approval of an arrangement by which the trustees would hold the farm on trust for her absolutely. The trustees opposed the variation. *Held*, the duty imposed by s. 1 of the 1958 Act required consideration of the interests of all persons who might have an interest under the protective trust, and not merely the interests of the person seeking the variation of the trust. If the plaintiff married, her husband would have an interest under the discretionary trust which would arise if the plaintiff attempted to alienate the property. It would not be in the interest of such a future husband for the court to approve the variation sought. "The court must regard the proposal as a whole, and . . . then ask itself whether . . . it should approve that proposal on behalf of the person who cannot give a consent, because he is not in a position to do so . . . the court is bound to look at the scheme as a whole, and . . . to consider . . . what really was the intention of the benefactor" (*per* Lord Evershed, M. R.). Any future husband was part of the testator's scheme. Further, it was the testator's intention that the plaintiff should have proper provision made for her during her life and that she should not be exposed to the risk that she should part with the capital. Approval of the variation was therefore withheld.

Stemson's Will Trusts, Re, Carpenter v. Treasury Solicitor,   [295]
[1969] 2 All E.R. 517

A testator, by his will, made in 1950, bequeathed his residuary estate to a charitable organisation, the Rationalist Endowment Fund, Ltd. (" REF "). In 1963, REF passed in accordance with its memorandum of association, a special resolution to wind up and it was dissolved in 1965. Its assets were thereupon, in accordance with its memorandum of association, passed to the Rationalist Press Association, Ltd., which also was a charitable organisation although, unlike REF, its objects did not include the relief of poverty. The testator died in 1966 without having amended his will. *Held*, (1) Where funds came into the hands of a charitable organisation such as REF which was founded, not as a perpetual charity, but as one liable to termination, and its constitution provided for the disposal of its funds in that event, then, if the organisation ceased to exist and its funds were disposed of, the charity or charitable trust itself ceased to exist. (2) The particular reliance of the testator (shown in the will) on REF carrying out his wishes negatived any general charitable intention. (3) The disposition being " impossible ", but no general intention having been shown, the property could not be applied *cy près* and therefore the residuary estate was undisposed by the will.

Stocks v. Dobson (1853), 4 De G.M. & G. 11   [296]

In 1836 P. brought an action against D. and recovered judgment for £146. In the same year D. assigned the judgment debt to W., who gave notice to P. In 1842 W. assigned the debt to S., who gave no notice to D. In 1848 W. and D. made a settlement under which, in return for consideration provided by D.,.W. released D. from claims by him in respect of the debt assigned to him in 1836 (and which he had assigned to S.). In 1850 S. sought to enforce the debt against W. *Held*, there was no distinction to be drawn between a case of actual payment and a case of a *bona fide* settlement of the debt on terms arranged between the debtor and the creditor. Thus D., having discharged his liability to W. before receiving notice of the assignment by W. to S., was under no liability to S.

Stockloser v. Johnson, [1954] 1 All E.R. 630 (Court of Appeal)   **[297]**

The defendant agreed to sell to the plaintiff certain plant and machinery in two quarries and the agreement provided that payment was to be made by instalments. The agreement further provided that if the plaintiff made default in payment of an instalment for a period exceeding twenty-eight days the defendant was entitled to re-take possession of the plant and machinery and that in such event all instalments paid should be forfeited to the defendant. Two years later the plaintiff failed to pay the instalments due from him and the defendant rescinded the agreement. *Held*, the plaintiff was not entitled to recover the instalments which he had paid as the forfeiture clause did not operate to exact a penalty and it was not unconscionable for the defendant to retain them. "In my judgment, there is no sufficient ground for interfering with the contractual rights of a vendor under forfeiture clauses of the nature which are now under consideration, while the contract is still subsisting, beyond giving a purchaser who is in default, but who is able and willing to proceed with the contract, a further opportunity of doing so; and no relief of any other nature can properly be given, in the absence of some special circumstances such as fraud, sharp practice, or other unconscionable conduct of the vendor, to a purchaser after the vendor has rescinded the contract" (*per* ROMER, L. J.).

Stott v. Milne (1884), 25 Ch.D. 710 (Court of Appeal)   **[298]**

Trustees found themselves out of pocket as a result of an action brought by them in connection with the trust property. *Held*, "the right of trustees to indemnity against all costs and expenses properly incurred by them in the execution of the trust is a first charge on all the trust property, both income and corpus. The trustees, therefore, had the right to retain the costs out of income until provision could be made for raising them out of the corpus" (*per* EARL OF SELBOURNE, L. C.).

Strakosch, Re, Temperley v. A.-G., [1949] 2 All E.R. 6   **[299]**
'   (Court of Appeal)

A testator by his will directed his trustees to apply part of his estate " to a fund for any purpose which in their opinion is designed to strengthen the bonds of unity between the Union of South Africa and the mother Country and which incidentally will conduce to the appeasement of racial feeling between the Dutch and English speaking sections of the South African community ". *Held*, (1) the purpose expressed in the disposition was not charitable, in the sense of the preamble to the statute 43 Eliz. c. 4, because it could be achieved by many methods which would not involve charitable benefits, such as the support of a political party or a newspaper. In particular, " the appeasement of racial feeling " was a political cause and was therefore not charitable.

Strahan, Re, (1856), 8 De G.M. & G. 291   **[300]**

P., a member of a banking firm of S., P. & B., was one of the trustees of a marriage settlement. The following events occurred.

(i) The trustees, in breach of the investment clause in the settlement, advanced £13,000 to the firm on the security of a mortgage of bonds in which some of the bankers were obligees.

(ii) P., in breach of trust, paid £3000 of trust money into his own account at the bank.

91

(iii) In 1852 S. was appointed a trustee of the settlement.

(iv) P., again in breach of trust, paid a further £1000 of trust money into his own account at the bank.

(v) S. did not enquire whether the old trustees received further trust money (the sums in (ii) and (iv)) under a covenant in the settlement to settle after-acquired property.

(vi) Some of the bonds assigned by the bank to the trustees were paid off and others substituted in their place.

(vii) In 1855 the bank became bankrupt and new trustees were appointed.

(viii) At the time of the bankruptcy, of the bonds assigned by the bank to the trustees only one remained not paid off. The right to sue on this had become vested in P.

(ix) All three members of the bank, S., P. & B. were obligees of the substituted bonds.

Held, regarding (i), the new trustees were entitled to prove against the separate estate of S. for the £13,000. Regarding (ii) and (v), S. was not liable, as a new trustee was entitled to assume that the former trustees had done their duty under a covenant to settle after-acquired property; and, in the absence of any reason for supposing that they had not, was not bound to look back to see whether they had received funds which ought to have been settled. Regarding (iv) and (v), S. was not liable, as a trustee was not under a duty to enquire whether any property, subject to be settled under a covenant, had fallen in, when there was nothing to lead him to suppose that there was such property. Regarding (viii), P. was the reputed and true owner of the bond, but subject to a trust in favour of the beneficiaries under the settlement, and the bond did not pass to the assignees in bankruptcy as being in the order and disposition of the bankrupt. Regarding (ix) the members of the bank were the reputed and true owners of the other bonds, but subject to a trust, as in the case of (viii), and so the bonds did not pass to the assignees in bankruptcy.

Stratheden and Campbell (Lord), Re, [1894] 3 Ch. 265   **[301]**

A testator bequeathed "an annuity of £100 to be provided to the Central London Rangers" (the 22nd Middlesex Rifle Volunteer Regiment) "on the appointment of the next lieutenant-colonel". *Held*, the gift failed as infringing the rule against perpetuities. "It is a gift conditional on the appointment of the next lieutenant-colonel. Now the next lieutenant-colonel may not be appointed for some time after the death of the present commanding officer, he may never be appointed at all; and, consequently, it appears to me that this is a gift conditional upon an event which transgresses the . . . law against perpetuities" (*per* ROMER, J.).

Stratton, Re, Knapman v. A.-G., [1930] All E.R. Rep. 255   **[302]**
(Court of Appeal)

A testatrix gave property to the vicar for the time being of Mortlake on trust "to be by him distributed at his discretion among such parochial institutions or purposes as he shall select". *Held*, not every parochial purpose was charitable in law: the gift could be applied to non-charitable purposes and was therefore not charitable.

Strong v. Bird (1874), L.R. 18 Eq. 315   **[303]**

F. B. lived in her step-son's house and paid him £212 10s. a quarter for board. In 1866 F. B. lent her step-son, B., £1100 and it was agreed that the loan should be paid off by a deduction of £100 from each quarter's payment. Deductions were made on two quarter days, but on the third quarter day, F.B. insisted on paying the full amount of £212 10s., and continued to pay this sum each quarter day until her death four years later. In her will F. B. appointed B. her sole executor. The question arose whether B. was liable to F. B.'s estate for the balance of £900 which had not been repaid by B. to F. B. during her life. *Held*, B. was not liable for the £900. There had been an effective gift of the amount to B. [Under the rule in *Strong* v. *Bird* an apparently imperfect gift of property is effective if (i) the donee becomes one of the donor's personal representatives, and (ii) the donor has manifested an intention to make a present of definite property (in the case of *Strong* v. *Bird*, by forgiving a debt) and this intention has continued until the donor's death.]

Tacon, Re, Public Trustee v. Tacon, [1958] 1 Ch. 449   [304]
(Court of Appeal)

A testator, who died in 1922, gave property to his daughter for life with remainder to her children, and, if she had none, he directed his trustees to apply a one-sixth part of the property in establishing a convalescent home. At the testator's death a one-sixth share of the property would have been sufficient to establish a convalescent home. If at that time the reversionary interest had been sold the sum realised would have been inadequate for the purpose. The daughter died without children in 1952. The value of a one-sixth share had by then increased, but, owing to the fall in the value of money and an increase in estate duty since the testator's death, was insufficient to establish a home. *Held*, in deciding whether a charitable gift was impracticable *ab initio* (in which case if there was no general charitable intention it would fail), in the case of a gift of a vested remainder liable to be defeated, the test was not merely (a) whether at the testator's death it was immediately practicable, but also (b) whether it could at that date be said that it would be practicable to give effect to such purpose at some future time. Under test (a) it was not practicable to give effect to the trust as the value of the reversionary interest was insufficient. Under test (b) as, at the testator's death, a one-sixth share would have been sufficient to establish a home, and as at that time there was no reason to anticipate the subsequent increase in estate duty and the fall in the value of money, there was at the testator's death a reasonable prospect that it would be practicable to give effect to the trust. Thus the trust took effect.

Tamplin v. James (1880), 15 Ch.D. 215   [305]
"The Ship Inn" and a saddler's shop adjoining were put up for sale by auction and the extent of the property to be sold was clearly marked on plans which were on view in the auction room. At the back of the property were two pieces of garden which originally belonged to the vendors, the plaintiffs, but which were now let to them by the present owners. The tenants of the inn and shop used and enjoyed these gardens and the defendant, who purchased the inn and shop at the auction, refused to complete his purchase on the ground that he believed that he was buying the freehold of all that was in the occupation of the plaintiffs' tenants. The defendant said that he had not seen the plans which correctly delineated the property to be sold. *Held*, the plaintiffs were entitled to specific performance as the fact that the purchaser had made this mistake without any excuse ought not to enable him to escape from his bargain.

Tancred v. Delagoa Bay Railway Co. (1889), 23 Q.B.D. 239   [306]
Sir Thomas Tancred borrowed money from Gosling and Sharpe. In the loan agreement he assigned to Gosling and Sharpe debts due to him by the Delagoa Bay Railway Co. The loan agreement contained a proviso that Gosling and Sharpe should reassign the debt back to Sir Thomas Tancred, when he had repaid Gosling and Sharpe the money borrowed from them. The question arose whether the assignment was "absolute" within the meaning of s. 25 (6) of the Judicature Act 1873 (replaced by s. 136 of the Law of Property Act 1925). *Held*, the assignment was not prevented from being "absolute" by reason of the fact that it was made subject to a proviso for reassignment on the repayment of money lent. The assignment was thus within the statute and therefore a valid legal assignment.

Tempest, Re (1866), 1 Ch. App. 485 (Court of Appeal in Chancery)   **[307]**

A testator devised property to S. and F. on certain trusts. He gave the power of appointing new trustees to F. and T. On the death of S., F. and T. were unable to agree in the choice of a new trustee. A beneficiary petitioned the court for the appointment of P. F. opposed the appointment of P., not from any personal objection to P., but because he was connected with a branch of the family with which the testator was not on friendly terms and which he had excluded from participation in the management of his property. *Held*, in appointing a trustee, the court will have regard to the wishes of the settlor expressed in, or deduced from, the instrument creating the trust. The court will not appoint a person with a view to the interest of some beneficiaries in opposition to the interest of others. The court will consider whether the appointment will promote or impede the execution of the trust. The testator would never have consented that P. should be appointed. Therefore he was not to be appointed. The court instead appointed C. trustee.

Tempest v. Lord Camoys (1882), 21 Ch.D. 571 (Court of Appeal)   **[308]**

A testator gave his trustees a discretionary power to sell certain property, and a discretionary power to purchase other property with the proceeds. The property was sold. One of the trustees then proposed that certain other property should be purchased. The other trustee refused to agree to the purchase. *Held*, the court will not interfere with a trustee's *bona fide* exercise of his discretion. The court would therefore not intervene to compel the dissenting trustee to agree to the purchase.

Thompson, Re, Public Trustee v. Lloyd, [1933]   **[309]**
    All E.R. Rep. 805

A testator bequeathed £1000 to a friend to be applied by him in such manner as in his discretion he might think fit towards the promotion and furtherance of fox-hunting. *Held*, the gift was not a gift to the friend personally; nor was it a charitable gift, but the object of the gift was sufficiently definite to enable the gift to be enforced by the court. The court ordered that, on the friend giving an undertaking to apply the money towards the promotion and furtherance of fox-hunting, the legacy should be paid to him; but that the residuary legatees might apply to the court if the legacy was not so applied. [Thus the case fell into the anomalous class of trusts of imperfect obligation which the court is nevertheless prepared to uphold.]

Thorndike v. Hunt (1859), 3 De G. & J. 563   **[310]**

A trustee held a sum of money on trust for A. and another sum on trust for B. In an action by A. the trustee was ordered to pay the money into court. The trustee paid the amount into court and it was treated as belonging to A.'s estate. It then appeared that the trustee had obtained the money by fraudulently misappropriating money which he held on trust for B. The question arose as to whether B. had the right to claim the money which had been paid into court. *Held*, as A. had in effect obtained the legal title, the money having vested in the Accountant General on A.'s behalf, B. could not claim the money, as B.'s right to recover the money was no greater than A.'s right to retain it. [Although not a *bona fide* purchaser for value of the legal estate, A. had a better title to the legal estate and this gave him the priority enjoyed by such a purchaser.]

Thorne v. Heard and Marsh, [1895] A.C. 495 (House of Lords)   **[311]**

Heard and Marsh were first mortgagees of certain property. In 1878 they exercised their power of sale. The proceeds of the sale amounted to more than the sum which they had lent on the security of the mortgage. (They therefore became trustees of the surplus on behalf of subsequent mortgagees and the mortgagor). They handed the surplus to their solicitor, Searle, to pass to the second mortgagee.

Searle gave them a receipt acknowledging payment to the second mortgagee, but retained the money for his own use and did not inform the second mortgagee of the sale. In 1892 Searle became bankrupt and the fraud was discovered. Thorne, a beneficiary under the will of the second mortgagee, sued Heard and Marsh as trustees of the surplus proceeds of sale for her. *Held*, Heard and Marsh were not liable for the surplus to Thorne, as they were not "party or privy" to the fraud of the solicitor. They believed that Searle was acting as agent of Thorne. "If that be the state of the facts, it seems to me to be idle to contend that money which is paid away by a trustee to another person, in the erroneous belief that he fills a particular character which it turns out he does not fill, is still retained by the trustee" (*per* LORD DAVEY).

Thynne v. Earl of Glengall (1848), 2 H.L.C. 131 [312]

A father, on the marriage of his daughter, agreed to give her a portion of £100,000. He transferred one-third of this sum in Consols to the trustees of his daughter's marriage settlement. He gave the trustees his bond for the transfer of the remainder on his death, to be held by the trustees on trust for the daughter for life with remainder to such children of the marriage as she and her husband should have appointed. The father by his will afterwards gave the trustees a moiety of the residue of his personalty, on trust for his daughter for life with remainder to such of her children as she should have appointed. *Held*, the moiety of the residue given by the will was, notwithstanding the difference in the trusts, in satisfaction of the sum of stock due under the bond. The daughter had to elect between the two provisions. As it was more advantageous to the daughter and her children, if any, to take under the will she was bound to elect so to take.

Tilley's Will Trusts, Re, Burgin v. Croad, [1967] 2 All E.R. 303 [313]

A testator, who died in 1932, left property to his widow as sole trustee on trust to the widow for life and on her death to C. and M., his children by a former marriage, in equal shares. The widow engaged in many property transactions both before and after the testator's death. Properties forming part of the testator's estate were realized in 1933, 1939, 1951 and 1952. From these the widow received a total of £2237 which was paid into her bank account and was mingled with her own moneys. Up until 1951 the widow's bank account was at various times substantially overdrawn (in 1945 to the extent of £23,536) and investments purchased by the widow financed by overdraft facilities at the bank. From 1951 her bank account was sufficiently in credit from her own personal contributions to it, without regard to any trust moneys credited to it, to pay for her later property purchases. In 1959 the widow died, her estate being valued at £94,000. The administrator of M., who had predeceased the widow, sued the widow's personal representatives for an account of the testator's estate, and claimed that M.'s estate was entitled to one-half of the proportion of profits of purchases made by the widow to the extent that the defendants could not show that such properties were purchased out of the widow's own money. *Held*, if a trustee mixes trust property with his own and purchases property with money drawn from the account, then (a) if the beneficiary makes a claim against the property so purchased, there is no presumption that the trustee withdrew his own money in order to make the purchase; (b) the beneficiary can claim a charge on the property for the amount of trust money expended on the purchase; (c) as regards any increase in value in the property, the beneficiary can claim that proportion of the profit attributable to the amount of trust money expended in the purchase.

Towndrow, Re, [1911] 1 Ch. 662 [314]

M. was a trustee of two trust funds. Under the first M. held a beneficial interest. Under the second he held no beneficial interest. M. settled part of the property in which he held a beneficial interest under the first trust, and mortgaged the remaining part to G. M. later misappropriated property which he held as trustee under the second trust. *Held*, as there were two distinct trusts, the court had no power to impound M.'s interest in the first to make good his default in the second. G., as M.'s assignee, therefore took free of any equity in respect of M.'s default.

Townley v. Sherborne (1634), Bridg. J. 35   [315]

T. joined with his co-trustee in signing receipts for rents due to the trust. The money was paid to the co-trustee, in whose hands T. allowed it to remain. The co-trustee became insolvent. *Held*, a trustee is not liable for breaches committed by a co-trustee unless he is himself in some way at fault. T. was not liable in respect of the breach by his co-trustee, but he was liable on the grounds that he had been at fault in allowing the money to remain in the hands of the co-trustee.

Tulk v. Moxhay (1848), 2 Ph. 774   [316]

The plaintiff, who owned several houses in Leicester Square, sold the garden in the centre of the square to one Elms who covenanted, for himself, his heirs, and assigns, that he would keep the gardens and railings around them in their present condition and continue to allow the inhabitants of the square to have the use and enjoyment of the gardens. The land in question was sold to the defendant and the conveyance to him did not contain a covenant in similar terms although he knew of the restriction contained in the deed to which the plaintiff and Elms were parties. The defendant announced that he intended to build on the land and the plaintiff, who still remained the owner of several adjacent houses, sought an injunction to restrain him from doing so. *Held*, the injunction would be granted as the covenant would be enforced in equity against all subsequent purchasers with notice.

Turner's Will Trusts, Re, District Bank Ltd. v. Turner,   [317]
[1936] 2 All E.R. 1435 (Court of Appeal)

A testator gave one-fifth of the residue of his property to such of the children of his late son C. H. T. as should be living at his death and should have then attained or should thereafter attain the age of twenty-eight. Clause 15 of the will provided ". . . my trustees may apply the whole or part . . . of the income of the expectant or presumptive share of any grandchild of mine in my residuary estate . . . for . . . his . . . education . . . during such time as such grandchildren shall be under the age of twenty-eight years . . . and shall during the suspense of absolute vesting of any such share accumulate the surplus if any of the income thereof . . . by investing the same and the resulting income thereof . . . so as to follow the destination of the share from which the same shall have proceeded but with power to apply any such accumulations . . . for . . . the . . . education . . . of the grandchild for the time being presumptively entitled . . . in the same manner as such accumulations might have been applied had they been income arising from the original share in the then current year . . ." At the testator's death on December 5, 1931, there were living three children of C. H. T., of whom two, Robert and Doris, had reached the age of 28. The third child, Geoffrey, reached the age of 21 on August 3, 1931 but died on November 23, 1934, intestate and unmarried. At his death the amount accumulated by the trustees, in respect of his share of the residue amounted to £3421. If this share passed under his intestacy, then the addition of this sum to the rest of his estate would raise the rate of estate duty payable with the result that the amount of tax payable would be increased by a much larger sum than £3421. The person entitled under Geoffrey's intestacy therefore claimed that the accumulation should go to Robert and Doris. *Held*, although s. 31 (1) (ii) of the Trustee Act 1925 is imperative in form, it is part of and ancillary to the statutory power of maintenance conferred on Trustees by the section, and s. 69 (2) of the 1925 Act therefore applies to it. Thus where a contrary intention is expressed in the instrument creating the trust, the contrary intention prevails. For these reasons the accumulations of the income of the presumptive share of Geoffrey made by the trustees did not form part of his estate, but accrued by way of addition to the shares of Robert and Doris in the residuary estate of the testator.

Tweddle v. Atkinson (1861), 1 B. & S. 393   [318]

The plaintiff's father and father-in-law agreed with each other to pay the plaintiff £100 and £200 respectively in consideration of his then intended marriage and after the marriage had taken place they confirmed their agreement in writing. The £200 was not paid and the plaintiff sued his father-in-law's executor to recover this sum. *Held*, his action must fail as no stranger to the consideration can take advantage of a contract, although made for his benefit. A promisee cannot bring a successful action unless the consideration for the promise moved from him.

Tyler, Re, Tyler v. Tyler, [1891] 3 Ch. 252   [319]

A testator bequeathed £42,000 in stock to the trustees for the time being of the London Missionary Society, with a gift over to the Blue Coat School, London, if the Society failed to keep the family vault in good repair. *Held*, the condition for the repair of the vault was valid and binding on the Society, and the gift over, on failure to comply with the condition, to the School was valid, on the principle that the rule against perpetuities had no application to a transfer, on the occurrence of a certain event, of property from one charity to another.

Tyler's Fund Trusts, Re, Graves v. King, [1967] 3 All E.R. 389   [320]

(i) In March 1951 T. made her will. She appointed K., who worked in a solicitor's office and G., to be her executors. The will included a legacy of £500 to K. (ii) At some time before May 9, 1951, T. transferred £1500 to K. (iii) On May 9, 1951 T. wrote to K. saying that she wished him to hold the £1500 which she had put in his control for certain specified purposes; these were, in substance, to pay to G. during her life such sums as K. thought desirable, and to dispose, after G.'s death, of any moneys remaining in K.'s hands in such manner as he should consider would carry out the wishes of which T. had told him. (iv) T. died in 1954. (v) Shortly before probate was granted K. signed a memorandum in which, after stating that the £1500 had been put in his hands by T. for the benefit of G., he stated that authority was given to him by T. to divide the funds available on the death of G. among institutions mentioned in the memorandum and among any other charitable institutions in the proportions that he thought desirable. The memorandum further stated that T. directed that one-third of the amount available for division should be paid to his executors and the remainder should be divided between the societies mentioned in the memorandum. (vi) K. died in 1960. (viii) G. died in 1966. On the validity of the trust created by T. in 1951, *Held*, (1) After the transfer at (ii) above, K. held the £1500 on trust for T., who thus then had an equitable interest in the property. T.'s letter of 9 May (at (iii) above) constituted a valid assignment (under s. 53 (1) (c) of the Law of Property Act 1925) of T.'s equitable interest in the property to those entitled according to directions in T.'s letter. (2) K.'s memorandum (at (v) above) was admissible in evidence by virtue of s. 1 of the Evidence Act 1938. The memorandum was, however, insufficient to establish a trust of £500 (i.e. one third of £1500) in favour of those claiming under K. having regard to the facts that there was a quasi-professional relationship between K. and T. and that T. had by will bequeathed a gift to K. of the like amount (£500) only two months previously. (3) Since an intention appeared from the memorandum that the whole balance of the funds should be distributed among charitable institutions, the balance of the fund would be applied by way of scheme for the benefit of charity.

Ulverston and District New Hospital Building Trusts, Re,   [321] Birkett v. Barrow and Furness Hospital Management Committee, [1956] Ch. 622 (Court of Appeal)

Subscriptions were invited for a fund to build a new hospital to serve the needs of Ulverstone and surrounding districts. Subscriptions were received from named donors, and money was collected from anonymous donors in street collections and at entertainments. The amount raised was insufficient to finance the building of a new hospital and, after the National Health Service was introduced, the trustees sought the direction of the court as to what should be done with the money in their hands. *Held*, as the fund had been collected for one particular purpose no general charitable intent was to be inferred. The particular purpose having failed, the trustees held the money collected on a resulting trust for the donors. [For the present law, see Charities Act 1960, s. 14.]

Vandepitte v. Preferred Accident Insurance Corporation   [322]
of New York, [1933] A.C. 70 (Privy Council)

Mrs. Vandepitte, the plaintiff, was being driven by her husband when their car was in collision with one driven by Jean Berry. Jean was driving her father's car with his permission and the plaintiff obtained a judgment, which was not satisfied, against her in respect of injuries which she received in the accident. Jean's father was insured with the defendants against third-party risks and the policy covered accidents which might occur while Jean was driving. The plaintiff sought to recover the amount of the judgment which she had previously obtained against Jean from the defendants and founded her claim on s. 24 of the British Columbia Insurance Act 1925, which enabled an injured person to avail himself of any rights possessed by the driver of the vehicle against the insurance company where an action against the negligent motorist had been unfruitful. *Held*, the plaintiff's action would fail as Jean was not a party to the contract of insurance and there was no evidence that her father had intended to create a trust in her favour.

Vandervell v. Inland Revenue Commissioners, [1967]   [323]
1 All E.R. 1 (House of Lords)

V. wishes to give £150,000 to the Royal College of Surgeons to found a chair of pharmacology. At V.'s direction a bank which held shares as nominee of V. transferred 100,000 of these shares to the Royal College of Surgeons. As part of the arrangement the College gave V.T. Ltd., the trustees of a family settlement, an option to purchase the shares for £5000 in five years time. Dividends on the shares were subsequently paid to the College. V.T. Ltd. later exercised the option to purchase and paid £5000 to the College. On the question whether V. had divested himself absolutely of the property in the shares, *Held*, (1) " section 53 (1) (c) of the Law of Property Act 1925 . . . refers to the disposition of an equitable interest as such. If, owning the entire estate, legal and beneficial, in a piece of property, and desiring to transfer that entire estate to another, I do so by means of a disposition which *ex facie* deals only with the legal estate, it would be ridiculous to argue that section 53 (1) (c) had not been complied with, and that therefore the legal estate alone passed. The present case, it is true, is different in its facts in that the legal and equitable estates in the shares were in separate ownership: but when [V.] . . . instructed the bank to transfer the shares to the college, and made it abundantly clear that he wanted to pass, by means of that transfer, his own beneficial, or equitable, interest, plus the bank's legal interest, he achieved the same result as if there had been no separation of interests. The transfer thus made . . . was a disposition not of the equitable interest alone, but of the entire estate in the shares. In such a case I see no room for the operation of section 53 (1) (c) ". (*Per* LORD DONOVAN). (2) The option to purchase the shares was vested in V.T. Ltd. on a resulting trust for V.; thus V. had failed to divest himself absolutely of the property in the shares [and had therefore failed to bring himself within the exempting provisions of 415 (1) (d) (2) of the Income Tax Act 1952].

Vatcher v. Paull, [1915] A.C. 372 (Privy Council)   [324]

Henry Vatcher married twice. He had two children by his first marriage and six children by his second marriage. In 1846 he made a settlement of property in contemplation of his second marriage. Under this funds were settled on himself and his second wife for their lives, and thereafter to such of his children by his first and second marriages as he and his wife should appoint, and in default of appointment to all his children equally. In 1882 Henry Vatcher and his wife made an appointment in favour of the children of the second marriage, with the proviso that if the children of the first marriage renounced any claims they might have to lands in Jersey (where Henry Vatcher had lived since 1863) then the appointment should be revoked (with the result that the settled property would pass, in default of appointment, to the children of both marriages). In 1886 the children of the first marriage renounced their entitlement to land in Jersey. The children of the first marriage later contended that the appointment of 1882 constituted a fraud on a power (*i.e.*, the exercise of a power for a purpose beyond the scope of or not justified by the instrument creating the power.) *Held*, the appointment did not constitute a fraud on a power. A condition in the appointment which lead to the property going to the persons entitled in default of appointment was not fraudulent as it did not defeat the intention of the donor of the appointment.

Vaughan, Re, Vaughan v. Thomas (1886), 33 Ch.D. 187   **[325]**

A testator bequeathed £500 to trustees on trust to invest the capital and use such part of the income as was necessary to keep in repair a family vault in the churchyard at Llansaintfread, and to use the remaining money to keep in repair the churchyard itself and a tomb in it. *Held*, (1) The gift to maintain the vault and the tomb were not charitable. (2) The gift to maintain the churchyard was charitable. (3) The gift to maintain the vault, being non-charitable, was void. The gift of the income intended to be applied for the maintenance of the vault did not fall into residue, but fell into the second residuary part of the disposition i.e. for the maintenance of the church yard and the tomb. (4) Regarding this residuary disposition, the amount needed to maintain the tomb was to be assessed, and the gift of that amount of capital required to produce such an annual sum failed. The balance of the £500 was to be applied, as a valid charitable gift, for the upkeep of the churchyard.

Verge v. Somerville, [1924] A.C. 406 (House of Lords)   **[326]**

A testator resident in New South Wales bequeathed his residuary estate to the trustees " . . . of the ' Repatriation Fund ' or other similar fund for the benefit of New South Wales returned soldiers ". *Held*, (1) " repatriation " (by which was meant restoring the soldiers to their native land and giving them a fresh start in life) was a charitable purpose. (2) The trust was a public trust as it was for the benefit of a class of the community. (3) A trust might be charitable notwithstanding that it benefited the rich as well as the poor. The gift was therefore charitable.

Vernon's Will Trusts, Re, Lloyds Bank, Ltd. v. Group 20,   **[327]**
   Hospital Management Committee (Coventry), [1971] 3 All E.R. 1061

A testatrix, who died in 1960, by her will directed that her residuary estate should be divided " among the following charitable institutions in equal shares, *viz*: Coventry Crippled Children's Guild; The National Life Boat Institution, The Royal Midland Counties Home for Incurables (at Leamington) ". At the date of the will there was in existence a body named the Coventry and District Crippled Children's Guild. This body had been incorporated as a company limited by guarantee under the Companies Act 1919. Its objects included the provision of orthopaedic clinics and convalescent homes for crippled children. In 1948 the assets of the Guild vested in the Minister of Health under the National Health Services Act 1946. In 1952 the guild was dissolved, and its name struck off the register of companies under s. 353 of the Companies Act 1948. A clinic (at 55 Holywood Road, Coventry) and a hospital (the Paybody Hospital) which had been established by the guild continued to be used, as part of the National Health Service, at the date of the testatrix's death in 1960. In 1949, an unincorporated body, named the Coventry and District Cripples' Guild, had been formed. Its objects included supporting work for the benefit of cripples. It never carried on any orthopaedic activities. On the effect of the gift to the " Coventry Crippled Children's Guild ", *Held*, (1) the testatrix intended to refer to an institution which she then believed to exist. Her words were a misdescription of Coventry and District Crippled Children's Guild, and the will was to be construed as a gift to that body. (2) " Every bequest to an unincorporated charity by name without more must take effect as a gift for a charitable purpose . . . i.e. that charitable purpose which the named charity exists to serve . . . ". (3) " A bequest to a named unincorporated charity, however, may on its true interpretation show that the testator's intention to make the gift at all was dependant on the named charitable organisation being available at the time when the gift takes effect to serve as the instrument for applying the subject-matter of the gift to the charitable purpose for which it is by inference given. If so and the named charity ceases to exist in the lifetime of the testator, the gift fails ". (4) " A bequest to a corporate body on the other hand, takes effect simply as a gift to the body beneficially, unless there are circumstances which show that the recipient is to take the gift as a trustee. There is no need in such a case to infer a trust for any particular purpose . . . the natural construction is that the bequest is made to the corporate body as part of its general funds, that is to say, beneficially and without the imposition of any trust ". (5) There was nothing in the will to indicate that the gift to the incorporated Guild was to be construed as a gift on trust for the purpose of the Guild. (6) The charity might be entitled, notwithstanding that its objects had been modified or changed in accordance with the law between the date of the will and the testator's death or any later date at which the gift took effect. " A change merely in its mechanical aspect could not involve the charity ceasing to exist ". (7) " . . . the true view is that the charity which at the date of the testatrix' will was being carried on by the incorporated guild continued in existence down to and after the date of her death in the form of the Orthopaedic clinic and hospital which were conducted by the first defendant at 55 Holyhead Road and the Paybody Hospital " (*per* BUCKLEY, J.) (8) The gift thus took effect as a valid charitable gift in favour of the charity consisting of the orthopaedic clinic at 55 Holyhead Road and the orthopaedic hospital carried on in the building known as the Paybody Hospital.

Vickery, Re, Vickery v. Stephens, [1931] All E.R. Rep. 562   **[328]**

A sole executor employed a solicitor to wind up the estate. Unknown to the executor the solicitor had at one time been suspended from practice. The solicitor absconded with £276 belonging to the estate. The beneficiaries under the will sought a declaration that the executor had been in breach of trust. *Held*, the executor had been guilty only of an error of judgment which in the circumstances did not amount to " wilful default " under s. 30 (1) of the Trustee Act 1925, by which trustees are not liable for losses due to the default of " any banker, broker or other person with whom any trust money or other securities may be deposited " unless the losses are caused by the trustees' own wilful default. The executor was therefore not liable.

Vinogradoff, Re, [1935] W.N. 68   **[329]**

In 1926 T. transferred £800 War Loan, then standing in her own name, to the joint names of herself and Laura Jackson, then aged four. By her will dated May 14, 1934 T. gave a life interest in the stock to Helen Lee. The executors brought the action to determine what beneficial interest, if any, Laura Jackson held in the stock. *Held*, by the transfer of the stock a resulting trust had been created, by which the joint-holders held the stock on trust for the transferor, T. The fact that

s. 20 of the Law of Property Act 1925 provided that the appointment of an infant trustee was void was not sufficient to rebut the presumption of a resulting trust. Laura Jackson thus held no beneficial interest in the stock, which passed under the will.

Wale, Re, Wale v. Harris, [1956] 3 All E.R. 280   **[330]**

Elizabeth Wale was entitled to certain "B" investments under her husband's will. These were registered in the names of the executors of her husband's will. She was also the absolute owner of certain "A" shares, registered in her own name. In 1939 Elizabeth Wale made a voluntary gift of the "A" and "B" shares to trustees on trust for her daughter, but did not take any steps to transfer the shares to the trustees and during the rest of her life showed no indication of remembering the creation of the settlement. In her will she left her property to her two sons. The two sons and the daughter were appointed her executors. When she died in 1953 the family solicitor produced the 1939 settlement. The question arose as to whether the shares should go to the daughter under the settlement or to the sons under the will. *Held*, regarding the "B" shares, as, at the time of the settlement in 1939, Elizabeth Wale held an equitable interest in the shares (an equitable chose in action), and as an assignment of an equitable chose in action need not be in any particular form [provided that s. 53 (1) (c) of the L.P.A. is complied with], there had been a valid assignment of her interest in the shares to the trustees. The absence of consideration did not affect the validity of the assignment. Thus the daughter was entitled to the "B" shares under the 1939 settlement. Regarding the "A" shares, as Elizabeth Wale held the legal title to these, the property in them had not passed to the trustees. The court considered whether the appointment of the daughter as one of the executors of her mother's will brought the case within the rule in *Strong* v. *Bird*, by which an imperfect gift of property may be made effective by the donee becoming the personal representative of the donor, but found that for the rule to apply the donor's intention to make the gift must have continued until the donor's death. This condition was not satisfied. Thus the gift to trustees on trust for the daughter remained ineffective and the "A" shares passed to the sons under the will.

Wallgrave v. Tebbs (1855), 2 K. & J. 313   **[331]**

A testator bequeathed T. and M. £12,000 and some freehold properties in Chelsea. The testator had contemplated devoting part of his property to charitable objects, and after the will was made G., one of his executors, prepared a draft letter from the testator to T. and M. setting out the charitable objects which the testator had in mind. The draft letter was not sent to T. and M., and they did not see it until after the testator's death. They at no time gave any undertaking to carry out the testator's wishes, and did not learn of these until after the testator's death. *Held*, "where a person, knowing that a testator in making a disposition in his favour intends it to be applied for purposes other than his own benefit, either expressly promises, or by silence implies, that he will carry the testator's intention into effect, and the property is left to him upon the faith of that promise or undertaking, it is in effect a case of trust . . . But the question here is totally different. Here there has been no such promise or undertaking on the part of the devisees. Here the devisees knew nothing of the testator's intention until after his death" (*per* WOOD, V.-C.). No trust had been created and the legatees took the properties absolutely.

Walsh v. Lonsdale (1882), 21 Ch. D. 9 (Court of Appeal)   **[332]**

W. entered into possession of a cotton mill, under a written agreement with L. for a seven years' lease. It was part of the agreement that a deed should be executed containing, *inter alia*, a provision that rent should be payable one year in advance upon L.'s demand. In the event no deed was executed. W. paid rent, quarterly, in arrear, for a year and a half. L. then demanded a year's rent in advance. When W. refused to pay, L. distrained for the amount. W. thereupon brought an action against L. for illegal distress. W. claimed that as he had been let into possession and had paid rent upon a yearly basis, he was in the position of a tenant from year to year. As a tenancy of this kind was determinable upon six months' notice, L.'s proposal that rent should be payable a year in advance was, he claimed, inconsistent with his position as a tenant from year to year. For this reason, W. claimed, L.'s distress was illegal. *Held*, since the agreement under which W. entered into possession was capable of specific performance, and since equity looked on that as done which ought to be done, the position was just the same as it would have been if the formal lease had actually been executed. W. thus held upon the full terms of the agreement to execute the lease. L. was therefore entitled to demand that rent should be payable one year in advance and his distress was lawful.

Ward v. Duncombe, [1893] A.C. 369 (House of Lords)   [333]

A testator, M. C. W., bequeathed property to trustees Sharp and Ellis on trust for sale for his son Matthew for life, with remainder to Matthew's children, of whom Mary was one. In contemplation of her marriage to D., Mary assigned her interest under M. C. W.'s will to F. W. upon certain trusts. Sharp had notice of the assignment to F. W.; Ellis did not. Later Mary proposed to mortgage her interest under the will of M. C. W. to the L. Insurance company as security for a loan, without disclosing to the company that the interest had already been assigned to F. W. The company enquired from Sharp and Ellis whether they had received notice of any prior incumbrance on Mary's interest. Sharp returned an evasive answer; Ellis replied that he knew of no incumbrance. The company advanced £300 to Mary on the security of the mortgage of her interest under the will. Notice of the mortgage was given to Sharp and Ellis. Sharp later died and was replaced as trustee by Evitt. On the death of M. C. W., Matthew also having died, the question arose as to whether F. W. or the company should take priority. *Held*, F. W. took priority. Notice to one of several trustees (Sharp) remained effective indefinitely, even after his death or retirement, as regards all transactions effected while he was still trustee. The company could have discovered the assignment to F. W. if it had made proper enquiries of Sharp. (But see *Re Phillips' Trusts*.)

Warner Brothers Pictures Inc. v. Nelson, [1936] 3 All E.R. 160   [334]

An actress entered into a contract with the plaintiffs, initially for a term of one year, but giving the plaintiffs the option of extending it, whereby she agreed that she would not undertake other film work without obtaining their written consent. The plaintiffs sought an injunction to restrain her from doing film work for another in breach of this agreement. *Held*, the injunction would be granted for the period of the continuance of the contract or for three years, whichever was the shorter.

Warren v. Gurney, [1944] 2 All E.R. 472 (Court of Appeal)   [335]

In 1929 a father purchased a house for £300. The house was conveyed into the name of his daughter. The father retained the title deeds. In 1943 the father signed a document headed "my wish" in which he directed that the house was to be divided between his three daughters. The father died in 1944, the title deeds still being in his possession at the time of his death. The daughter claimed to be owner of the house and so to be entitled to possession of the title deeds. The executors of the father's will contended that the daughter was a trustee of the property for her father. *Held*, (i) the document headed "my wish" was not admissible in evidence, as it was in the nature of a subsequent declaration by the donor, which was not against his own interest, and it was established that such declarations by a donor were only admissible if they were against his interest; (ii) the retention of the title deeds by the father, together with certain declarations of the father at the time of the purchase, were sufficient to rebut the presumption of advancement. Thus the daughter held the house as trustee for her father's estate.

Wasdale, Re, Brittin v. Partridge, [1899] 1 Ch. 163   [336]

A testator devised land to trustees, A. B. and R. B., on trust for sale and conversion. E. N. W. was entitled to a reversionary interest in the proceeds of sale. In 1871 E. N. W. assigned his interest to J. P., who gave notice to A. B. and R. B. A. B. and R. B. subsequently died and were replaced by fresh trustees. In 1897 E. N. W. assigned his interest to L. B. as security for a loan. L. B. gave notice of the assignment to the new trustees. Later, when the interest fell into possession, the question arose as to whether J. P. or L. B. should take priority. *Held,* J. P. took priority. Where notice is given to all of several trustees, the notice remains effective indefinitely even though they die or retire without communicating the notice to their successors. (But see *Phipps* v. *Lovegrove*.)

Webster v. Cecil (1861), 30 Beav. 62   [337]

The defendant wrote to offer to sell some property to the plaintiff for £1250. Although the defendant had already refused to sell this land to the plaintiff for £2000, the plaintiff, who therefore had knowledge of the mistake, wrote to accept the offer contained in the defendant's letter. The defendant had intended that the price should be £2250 and he immediately gave notice of the error. *Held,* a decree of specific performance would not be granted.

Wedgwood, Re, Allen v. Wedgwood, [1915] 1 Ch. 113   [338]
(Court of Appeal)

A testatrix, who died in 1913, by her will gave her residue to C.W. absolutely. On the evidence submitted to the court, it was *Held,* that C.W. held the property under a secret trust, on trust for the protection and benefit of animals; and, further, that this object constituted a valid charitable trust, on the grounds that it was calculated to promote public morality by checking the innate tendency to cruelty.

Weekes' Settlement, Re, [1897] 1 Ch. 289   [339]

A testatrix bequeathed certain real property to her husband for life, and gave "him power to dispose of all such property by will amongst our children". There was no gift over in default of appointment. There were children, but the husband died intestate without having exercised the power. *Held,* in the circumstances of the case the court was not bound to imply that a gift to the class was intended in default of the power being exercised [*i.e.,* that the power was a "trust power"]. In order for such a gift to be implied there must be a clear indication in the will that the testator intended the power to be regarded in the nature of a trust. There being no such evidence in the will, the power was a mere power and not a "trust power". Consequently the property was not to be divided among the children equally, but was to go to the heir of the testatrix.

Welsh Hospital (Netley) Fund, Re, [1921] 1 Ch. 655   [340]

In 1914 an appeal was made for money to build a hospital for sick or wounded Welsh soldiers. Large sums were received, partly by subscriptions from private individuals and partly from concerts and street collections in Wales. A hospital was built with the money so raised. In 1919 the hospital was closed and the property sold to the War Office. After winding up the affairs of the hospital there was a surplus of £9000. *Held,* " although all the contributions were in the first instance made for the particular purpose of building, equipping and maintaining the Welsh Hospital at Netley, the main underlying object of the contributors was to provide money for the comfort of sick and wounded Welshmen, and that all the subscribers intended to devote their contributions not only to the particular object, but generally for the benefit of their sick and wounded countrymen ". That being so the Court is . . . at liberty to apply the surplus of the fund *cy-près*. (*per* Lawrence, J.)

West Sussex Constabulary's Widows Children and Benevolent   **[341]**
(1930) Fund Trusts, Re, Barnett v. Ketteringham, [1970]
1 All E.R. 544

In 1930 the West Sussex Constabulary Widows, Children and Benevolent Fund Trusts were established to provide for the widows and orphans of deceased members of the West Sussex Constabulary. The Fund received revenue from (a) subscriptions from members of the Constabulary; (b) proceeds of entertainments, raffles and sweepstakes; (c) collecting boxes; (d) donations, including legacies. On January 1, 1968, the West Sussex Constabulary was (by authority of statute) amalgamated with other police forces in Sussex to form a single force. As a result of this amalgamation doubts arose as to how the funds, which then amounted to some £35,000, were to be dealt with. At the annual general meeting of members of the fund, on June 7th, 1968, it was decided to amend and add to the rules to enable them to wind up the fund and to apply the contents in accordance with a new rule. *Held*, (1) the meeting on 7 June 1968 was abortive and there were at no time after December 3, 1967 any members of the fund capable of holding a meeting amending the rules or winding up the fund. (2) The fund could not belong to the members themselves (as might be the result in the event of the dissolution of a members' club) because only third parties were entitled to benefit from the fund. (3) That part of the fund derived from (a) above was not held on a resulting trust for the donors since the money had been subscribed on a contractual, not a trust, basis. Apart from any claim which members might have in contract based on frustration or total failure of consideration, this part of the fund was *bona vacantia*. (4) That part of the fund derived from (b) above, having been subscribed on a contractual, not a trust basis, was *bona vacantia*. (5) That part of the fund derived from (c) above, since it should be regarded as having been made by donors intending to part out and out with their money, was *bona vacantia*. (6) That part of the fund derived from (d) above, since the purpose of the donation was unequivocal, was held on a resulting trust for the donors or their estates.

Westerton, Re, Public Trustee v. Gray, [1919] 2 Ch. 104   **[342]**

In 1914 W. placed £500 on deposit in his account at the London and County Westminster Bank and obtained a receipt. In 1916 W. gave his landlady, Mrs. G., an envelope addressed to her, saying it was a present. Before she was able to open it, W. took it from her and said he would keep it for her, and locked it up in his despatch box. After W.'s death in 1917, the envelope was found to contain the receipt for £500; an order in writing signed by W. directing the bank to pay the £500 on deposit to Mrs. G.; and a letter addressed to Mrs. G. saying "You have been very kind to me and I desire to make some return by giving you the amount of £500 now on deposit at the . . . Bank as per receipt enclosed". The bank did not receive any notice of any assignment until after W.'s death when the envelope was opened. *Held*, there had been a valid assignment to Mrs. G. of the amount on deposit at the bank under the Judicature Act, s. 25 (6) [now s. 136 of the Law of Property Act 1925]. Value or consideration was not necessary for an assignment under the section.

Westminster Bank v. Lee, [1955] 2 All E.R. 883   **[343]**

In September 1948 a husband deserted his wife, leaving her in occupation of the matrimonial home. In November 1948 the husband created an equitable mortgage of the matrimonial home in favour of the Westminster Bank to secure his overdraft. In 1951 the wife obtained an order of the court restraining the husband from ejecting her from the home until he had provided other suitable accommodation. In July, 1954 the Bank took out an originating summons to enforce the equitable mortgage against the husband and to seek possession against the wife. *Held*, (i) the right of a deserted wife to remain in the matrimonial home, put at its highest, was a mere equity, and no equitable estate or interest in that home was created in her favour upon desertion; (ii) the subsequent purchaser of an equitable estate without notice of mere equities attaching to the estate, took free of those mere equities; (iii) the bank could not be held to have had notice, actual or constructive, of the wife's mere equity; (iv) the bank's mortgage therefore took priority over the wife's equity. The Bank was thus entitled to an order for possession against the wife. (But see *National Provincial Bank* v. *Ainsworth*.)

Weston's Settlement, Re, [1968] 3 All E.R. 338   [344]
(Court of Appeal)

In 1964 W. made two settlements, one in favour of his son A. and the other in favour of his son R. Each trust fund was worth about £400,000. W. lived in England until 1967 when he, his wife, and A. went to live in a house which W. had bought in Jersey. In the same year R. sold his house in Sheffield and went with his family to live in a flat which he had leased in Jersey. W. sought the sanction of the court to a scheme to remove the settlements from England to Jersey, thus freeing the settled funds from liability to capital gains tax and to estate duty on the death of A or R. *Held*, the court was not prepared to sanction the proposed removal of the settlements to Jersey since the underlying purpose was the avoidance of tax and (a) the overall effect was not for the true benefit of the children born and yet to be born; (b) no good reason connected with the trusts themselves had been put forward for their removal.

Whistler v. Webster (1794), 2 Ves. Jun. 367   [345]

J. W. had power to appoint certain property to his children, to whom the property was to go in default of appointment. In his will J. W. gave certain legacies to his sons, but exercised the power of appointment in favour of his grand-children. *Held*, J. W.'s children were to be put to their election to take under the will (and take the legacies and allow the appointment to the grandchildren to take effect) or against the will (and, as the persons entitled in default of appointment, take the property appointed to the grandchildren, but compensate the grand-children for their loss out of the legacies received from their father).

William Brandt's Sons & Co. v. Dunlop Rubber Co., [1905]   [346]
A.C. 454 (House of Lords)

The Dunlop Rubber Co., the defendants, owed money to Kramrisch & Co., a firm of merchants. Kramrisch & Co. in turn owed money to William Brandt's Sons & Co., bankers. Kramrisch & Co. agreed with William Brandt's Sons and Co. that the money owing to Kramrisch & Co. by the Dunlop Rubber Co. should be paid direct to William Brandt's Sons & Co. William Brandt's Sons & Co. forwarded to the Dunlop Rubber Co. notice in writing that Kramrisch & Co. had assigned to them the right to receive the money owed by the Dunlop Rubber Co. to Kramrisch & Co., and requested the Dunlop Rubber Co. to sign an undertaking to remit the money. Later, when Kramrisch & Co. had become bankrupt, the Dunlop Rubber Co. by inadvertence paid the money to some one other than William Brandt's Sons and Co. *Held*, although the language of a formal assignment had not been used this was immaterial if the meaning was plain. There had been a valid equitable assign-ment of the debt to William Brandt's Sons & Co., with notice by William Brandt's Sons & Co. to the debtor, the Dunlop Rubber Co. Therefore the Dunlop Rubber Co. "must pay the money over again, and pay it to the right person" (*per* LORD MACNAGHTEN), *i.e.*, William Brandt's Sons & Co.

Williams v. Atlantic Assurance Co., [1933] 1 K.B. 81   [347]
(Court of Appeal)

C. V. & Co. insured certain goods, of which they were the owner or pledgee, for

£8000. The goods were lost at sea. In settlement of a claim by W., to whom the firm had incurred a liability of £7000, it was agreed that the firm should assign to W. the benefit of the insurance policy under which the goods had been insured, and that W. should pay the firm £1000 if he should receive that amount or more from the insurance company. W. brought an action in his own name against the insurance company to recover the value of the insured goods. *Held*, Williams had only acquired the policy subject to an equitable interest to the extent of £1000 retained by the firm. The assignment of a part of a debt or legal chose in action was not "absolute" and was therefore not within s. 136 of the Law of Property Act 1925. There had been no legal assignment to W. and W. was therefore not entitled to sue the insurance company, the debtor, in his own name.

Williams v. Barton, [1927] 2 Ch. 9   [348]

B. was employed as a clerk by a firm of stockbrokers on the basis that his salary should consist of half the commission earned by the firm on business introduced by B. On B.'s recommendation the firm was employed to value the securities of a testator, of whose will B. was one of two trustees. B. took no part in the work of valuation. The trustees paid the commission charged by the firm, and B. received one half of this. B.'s co-trustee claimed that B. held this money on trust for the beneficiaries under the will, and that the money must be paid over to the estate. *Held*, where a trustee makes a profit out of his position as a trustee he holds that profit as constructive trustee for the benefit of the *cestuis que trust*. B. would not have received the particular half share of commission but for his position as trustee and he was therefore bound to pay it over to the estate.

Williams, Re, Williams v. Williams, [1897] 2 Ch. 12   [349]

A testator bequeathed certain property to his sons and then directed "As to all the . . . residue of my estate . . . I bequeath the same unto my wife Lucy . . . absolutely, in the fullest confidence that she will carry out my wishes in the following particulars; namely, that she pays the premiums . . . in respect of the policy for £1000 on her own life and that she by her will leaves the moneys . . . payable under such policy and also the moneys to become payable . . . under the £300 on my own life to my daughter . . .". The widow in her will bequeathed the proceeds of the policy on the testator's life to the daughter, and the proceeds of the policy on her own life to another. *Held*, the words used in the will ("in the fullest confidence") being only precatory and not imperative were insufficient to create a trust by making the widow trustee of the proceeds of the policy on the testator's life for the daughter. The widow was therefore entitled to dispose of the proceeds as she wished, and the property passed according to the widow's will.

Williams' Trustees v. Inland Revenue Commissioners,   [350]
[1947] 1 All E.R. 513 (House of Lords)

A trust was created with the object of establishing and maintaining an institute ". . . with a view to creating a centre in London for promoting the moral, social, spiritual and educational welfare of Welsh people and fostering the study of the Welsh language and of Welsh history, literature music and art". *Held*, the trust was not charitable as it was not beneficial to the community in a way the law regards as charitable.

Wilson v Duguid (1883) Ch. 24   [351]

By a settlement dated 1833 leasehold property was assigned to trustees on trust for A. for life with remainder to B. (her husband) for life, with remainder on trust to assign the property among such of their children in such shares as the survivor should appoint, and if there were no children then on trust for C. for life with remainder on trust to assign the property among such of C.'s children in such shares as C. should appoint. A. died in 1876 and B. in 1880. They left no children. C. died in 1863 without having exercised the power of appointment. Of C.'s ten children, three died before him, two died between his death and A.'s death, and one between the death of A. and B.; four of C.'s children were living at B.'s death. *Held*, that all the children of C. took as tenants in common in equal shares.

Wise, Re, Ex parte Mercer (1886), 17 Q.B.D. 290   [352]
(Court of Appeal)

In 1881 Wise became engaged to Miss Vyse. In May of the same year he married someone else. Miss Vyse brought an action against him for breach of promise. The writ was served on Wise on October 8. A few days later Wise heard that he had become entitled to a legacy of £500. On October 17, he made a voluntary settlement of the legacy on trust for his wife for life, with remainder to the children of the marriage. On July 20, 1882 Miss Vyse was awarded £500 damages in her action for breach of promise. On November 14, Wise was adjudicated bankrupt on a petition presented by Miss Vyse who had failed to obtain the damages awarded to her. The trustee in bankruptcy applied to have the settlement of October 17 set aside. Wise was able to show that at the time when he made the settlement he was in a position to pay his debts. He was also able to satisfy the court that in making the settlement he had not been influenced by the possibility of having damages awarded against him in the action brought by Miss Vyse. *Held*, as Wise had not made the settlement with the intention of defrauding his creditors, there was no ground for setting the settlement aside. The fact that the creation of the settlement resulted, in the event, in creditors being defeated was not relevant. What mattered was an intention to defeat creditors, and this intention was not proved.

Wise v. Perpetual Trustee Company, [1903] A.C. 139   [353]
(Privy Council)

In 1888 the trustees of a club in Sydney, Australia, the Cercle Français took a lease of property for use as club premises. After the club was dissolved in 1891, the trustees sub-let the premises, but the rent received was not sufficient to pay the rent due under the original lease taken by the club. P., one of the trustees, made up the difference out of his own pocket and by his death had paid £2350. After his death his executors sought to make the persons who had been members of the club in 1888 liable to indemnify P.'s estate in respect of the money paid by P. *Held*, in the absence of any rule of a club to the contrary, a member was not liable to pay more than the subscription required by the rules. Thus, in the absence of any rule to the contrary, a member was not liable to indemnify the trustees of the club in respect of liabilities incurred by them. The Cercle Français had no such rule and the executors therefore failed in their claim.

Wootton's Will Trusts, Re, Trotter v. Duffin, [1968]   [354]
2 All E.R. 618

By clause 13 (iii) of her will a testatrix who died in 1962 directed her trustees to hold certain property on trust for " (a) any charitable institution or other charitable body in England or (b) such other organisation or body not being registered as a charity but in the opinion of my trustees as having charitable objects or such other person or persons who owing to age or ill health shall be in need of financial help for their respective care or maintenance as my trustees shall in their absolute discretion from time to time select or determine ". *Held*, the objects under (b) were not charitable, since the qualification was not the intrinsic character of the organisation or body but the opinion of the trustees. Since the objects of the trust under clause 13 (iii) were not exclusively charitable, the trust failed. By clause 13 (ii) of her will, the testatrix gave to her trustees a power of appointment over certain property, the objects of the power being the same as the beneficiaries set out under (a) and (b) above. *Held,* as it would be possible to determine (i) whether any organisation or body was charitable (ii) what was the opinion of the trustees as regards any organisation or body, and whether any person complied with the requirements of that clause, the test for the validity of a power was complied with (*viz.,* that it must be possible to ascertain with certainty whether any particular person fell within the description given). The power of appointment was therefore valid.

Wright, Re, Blizard v. Lockhart, [1954] 2 All E.R. 98   [355]
(Court of Appeal)

A testatrix who died in 1933 gave her residuary estate to trustees on trust for a tenant for life, who died in 1942, with remainder on trust to found and maintain a convalescent home. On the question of the proper date to determine the practicability of the trust, it was found that the proper date was that of the death of the testatrix. *Held,* confirming the decision of the High Court, once money has been effectively dedicated to charity, whether in pursuance of a general or particular intention, the testator's next-of-kin or residuary legatees are excluded and no question of lapse, or anything analogous to lapse, between the date of the testator's death and the time when the money becomes available for the application of the testator's charitable purpose can affect the matter so far as they are concerned.

Wykes' Will Trusts, Re, Riddington v. Spencer,   [356]
[1961] 1 All E.R. 470

By his will, a testator who died in 1954, bequeathed one third of his residuary estate " . . . to the board of directors of E. Wykes (Leicester), Ltd. to be used at their descretion as a benevolent or welfare fund or for welfare purposes for the sole benefit of the past, present and future employees of the company ". On the question whether this bequest, which would otherwise be invalid was validated by the Charitable Trusts (Validation) Act 1954. *Held,* (1) the words of s. 1 (1) of the Charitable Trusts (Validation) Act 1954 should not be restricted so as to limit their application to trusts that include express reference both to a charitable purpose and to a non-charitable purpose (*e.g.* for charitable or benevolent purposes), as distinct from a trust expressed by a general description (e.g. " for public purposes ") which would embrace both charitable and non-charitable purposes. (2) Since the wording of the bequest described the objects of the trust established by the bequest in such a way that the trust property could be used exclusively for charitable purposes (*e.g.,* the relief of poverty) notwithstanding that it could be used for purposes that were not charitable, the bequest was an imperfect trust provision within s. 1 (1), and was validated by s. 1 (2).

Young, Re, Young v. Young, [1950] 2 All E.R. 1040   [357]

A testator, who died in 1943, by his will provided " This is the last will and testament of R.P.Y. and is to the effect that he leaves his worldly goods and chattels unto his wife E.M.Y. for her life-time only and he appoints the said E.M.Y. together with J.T.M. . . . to be his executors it being a condition of this will that after the testator's death the said E.M.Y. makes a new will leaving R.P.Y's estate for the purposes she knows he desires it to be used for—for the permanent aid of distressed gentlefolk and similar purposes such will to be held by and administered by Messrs. M. & Co. . . . leaving such small legacies as she knows I wish to be paid and Messrs. M. & Co. to be allowed to charge reasonable fees for the work they do ". J.T.M. died soon after the testator's death and probate of the testator's will was granted to E.M.Y. Questions of construction of the will arose, and, in applying to the court for directions, E.M.Y. deposed: " Prior to executing his said will the testator discussed with me the devolution of his estate after my death and I was well aware of his wishes in regard thereto, which were as follows, namely, that T.C. . . . should receive a legacy of £2000 and that G.S. . . . should receive a legacy of £1000, and that, subject thereto, his estate should be used to found and endow a home for distressed gentlefolk ". T.C. was one of the witnesses who attested the testator's will.

Held, (1) having regard to the imperative terms of the will and especially to the words " it being a condition of the will " the testator intended to impose a trust on his executors with regard to the dispositions of his estate after his widow's death, and notwithstanding, that the testator's wishes were not made known to both his executors and that the dispositions were not intended to take effect until after the death of the widow, the trust so created was an effective secret trust established by affidavit evidence of the widow. (2) the gift " for the permanent aid of distressed gentlefolk and similar purposes " was charitable, being for the relief of poor persons, and its charitable nature was unaffected by the reference to " similar purposes ". (3) although T.C. was an attesting witness, his beneficial interest was not rendered ineffective by s. 15 of the Wills Act, because he became entitled under the secret trust and not under the will.

Young v. Sealey, [1949] 1 All E.R. 92   [358]

An aunt paid money of her own into a joint banking account in the names of herself and her nephew. During her life time she alone made payments and withdrawals. There was evidence that the aunt intended the money in the account to belong to the nephew on her death. On the aunt's death intestate the personal representatives sought a declaration that the nephew held the money as trustee for the estate. They contended that if the aunt had intended the money to pass to the nephew on her death it constituted a testamentary disposition, which was invalid for failure to comply with the Wills Act 1837. *Held*, the disposition was not invalid by reason of failure to comply with the requirements of the Wills Act 1837. The nephew had the beneficial title to the money.

STATUTES

CHARITIES ACT 1601 [359]
(43 Eliz. 1, c. 4; 2 Statutes at Large 708)

Preamble

WHEREAS Lands, Tenements, Rents, Annuities, Profits, Hereditaments, Goods, Chattels, Money and Stocks of Money, have been heretofore given, limited, appointed and assigned, as well by the Queen's most excellent Majesty, and her most noble Progenitors, as by sundry other well-disposed Persons; some for Relief of aged, impotent and poor People, some for Maintenance of sick and maimed Soldiers and Mariners, Schools of Learning, Free Schools, and Scholars in Universities, some for Repair of Bridges, Ports, Havens, Causways, Churches, Sea-banks and Highways, some for Education and Preferment of Orphans, some for or towards Relief, Stock, or Maintenance for House of Correction, some for Marriages of poor Maids, some for Supportation, Aid and Help of young Trades-men, Handicraftsmen and Persons decayed, and others for Relief or Redemption of Prisoners or Captives, and for Aid or Ease of any poor Inhabitants concerning Payments of Fifteens, setting out of Solders and other Taxes; which Lands, Tenements, Rents, Annuities, Profits, Hereditaments, Goods, Chattels, Money and Stocks of Money, nevertheless have not been employed according to the charitable Intent of the Givers and Founders thereof, by reason of Frauds, Breaches of Trust, and Negligence in those that should pay, deliver and employ the same: (2) For Redress and Remedy whereof, Be it enacted by Authority of this present Parliament, . . .

(**Note:** The 1601 Act was repealed by the Mortmain and Charitable Uses Act 1888, but the preamble to the 1601 Act was repeated in s. 13 (2) of the 1888 Act, which was itself repealed by the Charities Act 1960, s. 48 (2), 7th Sched. Though the preamble to the 1601 Act is thus no longer on the statute book, it remains a guide to the courts as to the legal meaning of charity.)

WILLS ACT 1837 [360]
(7 Will. IV & 1 Vict. c. 26; 39 Halsbury's Statutes (3rd Edn.) 859)

9. Every will shall be in writing, and signed or acknowledged by the testator in the presence of two witnesses at one time, who shall attest the will.

And be it further enacted, That no Will shall be valid unless it shall be in writing and executed in manner herein-after mentioned; (that is to say,) it shall be signed at the foot or end thereof by the testator, or by some other person in his presence and by his direction; and such signature shall be made or acknowledged by the testator in the presence of two or more witnesses present at the same time, and such witnesses shall attest and shall subscribe the will in the presence of the testator, but no form of attestation shall be necessary.

APPORTIONMENT ACT 1870
(33 & 34 Vict. c. 35; 18 Halsbury's Statutes (3rd Edn.) 434)

**2. Rents, etc. to be apportionable in [361]
respect of time**

. . . . All rents, annuities, dividends, and other periodical payments in the nature of income (whether reserved or made payable under an instrument in writing or otherwise) shall, like interest on money lent, be considered as accruing from day to day, and shall be apportionable in respect of time accordingly.

7. Nor where stipulation made to the contrary [362]

The provisions of this Act shall not extend to any case in which it is or shall be expressly stipulated that no apportionment shall take place.

MARRIED WOMEN'S PROPERTY ACT 1882
(45 & 46 Vict. c. 75; 17 Halsbury's Statutes (3rd Edn.) 120)

17. Questions between husband and wife as to [363]
property to be decided in a summary way

In any question between husband and wife as to the title or possession of property, either party, or any such bank, corporation, company, public body, or society as aforesaid in whose books any stocks, funds, or shares of either party are standing, may apply by summons or otherwise in a summary way to any judge of the High Court of Justice in England or in Ireland, according as such property is in England or Ireland, or (at the option of the applicant irrespectively of the value of the property in dispute) in England to the judge of the county court of the district, or in Ireland to the chairman of the civil bill court of the division in which either party resides, and the judge of the High Court of Justice or of the county court, or the chairman of the civil bill court (as the case may be) may make such order with respect to the property in dispute, and as to the costs of and consequent on the application as he thinks fit, or may direct such application to stand over from time to time, and any inquiry touching the matters in question to be made in such manner as he shall think fit: Provided always, that any such order of a judge of the High Court of Justice to be made under the provisions of this section shall be subject to appeal in the same way as an order made by the same judge in a suit pending or on an equitable plaint in the said court would be; and any order of a county or civil bill court under the provisions of this section shall be subject to appeal in the same way as any other order made by the same court would be, and all proceedings in a county court or civil bill court under this section in which, by reason of the value of the property in dispute, such court would not have had jurisdiction if this Act or the Married Women's Property Act, 1870, had not passed, may, at the option of the defendant or respondent to such proceedings, be removed as of right into the High Court of Justice in England or Ireland (as the case may be), by writ of *certiorari* or otherwise as may be prescribed by any rule of such High Court; but any order made or act done in the course of such proceedings prior to such removal shall be valid, unless order shall be made to the contrary by such High Court: Provided also that the judge of the High Court of Justice or of the county court, or the chairman of the civil bill court, if either party so require, may hear any such application in his private room; Provided also, that any such bank, corporation, company, public body, or society as aforesaid, shall, in the matter of any such application for the purposes of costs or otherwise, be treated as a stakeholder only.

TRUSTEE ACT 1925
(15 & 16 Geo. 5 c. 19; 38 Halsbury's Statutes (3rd Edn.) 106)

PART I

INVESTMENTS

2. Purchase at a premium of redeemable stocks; [364]
change of character of investment

(1) A trustee may under the powers of this Act invest in any of the securities

112

mentioned or referred to in section one of this Act, notwithstanding that the same may be redeemable, and that the price exceeds the redemption value. . . .

(2) A trustee may retain until redemption any redeemable stock, fund, or security which may have been purchased in accordance with the powers of this Act, or any statute replaced by this Act.

(The words omitted were repealed by the Trustee Investments Act 1961.)

3. Discretion of trustees [365]

Every power conferred by the preceding sections shall be exercised according to the discretion of the trustee, but subject to any consent or direction required by the instrument, if any, creating the trust or by statute with respect to the investment of the trust funds.

4. Power to retain investment which has ceased to be authorised [366]

A trustee shall not be liable for breach of trust by reason only of his continuing to hold an investment which has ceased to be an investment authorised by the trust instrument or by the general law.

5. Enlargement of powers of investment [367]

(1) A trustee having power to invest in real securities may invest and snall be deemed always to have had power to invest . . . on any charge, or upon mortgage of any charge, made under the Improvement of Land Act 1864.

(2) A trustee having power to invest in real securities may accept the security in the form of a charge by way of legal mortgage, and may, in exercise of the statutory power, convert an existing mortgage into a charge by way of legal mortgage.

(The words omitted were repealed by the Trustee Investments Act 1961.)

7. Investment in bearer securities [368]

(1) A trustee may, unless expressly prohibited by the instrument creating the trust, retain or invest in securities payable to bearer which, if not so payable, would have been authorised investments:

Provided that securities to bearer retained or taken as an investment by a trustee (not being a trust corporation) shall, until sold, be deposited by him for safe custody and collection of income with a banker or banking company.

A direction that investments shall be retained or made in the name of a trustee shall not, for the purposes of this subsection, be deemed to be such an express prohibition as aforesaid.

(2) A trustee shall not be responsible for any loss incurred by reason of such deposit, and any sum payable in respect of such deposit and collection shall be paid out of the income of the trust property.

8. Loans and investments by trustees not chargeable as breaches of trust [369]

(1) A trustee lending money on the security of any property on which he can properly lend shall not be chargeable with breach of trust by reason only of the proportion borne by the amount of the loan to the value of the property at the time when the loan was made, if it appears to the court—

(a) that in making the loan the trustee was acting upon a report as to the value of the property made by a person whom he reasonably believed to be an able practical surveyor or valuer instructed and employed independently of any owner of the property, whether such surveyor or valuer carried on business in the locality where the property is situate or elsewhere; and

(b) that the amount of the loan does not exceed two third parts of the value of the property as stated in the report; and

(c) that the loan was made under the advice of the surveyor or valuer expressed in the report.

(2) A trustee lending money on the security of any leasehold property shall not be chargeable with breach of trust only upon the ground that in making such loan

113

he dispensed either wholly or partly with the production or investigation of the lessor's title.

(3) A trustee shall not be chargeable with breach of trust only upon the ground that in effecting the purchase, or in lending money upon the security, of any property he has accepted a shorter title than the title which a purchaser is, in the absence of a special contract, entitled to require, if in the opinion of the court the title accepted be such as a person acting with prudence and caution would have accepted.

(4) This section applies to transfers of existing securities as well as to new securities and to investments made before as well as after the commencement of this Act.

9. Liability for loss by reason of improper investment [370]

(1) Where a trustee improperly advances trust money on a mortgage security which would at the time of the investment be a proper investment in all respects for a smaller sum than is actually advanced thereon, the security shall be deemed an authorised investment for the smaller sum, and the trustee shall only be liable to make good the sum advanced in excess thereof with interest.

(2) This section applies to investments made before as well as after the commencement of this Act.

10. Powers supplementary to powers of investment [371]

(1) Trustees lending money on the security of any property on which they can lawfully lend may contract that such money shall not be called in during any period not exceeding seven years from the time when the loan was made, provided interest be paid within a specified time not exceeding thirty days after every half-yearly or other day on which it becomes due, and provided there be no breach of any covenant by the mortgagor contained in the instrument of mortgage or charge for the maintenance and protection of the property.

(2) On a sale of land for an estate in fee simple or for a term having at least five hundred years to run by trustees or by a tenant for life or statutory owner, the trustees, or the tenant for life or statutory owner on behalf of the trustees of the settlement, may, where the proceeds are liable to be invested, contract that the payment of any part, no exceeding two-thirds, of the purchase money shall be secured by a charge by way of legal mortgage or a mortgage by demise or sub-demise for a term of at least five hundred years (less a nominal reversion when by sub-demise), of the land sold, with or without the security of any other property, such charge or mortgage, if any buildings are comprised in the mortgage, to contain a covenant by the mortgagor to keep them insured against loss or damage by fire to the full value thereof.

The trustees shall not be bound to obtain any report as to the value of the land or other property to be comprised in such charge or mortgage, or any advice as to the making of the loan, and shall not be liable for any loss which may be incurred by reason only of the security being insufficient at the date of the charge or mortgage; and the trustees of the settlement shall be bound to give effect to such contract made by the tenant for life or statutory owner.

(3) Where any securities of a company are subject to a trust, the trustees, may concur in any scheme or arrangement—

(a) for the reconstruction of the company;
(b) for the sale of all or any part of the property and undertaking of the company to another company;
(bb) for the acquisition of the securities of the company, or of control thereof, by another company;
(c) for the amalgamation of the company with another company;
(d) for the release, modification, or variation of any rights, privileges or liabilities attached to the securities or any of them;

in like manner as if they were entitled to such securities beneficially, with power to accept any securities of any denomination or description of the reconstructed or purchasing or new company in lieu of or in exchange for all or any of the first-mentioned securities; and the trustees shall not be responsible for any loss occasioned by any act or thing so done in good fatih, and may retain any securities so accepted as aforesaid for any period for which they could have properly retained the original securities.

(4) If any conditional or preferential right to subscribe for any securities in any company is offered to trustees in respect of any holding in such company, they may as to all or any of such securities, either exercise such right and apply capital money subject to the trust in payment of the consideration, or renounce such right, or assign for the best consideration that can be reasonably obtained the benefit of such right or the title thereto to any person, including any beneficiary under the trust, without being responsible for any loss occasioned by any act or thing so done by them in good faith:

Provided that the consideration for any such assignment shall be held as capital money of the trust.

(5) The powers conferred by this section shall be exercisable subject to the consent of any person whose consent to a change of investment is required by law or by the instrument, if any, creating the trust.

(6) Where the loan referred to in subsection (1), or the sale referred to in subsection (2), of this section is made under the order of the court, the powers conferred by those subsections respectively shall apply only if and as far as the court may by order direct.

(As amended by s. 9 (1) of the Trustee Investments Act 1961.)

11. Power to deposit money at bank and to pay calls [372]

(1) Trustees may, pending the negotiation and preparation of any mortgage or charge, or during any other time while an investment is being sought for, pay any trust money into a bank to a deposit or other account, and all interest, if any, payable in respect thereof shall be applied as income.

(2) Trustees may apply capital money subject to a trust in payment of the calls on any shares subject to the same trust.

PART II

GENERAL POWERS OF TRUSTEES AND PERSONAL REPRESENTATIVES

General Powers

12. Power of trustees for sale to sell by auction, &c. [373]

(1) Where a trust for sale or a power of sale of property is vested in a trustee, he may sell or concur with any other person in selling all or any part of the property, either subject to prior charges or not, and either together or in lots, by public auction or by private contract, subject to any such conditions respecting title or evidence of title or other matter as the trustee thinks fit, with power to vary any contract for sale, and to buy in at any auction, or to rescind any contract for sale and to re-sell, without being answerable for any loss.

(2) A trust or power to sell or dispose of land includes a trust or power to sell or dispose of part thereof, whether the division is horizontal, vertical, or made in any other way.

(3) This section does not enable an express power to sell settled land to be exercised where the power is not vested in the tenant for life or statutory owner.

13. Power to sell subject to depreciatory conditions [374]

(1) No sale made by a trustee shall be impeached by any beneficiary upon the ground that any of the conditions subject to which the sale was made may have been unnecessarily depreciatory, unless it also appears that the consideration for the sale was thereby rendered inadequate.

(2) No sale made by a trustee shall, after the execution of the conveyance, be impeached as against the purchaser upon the ground that any of the conditions subject to which the sale was made may have been unnecessarily depreciatory, unless it appears that the purchaser was acting in collusion with the trustee at the time when the contract for sale was made.

(3) No purchaser, upon any sale made by a trustee, shall be at liberty to make any objection against the title upon any of the grounds aforesaid.

(4) This section applies to sales made before or after the commencement of this Act.

14. Power of trustees to give receipts   [375]

(1) The receipt in writing of a trustee for any money, securities, or other personal property or effects payable, transferable, or deliverable to him under any trust or power shall be a sufficient discharge to the person paying, transferring, or delivering the same and shall effectually exonerate him from seeing to the application or being answerable for any loss or misapplication thereof.

(2) This section does not, except where the trustee is a trust corporation, enable a sole trustee to give a valid receipt for—

    (a) the proceeds of sale or other capital money arising under a . . . . disposition on trust for sale of land;

    (b) capital money arising under the Settled Land Act 1925.

(3) This section applies notwithstanding anything to the contrary in the instrument, if any, creating the trust.

(The words omitted were repealed by the Law of Property (Amendment) Act 1926.)

15. Power to compound liabilities   [376]

A personal representative, or two or more trustees acting together, or, subject to the restrictions imposed in regard to receipts by a sole trustee not being a trust corporation, a sole acting trustee where by the instrument, if any, creating the trust, or by statute, a sole trustee is authorised to execute the trusts and powers reposed in him, may, if and as he or they think fit—

    (a) accept any property, real or personal, before the time at which it is made transferable or payable; or

    (b) sever and apportion any blended trust funds or property; or

    (c) pay or allow any debt or claim on any evidence that he or they think sufficient; or

    (d) accept any composition or any security, real or personal, for any debt or for any property, real or personal, claimed; or

    (e) allow any time of payment of any debt; or

    (f) compromise, compound, abandon, submit to arbitration, or otherwise settle any debt, account, claim, or thing whatever relating to the testator's or intestate's estate or to the trust;

and for any of those purposes may enter into, give, execute, and do such agreements, instruments of composition or arrangement, releases, and other things as to him or them seem expedient, without being responsible for any loss occasioned by any act or thing so done by him or them in good faith.

16. Power to raise money by sale, mortgage, &c.   [377]

(1) Where trustees are authorised by the instrument, if any, creating the trust or by law to pay or apply capital money subject to the trust for any purpose or in any manner, they shall have and shall be deemed always to have had power to raise the money required by sale, conversion, calling in, or mortgage of all or any part of the trust property for the time being in possession.

(2) This section applies notwithstanding anything to the contrary contained in the instrument, if any, creating the trust, but does not apply to trustees of property

held for charitable purposes, or to trustees of a settlement for the purposes of the Settled Land Act 1925, not being also the statutory owners.

17. Protection to purchasers and mortgagees dealing with trustees   [378]

No purchaser or mortgagee, paying or advancing money on a sale or mortgage purporting to be made under any trust or power vested in trustees, shall be concerned to see that such money is wanted, or that no more than is wanted is raised, or otherwise as to the application thereof.

18. Devolution of powers or trusts   [379]

(1) Where a power or trust is given to or imposed on two or more trustees jointly, the same may be exercised or performed by the survivors or survivor of them for the time being.

(2) Until the appointment of new trustees, the personal representatives or representative for the time being of a sole trustee, or, where there were two or more trustees of the last surviving or continuing trustee, shall be capable of exercising or performing any power or trust which was given to, or capable of being exercised by, the sole or last surviving or continuing trustee, or other the trustees or trustee for the time being of the trust.

(3) This section takes effect subject to the restrictions imposed in regard to receipts by a sole trustee, not being a trust corporation.

(4) In this section "personal representative" does not include an executor who has renounced or has not proved.

19. Power to insure   [380]

(1) A trustee may insure against loss or damage by fire any building or other insurable property to any amount, including the amount of any insurance already on foot, not exceeding three fourth parts of the full value of the building or property, and pay the premiums for such insurance out of the income thereof or out of the income of any other property subject to the same trusts without obtaining the consent of any person who may be entitled wholly or partly to such income.

(2) This section does not apply to any building or property which a trustee is bound forthwith to convey absolutely to any beneficiary upon being requested to do so.

20. Application of insurance money where policy kept up under any trust, power or obligation   [381]

(1) Money receivable by trustees or any beneficiary under a policy of insurance against the loss or damage of any property subject to a trust or to a settlement within the meaning of the Settled Land Act 1925, whether by fire or otherwise, shall, where the policy has been kept up under any trust in that behalf or under any power statutory or otherwise, or in performance of any covenant or of any obligation statutory or otherwise, or by a tenant for life impeachable for waste, be capital money for the purposes of the trust or settlement, as the case may be.

(2) If any such money is receivable by any person, other than the trustees of the trust or settlement, that person shall use his best endeavours to recover and receive the money, and shall pay the net residue thereof, after discharging any costs of recovering and receiving it, to the trustees of the trust or settlement, or, if there are no trustees capable of giving a discharge therefor, into court.

(3) Any such money—

(a) if it was receivable in respect of settled land within the meaning of the Settled Land Act 1925, or any building or works thereon, shall be deemed to be capital money arising under that Act from the settled land, and shall be invested or applied by the trustees, or, if in court, under the direction of the court, accordingly;

(b) if it was receivable in respect of personal chattels settled as heirlooms within

117

the meaning of the Settled Land Act 1925, shall be deemed to be capital money arising under that Act, and shall be applicable by the trustees, or, if in court, under the direction of the court, in like manner as provided by that Act with respect to money arising by a sale of chattels settled as heirlooms as aforesaid;

(c) if it was receivable in respect of property held upon trust for sale, shall be held upon the trusts and subject to the powers and provisions applicable to money arising by a sale under such trust;

(d) in any other case, shall be held upon trusts corresponding as nearly as may be with the trusts affecting the property in respect of which it was payable.

(4) Such money, or any part thereof, may also be applied by the trustees, or, if in court, under the direction of the court, in rebuilding, reinstating, replacing, or repairing the property lost or damaged, but any such application by the trustees shall be subject to the consent of any person whose consent is required by the instrument, if any, creating the trust to the investment of money subject to the trust, and, in the case of money which is deemed to be capital money arising under the Settled Land Act 1925, be subject to the provisions of that Act with respect to the application of capital money by the trustees of the settlement.

(5) Nothing contained in this section prejudices or affects the right of any person to require any such money or any part thereof to be applied in rebuilding, reinstating, or repairing the property lost or damaged, or the rights of any mortgagee, lessor, or lessee, whether under any statute or otherwise.

(6) This section applies to policies effected either before or after the commencement of this Act, but only to money received after such commencement.

21. Deposit of documents for safe custody [382]

Trustees may deposit any documents held by them relating to the trust, or to the trust property, with any banker or banking company or any other company whose business includes the undertaking of the safe custody of documents, and any sum payable in respect of such deposit shall be paid out of the income of the trust property.

22. Reversionary interests, valuations, and audit [383]

(1) Where trust property includes any share or interest in property not vested in the trustees, or the proceeds of the sale of any such property, or any other thing in action, the trustees on the same falling into possession, or becoming payable or transferable may—

(a) agree or ascertain the amount or value thereof or any part thereof in such manner as they may think fit:

(b) accept in or towards satisfaction thereof, at the market or current value, or upon any valuation or estimate of value which they may think fit, any authorised investments;

(c) allow any deductions for duties, costs, charges and expenses which they may think proper or reasonable;

(d) execute any release in respect of the premises so as effectually to discharge all accountable parties from all liability in respect of any matters coming within the scope of such release;

without being responsible in any such case for any loss occasioned by any act or thing so done by them in good faith.

(2) The trustees shall not be under any obligation and shall not be chargeable with any breach of trust by reason of any omission—

(a) to place any distringas notice or apply for any stop or other like order upon any securities or other property out of or on which such share or interest or other thing in action as aforesaid is derived, payable or charged; or

(b) to take any proceedings on account of any act, default, or neglect on the part of the persons in whom such securities or other property or any of them or any part thereof are for the time being, or had at any time been, vested;

unless and until required in writing so to do by some person, or the guardian of some person, beneficially interested under the trust, and unless also due provision is made to their satisfaction for payment of the costs of any proceedings required to be taken:

Provided that nothing in this subsection shall relieve the trustees of the obligation to get in and obtain payment or transfer of such share or interest or other thing in action on the same falling into possession.

(3) Trustees may, for the purpose of giving effect to the trust, or any of the provisions of the instrument, if any, creating the trust or of any statute, from time to time (by duly qualified agents) ascertain and fix the value of any trust property in such manner as they think proper, and any valuation so made in good faith shall be binding upon all persons interested under the trust.

(4) Trustees may, in their absolute discretion, from time to time, but not more than once in every three years unless the nature of the trust or any special dealings with the trust property make a more frequent exercise of the right reasonable, cause the accounts of the trust property to be examined or audited by an independent accountant, and shall, for that purpose, produce such vouchers and give such information to him as he may require; and the costs of such examination or audit, including the fee of the auditor, shall be paid out of the capital or income of the trust property, or partly in one way and partly in the other, as the trustees, in their absolute discretion, think fit, but, in default of any direction by the trustees to the contrary in any special case, costs attributable to capital shall be borne by capital and those attributable to income by income.

23. Power to employ agents [384]

(1) Trustees or personal representatives may, instead of acting personally, employ and pay an agent, whether a solicitor, banker, stockbroker, or other person, to transact any business or do any act required to be transacted or done in the execution of the trust, or the administration of the testator's or intestate's estate, including the receipt and payment of money, and shall be entitled to be allowed and paid all charges and expenses so incurred, and shall not be responsible for the default of any such agent if employed in good faith.

(2) Trustees or personal representatives may appoint any person to act as their agent or attorney for the purpose of selling, converting, collecting, getting in, and executing and perfecting insurances of, or managing or cultivating, or otherwise administering any property, real or personal, moveable or immoveable, subject to the trust or forming part of the testator's or intestate's estate, in any place outside the United Kingdom or executing or exercising any discretion or trust or power vested in them in relation to any such property, with such ancillary powers, and with and subject to such provisions and restrictions as they may think fit, including a power to appoint substitutes, and shall not, by reason only of their having made such appointment, be responsible for any loss arising thereby.

(3) Without prejudice to such general power of appointing agents as aforesaid—
(a) A trustee may appoint a solicitor to be his agent to receive and give a discharge for any money or valuable consideration or property receivable by the trustee under the trust, by permitting the solicitor to have the custody of, and to produce, a deed having in the body thereof or endorsed thereon a receipt for such money or valuable consideration or property, the deed being executed, or the endorsed receipt being signed, by the person entitled to give a receipt for that consideration;
(b) A trustee shall not be chargeable with breach of trust by reason only of his having made or concurred in making any such appointment; and the production of any such deed by the solicitor shall have the same statutory validity and effect as if the person appointing the solicitor had not been a trustee;
(c) A trustee may appoint a banker or solicitor to be his agent to receive and give a discharge for any money payable to the trustee under or by virtue of a policy of insurance, by permitting the banker or solicitor to have the custody

119

of and to produce the policy of insurance with a receipt signed by the trustee, and a trustee shall not be chargeable with a breach of trust by reason only of his having made or concurred in making any such appointment:

Provided that nothing in this subsection shall exempt a trustee from any liability which he would have incurred if this Act and any enactment replaced by this Act had not been passed, in case he permits any such money, valuable consideration, or property to remain in the hands or under the control of the banker or solicitor for a period longer than is reasonably necessary to enable the banker or solicitor, as the case may be, to pay or transfer the same to the trustee.

This subsection applies whether the money or valuable consideration or property was or is received before or after the commencement of this Act.

25. Power to delegate trusts during absence abroad [385]

[(1) Notwithstanding any rule of law or equity to the contrary, a trustee may, by power of attorney, delegate for a period not exceeding twelve months the execution or exercise of all or any of the trusts, powers and discretions vested in him as trustee either alone or jointly with any other person or persons.

(2) The persons who may be donees of a power of attorney under this section include a trust corporation but not (unless a trust corporation) the only other co-trustee of the donor of the power.

(3) An instrument creating a power of attorney under this section shall be attested by at least one witness.

(4) Before or within seven days after giving a power of attorney under this section the donor shall give written notice thereof (specifying the date on which the power comes into operation and its duration, the donee of the power, the reason why the power is given and, where some only are delegated, the trusts, powers and discretions delegated) to—

(a) each person (other than himself), if any, who under any instrument creating the trust has power (whether alone or jointly) to appoint a new trustee; and

(b) each of the other trustees, if any;

but failure to comply with this subsection shall not, in favour of a person dealing with the donee of the power, invalidate any act done or instrument executed by the donee.

(5) The donor of a power of attorney given under this section shall be liable for the acts or defaults of the donee in the same manner as if they were the acts or defaults of the donor.]

[(6) For the purpose of executing or exercising the trusts or powers delegated to him, the donee may exercise any of the powers conferred on the donor as trustee by statute or by the instrument creating the trust, including power, for the purpose of the transfer of any inscribed stock, himself to delegate to an attorney power to transfer but not including the power of delegation conferred by this section.

[(7) The fact that it appears from any power of attorney given under this section, or from any evidence required for the purposes of any such power of attorney or otherwise, that in dealing with any stock the donee of the power is acting in the execution of a trust shall not be deemed for any purpose to affect any person in whose books the stock is inscribed or registered with any notice of the trust.

[(8) This section applies to a personal representative, tenant for life and statutory owner as it applies to a trustee except that subsection (4) shall apply as if it required the notice there mentioned to be given—

(a) in the case of a personal representative, to each of the other personal representatives, if any, except any executor who has renounced probate;

(b) in the case of a tenant for life, to the trustees of the settlement and to each person, if any, who together with the person giving the notice constitutes the tenant for life;

(c) in the case of a statutory owner, to each of the persons, if any, who together

with the person giving the notice constitute the statutory owner and, in the case of a statutory owner by virtue of section 23 (1) (a) of the Settled Land Act 1925, to the trustees of the settlement.]
[As substituted by the Powers of Attorney Act 1971, s. 9 (1)-(3).]

Indemnities
26. Protection against liability in respect of [386]
rents and covenants
(1) Where a personal representative or trustee liable as such for—
(a) any rent, covenant, or agreement reserved by or contained in any lease; or
(b) any rent, covenant or agreement payable under or contained in any grant made in consideration of a rentcharge; or
(c) any indemnity given in respect of any rent, covenant or agreement referred to in either of the foregoing paragraphs;
satisfies all liabilities under the lease or grant which may have accrued, and been claimed, up to the date of the conveyance hereinafter mentioned, and, where necessary, sets apart a sufficient fund to answer any future claim that may be made in respect of any fixed and ascertained sum which the lessee or grantee agreed to lay out on the property demised or granted, although the period for laying out the same may not have arrived, then and in any such case the personal representative or trustee may convey the property demised or granted to a purchaser, legatee, devisee, or other person entitled to call for a conveyance thereof and thereafter—
(i) he may distribute the residuary real and personal estate of the deceased testator or intestate, or, as the case may be, the trust estate (other than the fund, if any, set apart as aforesaid) to or amongst the persons entitled thereto, without appropriating any part, or any further part, as the case may be, of the estate of the deceased or of the trust estate to meet any future liability under the said lease or grant;
(ii) notwithstanding such distribution, he shall not be personally liable in respect of any subsequent claim under the said lease or grant.
(2) This section operates without prejudice to the right of the lessor or grantor, or the persons deriving title under the lessor or grantor, to follow the assets of the deceased or the trust property into the hands of the persons amongst whom the same may have been respectively distributed, and applies notwithstanding anything to the contrary in the will or other instrument, if any, creating the trust.
(3) In this section "lease" includes an underlease and an agreement for a lease or underlease and any instrument giving any such indemnity as aforesaid or varying the liabilities under the lease; "grant" applies to a grant whether the rent is created by limitation, grant, reservation, or otherwise, and includes an agreement for a grant and any instrument giving any such indemnity as aforesaid or varying the liabilities under the grant; "lessee" and "grantee" include persons respectively deriving title under them.

27. Protection by means of advertisements [387]
(1) With a view to the conveyance to or distribution among the persons entitled to any real or personal property, the trustees of a settlement or of a disposition on trust for sale or personal representatives, may give notice by advertisement in the Gazette, and in a newspaper circulating in the district in which the land is situated, and such other like notices, including notices elsewhere than in England and Wales, as would, in any special case, have been directed by a court of competent jurisdiction in an action for administration, of their intention to make such conveyance or distribution as aforesaid, and requiring any person interested to send to the trustees or personal representatives within the time, not being less than two months, fixed in the notice or, where more than one notice is given, in the last of the notices, particulars of his claim in respect of the property or any part thereof to which the notice relates.
(2) At the expiration of the time fixed by the notice the trustees or personal representatives may convey or distribute the property or any part thereof to which the notice relates, to or among the persons entitled thereto, having regard only to

the claims, whether formal or not, of which the trustees or personal representatives then had notice and shall not, as respects the property so conveyed or distributed, be liable to any person of whose claim the trustees or personal representatives have not had notice at the time of conveyance or distribution; but nothing in this section—

(a) prejudices the right of any person to follow the property, or any property representing the same, into the hands of any person, other than a purchaser, who may have received it; or

(b) frees the trustees or personal representatives from any obligation to make searches or obtain official certificates of search similar to those which an intending purchaser would be advised to make or obtain.

(3) This section applies notwithstanding anything to the contrary in the will or other instrument, if any, creating the trust.

(As amended by the Law of Property (Amendment) Act 1926.)

28. Protection in regard to notice [388]

A trustee or personal representative acting for the purposes of more than one trust or estate shall not, in the absence of fraud, be affected by notice of any instrument, matter, fact or thing in relation to any particular trust or estate if he has obtained notice thereof merely by reason of his acting or having acted for the purposes of another trust or estate.

30. Implied indemnity of trustees [389]

(1) A trustee shall be chargeable only for money and securities actually received by him notwithstanding his signing any receipt for the sake of conformity, and shall be answerable and accountable only for his own acts, receipts, neglects, or defaults, and not for those of any other trustee, nor for any banker, broker, or other person with whom any trust money or securities may be deposited nor for the insufficiency or deficiency of any securities, nor for any other loss, unless the same happens through his own wilful default.

(2) A trustee may reimburse himself or pay or discharge out of the trust premises all expenses incurred in or about the execution of the trusts or powers.

Maintenance, Advancement and Protective Trusts

31. Power to apply income for maintenance and to [390] accumulate surplus income during a minority

(1) Where any property is held by trustees in trust for any person for any interest whatsoever, whether vested or contingent, then, subject to any prior interests or charges affecting that property—

(i) during the infancy of any such person, if his interest so long continues, the trustees may, at their sole discretion, pay to his parent or guardian, if any, or otherwise apply for or towards his maintenance, education, or benefit, the whole or such part, if any, of the income of that property as may, in all the circumstances, be reasonable, whether or not there is—

(a) any other fund applicable to the same purpose; or

(b) any person bound by law to provide for his maintenance or education; and

(ii) if such person on attaining the age of eighteen years has not a vested interest in such income, the trustees shall thenceforth pay the income of that property and of any accretion thereto under subsection (2) of this section to him, until he either attains a vested interest therein or dies, or until failure of his interest:

Provided that, in deciding whether the whole or any part of the income of the property is during a minority to be paid or applied for the purposes aforesaid, the trustees shall have regard to the age of the infant and his requirements and generally to the circumstances of the case, and in particular to what other income, if any, is applicable for the same purposes; and where trustees have notice that the income of more than one fund is applicable for those purposes, then, so far as practicable, unless the entire income of the funds is paid or applied as aforesaid or the court otherwise directs, a proportionate part only of the income of each fund shall be so paid or applied.

(2) During the infancy of any such person, if his interest so long continues, the trustees shall accumulate all the residue of that income in the way of compound interest by investing the same and the resulting income thereof from time to time in authorised investments, and shall hold those accumulations as follows:—

 (i) If any such person—

  (a) attains the age of eighteen years, or marries under that age, and his interest in such income during his infancy or until his marriage is a vested interest; or

  (b) on attaining the age of eighteen years or on marriage under that age becomes entitled to the property from which such income arose in fee simple, absolute or determinable, or absolutely, or for an entailed interest; the trustees shall hold the accumulations in trust for such person absolutely, but without prejudice to any provision with respect thereto contained in any settlement by him made under any statutory powers during his infancy, and so that the receipt of such person after marriage, and though still an infant, shall be a good discharge; and

 (ii) In any other case the trustees shall, notwithstanding that such person had a vested interest in such income, hold the accumulations as an accretion to the capital of the property from which such accumulations arose, and as one fund with such capital for all purposes, and so that, if such property is settled land, such accumulations shall be held upon the same trusts as if the same were capital money arising therefrom;

but the trustees may, at any time during the infancy of such person if his interest so long continues, apply those accumulations, or any part thereof, as if they were income arising in the then current year.

(3) This section applies in the case of a contingent interest only if the limitation or trust carries the intermediate income of the property, but it applies to a future or contingent legacy by the parent of, or a person standing in *loco parentis* to, the legatee, if and for such period as, under the general law, the legacy carries interest for the maintenance of the legatee, and in any such case as last aforesaid the rate of interest shall (if the income available is sufficient, and subject to any rules of court to the contrary) be five pounds per centum per annum.

(4) This section applies to a vested annuity in like manner as if the annuity were the income of property held by trustees in trust to pay the income thereof to the annuitant for the same period for which the annuity is payable, save that in any case accumulations made during the infancy of the annuitant shall be held in trust for the annuitant or his personal representatives absolutely.

(5) This section does not apply where the instrument, if any, under which the interest arises came into operation before the commencement of this Act.

32. Power of advancement [391]

(1) Trustees may at any time or times pay or apply any capital money subject to a trust, for the advancement or benefit, in such manner as they may, in their absolute discretion, think fit, of any person entitled to the capital of the trust property or of any share thereof, whether absolutely or contingently on his attaining any specified age or on the occurrence of any other event, or subject to a gift over on his death under any specified age or on the occurrence of any other event, and whether in possession or in remainder or reversion, and such payment or application may be made notwithstanding that the interest of such person is liable to be defeated by the exercise of a power of appointment or revocation, or to be diminished by the increase of the class to which he belongs:

Provided that—

 (a) the money so paid or applied for the advancement or benefit of any person shall not exceed altogether in amount one-half of the presumptive or vested share or interest of that person in the trust property; and

(b) if that person is or becomes absolutely and indefeasibly entitled to a share in the trust property the money so paid or applied shall be brought into account as part of such share; and

(c) no such payment or application shall be made so as to prejudice any person entitled to any prior life or other interest, whether vested or contingent, in the money paid or applied unless such person is in existence and of full age and consents in writing to such payment or application.

(2) This section applies only where the trust property consists of money or securities or of property held upon trust for sale calling in and conversion, and such money or securities, or the proceeds of such sale calling in and conversion are not by statute or in equity considered as land, or applicable as capital money for the purposes of the Settled Land Act 1925.

(3) This section does not apply to trusts constituted or created before the commencement of this Act.

33. Protective trusts   [392]

(1) Where any income, including an annuity or other periodical income payment, is directed to be held on protective trusts for the benefit of any person (in this section called "the principal beneficiary") for the period of his life or for any less period, then, during that period (in this section called the "trust period") the said income shall, without prejudice to any prior interest, be held on the following trusts, namely:—

(i) Upon trust for the principal beneficiary during the trust period or until he, whether before or after the termination of any prior interest, does or attempts to do or suffers any act or thing, or until any event happens, other than an advance under any statutory or express power, whereby, if the said income were payable during the trust period to the principal beneficiary absolutely during that period, he would be deprived of the right to receive the same or any part thereof, in any of which cases, as well as on the termination of the trust period, whichever first happens, this trust of the said income shall fail or determine;

(ii) If the trust aforesaid fails or determines during the subsistence of the trust period, then, during the residue of that period, the said income shall be held upon trust for the application thereof for the maintenance or support, or otherwise for the benefit, of all or any one or more exclusively of the other or others of the following persons (that is to say)—

(a) the principal beneficiary and his or her wife or husband, if any, and his or her children or more remote issue, if any; or

(b) if there is no wife or husband or issue of the principal beneficiary in existence, the principal beneficiary and the persons who would, if he were actually dead, be entitled to the trust property or the income thereof or to the annuity fund, if any, or arrears of the annuity, as the case may be;

as the trustees in their absolute discretion, without being liable to account for the exercise of such discretion, think fit.

(2) This section does not apply to trusts coming into operation before the commencement of this Act, and has effect subject to any variation of the implied trusts aforesaid contained in the instrument creating the trust.

(3) Nothing in this section operates to validate any trust which would, if contained in the instrument creating the trust, be liable to be set aside.

PART III

APPOINTMENT AND DISCHARGE OF TRUSTEES

34. Limitation of the number of trustees   [393]

(1) Where, at the commencement of this Act, there are more than four trustees of a settlement of land, or more than four trustees holding land on trust for sale,

no new trustees shall (except where as a result of the appointment the number is reduced to four or less) be capable of being appointed until the number is reduced to less than four, and thereafter the number shall not be increased beyond four.

(2) In the case of settlements and dispositions on trust for sale of land made or coming into operation after the commencement of this Act—

(a) the number of trustees thereof shall not in any case exceed four, and where more than four persons are named as such trustees, the four first named (who are able and willing to act) shall alone be the trustees, and the other persons named shall not be trustees unless appointed on the occurrence of a vacancy;

(b) the number of the trustees shall not be increased beyond four.

(3) This section only applies to settlements and dispositions of land, and the restrictions imposed on the number of trustees do not apply—

(a) in the case of land vested in trustees for charitable, ecclesiastical, or public purposes; or

(b) where the net proceeds of the sale of the land are held for like purposes; or

(c) to the trustees of a term of years absolute limited by a settlement on trusts for raising money, or of a like term created under the statutory remedies relating to annual sums charged on land.

35. Appointments of trustees of settlements and   [394] dispositions on trust for sale of land

(1) Appointments of new trustees of conveyances on trust for sale on the one hand and of the settlement of the proceeds of sale on the other hand, shall, subject to any order of the court, be effected by separate instruments, but in such manner as to secure that the same persons shall become the trustees of the conveyance on trust for sale as become the trustees of the settlement of the proceeds of sale.

(2) Where new trustees of a settlement are appointed, a memorandum of the names and addresses of the persons who are for the time being the trustees thereof for the purposes of the Settled Land Act 1925, shall be endorsed on or annexed to the last or only principal vesting instrument by or on behalf of the trustees of the settlement, and such vesting instrument shall, for that purpose, be produced by the person having the possession thereof to the trustees of the seettlment when so required.

(3) Where new trustees of a conveyance on trust for sale relating to a legal estate are appointed, a memorandum of the persons who are for the time being the trustees for sale shall be endorsed on or annexed thereto by or on behalf of the trustees of the settlement of the proceeds of sale, and the conveyance shall, for that purpose, be produced by the person having the possession thereof to the last-mentioned trustees when so required.

(4) This section applies only to settlements and dispositions of land.

36. Power of appointing new or additional trustees   [395]

(1) Where a trustee, either original or substituted, and whether appointed by a court or otherwise, is dead, or remains out of the United Kingdom for more than twelve months, or desires to be discharged from all or any of the trusts or powers reposed in or conferred on him, or refuses or is unfit to act therein, or is incapable of acting therein, or is an infant, then, subject to the restrictions imposed by this Act on the number of trustees,—

(a) the person or persons nominated for the purpose of appointing new trustees by the instrument, if any, creating the trust; or

(b) if there is no such person, or no such person able and willing to act, then the surviving or continuing trustees or trustee for the time being, or the personal representatives of the last surviving or continuing trustee;

may, by writing, appoint one or more other persons (whether or not being the persons exercising the power) to be a trustee or trustees in the place of the trustee so deceased remaining out of the United Kingdom, desiring to be discharged, refusing, or being unfit or being incapable, or being an infant, as aforesaid.

(2) Where a trustee has been removed under a power contained in the instrument creating the trust, a new trustee or new trustees may be appointed in the place of the trustee who is removed, as if he were dead, or, in the case of a corporation, as if the corporation desired to be discharged from the trust, and the provisions of this section shall apply accordingly, but subject to the restrictions imposed by this Act on the number of trustees.

(3) Where a corporation being a trustee is or has been dissolved, either before or after the commencement of this Act, then, for the purposes of this section and of any enactment replaced thereby, the corporation shall be deemed to be and to have been from the date of the dissolution incapable of acting in the trusts or powers reposed in or conferred on the corporation.

(4) The power of appointment given by subsection (1) of this section or any similar previous enactment to the personal representatives of a last surviving or continuing trustee shall be and shall be deemed always to have been exercisable by the executors for the time being (whether original or by representation) of such surviving or continuing trustee who have proved the will of their testator or by the administrators for the time being of such trustee without the concurrence of any executor who has renounced or has not proved.

(5) But a sole or last surviving executor intending to renounce, or all the executors where they all intend to renounce, shall have and shall be deemed always to have had power, at any time before renouncing probate, to exercise the power of appointment given by this section, or by any similar previous enactment, if willing to act for that purpose and without thereby accepting the office of executor.

(6) Where a sole trustee, other than a trust corporation, is or has been originally appointed to act in a trust, or where, in the case of any trust, there are not more than three trustees (none of them being a trust corporation) either original or substituted and whether appointed by the court or otherwise, then and in any such case—

(a) the person or persons nominated for the purpose of appointing new trustees by the instrument, if any, creating the trust; or

(b) if there is no such person, or no such person able and willing to act, then the trustee or trustees for the time being;

may, by writing, appoint another person or other persons to be an additional trustee or additional trustees, but it shall not be obligatory to appoint any additional trustee, unless the instrument, if any, creating the trust, or any statutory enactment provides to the contrary, nor shall the number of trustees be increased beyond four by virtue of any such appointment.

(7) Every new trustee appointed under this section as well before as after all the trust property becomes by law, or by assurance, or otherwise, vested in him, shall have the same powers, authorities, and discretions, and may in all respects act as if he had been originally appointed a trustee by the instrument, if any, creating the trust.

(8) The provisions of this section relating to a trustee who is dead include the case of a person nominated trustee in a will but dying before the testator, and those relative to a continuing trustee include a refusing or retiring trustee, if willing to act in the execution of the provisions of this section.

(9) Where a trustee is incapable, by reason of mental disorder within the meaning of the Mental Health Act 1959, of exercising his functions as trustee and is also entitled in possession to some beneficial interest in the trust property, no appointment of a new trustee in his place shall be made by virtue of paragraph (b) of subsection (1) of this section unless leave to make the appointment has been given by the authority having jurisdiction under Part VIII of the Mental Health Act 1959.

(As amended by the Mental Health Act 1959.)

37. Supplemental provisions as to appointment of trustees   [396]

(1) On the appointment of a trustee for the whole or any part of trust property—

(a) the number of trustees may, subject to the restrictions imposed by this Act on the number of trustees, be increased; and

(b) a separate set of trustees, not exceeding four, may be appointed for any part of the trust property held on trusts distinct from those relating to any other part or parts of the trust property, notwithstanding that no new trustees or trustee are or is to be appointed for other parts of the trust property, and any existing trustee may be appointed or remain one of such separate set of trustees, or, if only one trustee was originally appointed, then, save as hereinafter provided, one separate trustee may be so appointed; and

(c) it shall not be obligatory, save as hereinafter provided, to appoint more than one new trustee where only one trustee was originally appointed, or to fill up the original number of trustees where more than two trustees were originally appointed, but, except where only one trustee was originally appointed, and a sole trustee when appointed will be able to give valid receipts for all capital money, a trustee shall not be discharged from his trust unless there will be either a trust corporation or at least two individuals to act as trustees to perform the trust; and

(d) any assurance or thing requisite for vesting the trust property, or any part thereof, in a sole trustee, or jointly in the persons who are the trustees, shall be executed or done.

(2) Nothing in this Act shall authorise the appointment of a sole trustee, not being a trust corporation, where the trustee, when appointed, would not be able to give valid receipts for all capital money arising under the trust.

38. Evidence as to a vacancy in a trust [397]

(1) A statement, contained in any instrument coming into operation after the commencement of this Act by which a new trustee is appointed for any purpose connected with land, to the effect that a trustee has remained out of the United Kingdom for more than twelve months or refuses or is unfit to act, or is incapable of acting, or that he is not entitled to a beneficial interest in the trust property in possession, shall, in favour of a purchaser of a legal estate, be conclusive evidence of the matter stated.

(2) In favour of such purchaser any appointment of a new trustee depending on that statement, and any vesting declaration, express or implied, consequent on the appointment, shall be valid.

39. Retirement of trustee without a new appointment [398]

(1) Where a trustee is desirous of being discharged from the trust, and after his discharge there will be either a trust corporation or at least two individuals to act as trustees to perform the trust, then, if such trustee as aforesaid by deed declares that he is desirous of being discharged from the trust, and if his co-trustees and such other person, if any, as is empowered to appoint trustees, by deed consent to the discharge of the trustee, and to the vesting in the co-trustees alone of the trust property, the trustee desirous of being discharged shall be deemed to have retired from the trust, and shall, by the deed, be discharged therefrom under this Act, without any new trustee being appointed in his place.

(2) Any assurance or thing requisite for vesting the trust property in the continuing trustees alone shall be executed or done.

40. Vesting of trust property in new or continuing trustees [399]

(1) Where by a deed a new trustee is appointed to perform any trust, then—

(a) if the deed contains a declaration by the appointor to the effect that any estate or interest in any land subject to the trust, or in any chattel so subject, or the right to recover or receive any debt or other thing in action so subject, shall vest in the persons who by virtue of the deed become or are the trustees for performing the trust, the deed shall operate, without any conveyance or assignment, to vest in those persons as joint tenants and for the purposes of the trust the estate interest or right to which the declaration relates; and

(b) if the deed is made after the commencement of this Act and does not contain such a declaration, the deed shall, subject to any express provision to the

127

contrary therein contained, operate as if it had contained such a declaration by the appointor extending to all the estates interests and rights with respect to which a declaration could have been made.

(2) Where by a deed a retiring trustee is discharged under the statutory power without a new trustee being appointed, then—

(a) if the deed contains such a declaration as aforesaid by the retiring and continuing trustees, and by the other person, if any, empowered to appoint trustees, the deed shall, without any conveyance or assignment, operate to vest in the continuing trustees alone, as joint tenants, and for the purposes of the trust, the estate, interest, or right to which the declaration relates; and

(b) if the deed is made after the commencement of this Act and does not contain such a declaration, the deed shall, subject to any express provision to the contrary therein contained, operate as if it had contained such a declaration by such persons as aforesaid extending to all the estates, interests and rights with respect to which a declaration could have been made.

(3) An express vesting declaration, whether made before or after the commencement of this Act, shall, notwithstanding that the estate, interest or right to be vested is not expressly referred to, and provided that the other statutory requirements were or are complied with, operate and be deemed always to have operated (but without prejudice to any express provision to the contrary contained in the deed of appointment or discharge) to vest in the persons respectively referred to in subsections (1) and (2) of this section, as the case may require, such estates, interests and rights as are capable of being and ought to be vested in those persons.

(4) This section does not extend—

(a) to land conveyed by way of mortgage for securing money subject to the trust, except land conveyed on trust for securing debentures or debenture stock;

(b) to land held under a lease which contains any covenant, condition or agreement against assignment or disposing of the land without licence or consent, unless, prior to the execution of the deed containing expressly or impliedly the vesting declaration, the requisite licence or consent has been obtained, or unless, by virtue of any statute or rule of law, the vesting declaration, express or implied, would not operate as a breach of covenant or give rise to a forfeiture;

(c) to any share, stock, annuity or property which is only transferable in books kept by a company or other body, or in manner directed by or under an Act of Parliament.

In this subsection "lease" includes an underlease and an agreement for a lease or underlease.

(5) For purposes of registration of the deed in any registry, the person or persons making the declaration expressly or impliedly, shall be deemed the conveying party or parties, and the conveyance shall be deemed to be made by him or them under a power conferred by this Act.

(6) This section applies to deeds of appointment or discharge executed on or after the first day of January, eighteen hundred and eighty-two.

PART IV

POWERS OF THE COURT

Appointment of new Trustees

41. Power of court to appoint new trustees   **[400]**

(1) The court may, whenever it is expedient to appoint a new trustee or new trustees, and it is found inexpedient difficult or impracticable so to do without the assistance of the court, make an order appointing a new trustee or new trustees either in substitution for or in addition to any existing trustee or trustees, or although there is no existing trustee.

In particular and without prejudice to the generality of the foregoing provision, the court may make an order appointing a new trustee in substitution for a trustee who is incapable, by reason of mental disorder within the meaning of the Mental Health Act 1959, of exercising his functions as trustee, or is a bankrupt, or is a corporation which is in liquidation or has been dissolved.

(2) The power conferred by this section may, in the case of a deed of arrangement within the meaning of the Deeds of Arrangement Act 1914, be exercised either by the High Court or by the court having jurisdiction in bankruptcy in the district in which the debtor resided or carried on business at the date of the execution of the deed.

(3) An order under this section, and any consequential vesting order or conveyance, shall not operate further or otherwise as a discharge to any former or continuing trustee than an appointment of new trustees under any power for that purpose contained in any instrument would have operated.

(4) Nothing in this section gives power to appoint an executor or administrator. (As amended by the Mental Health Act 1959.)

42. Power to authorise remuneration [401]

Where the court appoints a corporation, other than the Public Trustee, to be a trustee either solely or jointly with another person, the court may authorise the corporation to charge such remuneration for its services as trustee as the court may think fit.

43. Powers of new trustee appointed by the court [402]

Every trustee appointed by a court of competent jurisdiction shall, as well before as after the trust property becomes by law, or by assurance, or otherwise, vested in him, have the same powers, authorities, and discretions, and may in all respects act as if he had been originally appointed a trustee by the instrument, if any, creating the trust.

Vesting Orders

44. Vesting orders of land [403]

In any of the following cases, namely:—

(i) Where the court appoints or has appointed a trustee, or where a trustee has been appointed out of court under any statutory or express power;

(ii) Where a trustee entitled to or possessed of any land or interest therein, whether by way of mortgage or otherwise, or entitled to a contingent right therein, either solely or jointly with any other person—

(a) is under disability; or

(b) is out of the jurisdiction of the High Court; or

(c) cannot be found, or, being a corporation, has been dissolved;

(iii) Where it is uncertain who was the survivor of two or more trustees jointly entitled to or possessed of any interest in land;

(iv) Where it is uncertain whether the last trustee known to have been entitled to or possessed of any interest in land is living or dead;

(v) Where there is no personal representative of a deceased trustee who was entitled to or possessed of any interest in land, or where it is uncertain who is the personal representative of a deceased trustee who was entitled to or possessed of any interest in land;

(vi) Where a trustee jointly or solely entitled to or possessed of any interest in land, or entitled to a contingent right therein, has been required, by or on behalf of a person entitled to require a conveyance of the land or interest or a release of the right, to convey the land or interest or to release the right, and has wilfully refused or neglected to convey the land or interest or release the right for twenty-eight days after the date of the requirement;

(vii) Where land or any interest therein is vested in a trustee whether by way of mortgage or otherwise, and it appears to the court to be expedient;

the court may make an order (in this Act called a vesting order) vesting the land or interest therein in any such person in any such manner and for any such estate or interest as the court may direct, or releasing or disposing of the contingent right to such person as the court may direct:

Provided that—

(a) Where the order is consequential on the appointment of a trustee the land or interest therein shall be vested for such estate as the court may direct in the persons who on the appointment are the trustees; and

(b) Where the order relates to a trustee entitled or formerly entitled jointly with another person, and such trustee is under disability or out of the jurisdiction of the High Court or cannot be found, or being a corporation has been dissolved, the land interest or right shall be vested in such other person who remains entitled, either alone or with any other person the court may appoint.

45. Orders as to contingent rights of unborn persons [404]

Where any interest in land is subject to a contingent right in an unborn person or class of unborn persons who, on coming into existence would, in respect thereof, become entitled to or possessed of that interest on any trust, the court may make an order releasing the land or interest therein from the contingent right, or may make an order vesting in any person the estate or interest to or of which the unborn person or class of unborn persons would, on coming into existence, be entitled or possessed in the land.

46. Vesting order in place of conveyance by infant mortgagee [405]

Where any person entitled to or possessed of any interest in land, or entitled to a contingent right in land, by way of security for money, is an infant, the court may make an order vesting or releasing or disposing of the interest in the land or the right in like manner as in the case of a trustee under disability.

47. Vesting order consequential on order for sale or mortgage of land [406]

Where any court gives a judgment or makes an order directing the sale or mortgage of any land, every person who is entitled to or possessed of any interest in the land, or entitled to a contingent right therein, and is a party to the action or proceeding in which the judgment or order is given or made or is otherwise bound by the judgment or order, shall be deemed to be so entitled or possessed, as the case may be, as a trustee for the purposes of this Act, and the court may, if it thinks expedient, make an order vesting the land or any part thereof for such estate or interest as that court thinks fit in the purchaser or mortgagaee or in any other person:

Provided that, in the case of a legal mortgage, the estate to be vested in the mortgagee shall be a term of years absolute.

48. Vesting order consequential on judgment for specific performance, &c. [407]

Where a judgment is given for the specific performance of a contract concerning any interest in land, or for sale or exchange of any interest in land, or generally where any judgment is given for the conveyance of any interest in land either in cases arising out of the doctrine of election or otherwise, the court may declare—

(a) that any of the parties to the action are trustees of any interest in the land or any part thereof within the meaning of this Act; or

(b) that the interests of unborn persons who might claim under any party to the action, or under the will or voluntary settlement of any deceased person who was during his lifetime a party to the contract or transaction concerning which the judgment is given, are the interests of persons who, on coming into existence, would be trustees within the meaning of this Act;

and thereupon the court may make a vesting order relating to the rights of those persons, born and unborn, as if they had been trustees.

49. Effect of vesting order [408]

A vesting order under any of the foregoing provisions shall in the case of a vesting order consequential on the appointment of a trustee, have the same effect—

(a) as if the persons who before the appointment were the trustees, if any, had duly executed all proper conveyances of the land for such estate or interest as the court directs; or

(b) if there is no such person, or no such person of full capacity, as if such person had existed and been of full capacity and had duly executed all proper conveyances of the land for such estate or interest as the court directs;

and shall in every other case have the same effect as if the trustee or other person or description or class of persons to whose rights or supposed rights the said provisions respectively relate had been an ascertained and existing person of full capacity, and had executed a conveyance or release to the effect intended by the order.

53. Vesting orders in relation to infant's beneficial interests [409]

Where an infant is beneficially entitled to any property the court may, with a view to the application of the capital or income thereof for the maintenance, education, or benefit of the infant, make an order—

(a) appointing a person to convey such property; or

(b) in the case of stock, or a thing in action, vesting in any person the right to transfer or call for a transfer of such stock, or to receive the dividends or income thereof, or to sue for and recover such thing in action, upon such terms as the court may think fit.

Jurisdiction to make other Orders

57. Power of court to authorise dealings with trust property [410]

(1) Where in the management or administration of any property vested in trustees, any sale, lease, mortgage, surrender, release, or other disposition, or any purchase, investment, acquisition, expenditure, or other transaction, is in the opinion of the court expedient, but the same cannot be effected by reason of the absence of any power for that purpose vested in the trustees by the trust instrument, if any, or by law, the court may by order confer upon the trustees, either generally or in any particular instance, the necessary power for the purpose, on such terms, and subject to such provisions and conditions, if any, as the court may think fit and may direct in what manner any money authorised to be expended, and the costs of any transaction, are to be paid or borne as between capital and income.

(2) The court may, from time to time, rescind or vary any order made under this section, or may make any new or further order.

(3) An application to the court under this section may be made by the trustees, or by any of them, or by any person beneficially interested under the trust.

(4) This section does not apply to trustees of a settlement for the purposes of the Settled Land Act 1925.

58. Persons entitled to apply for orders [411]

(1) An order under this Act for the appointment of a new trustee or concerning any interest in land, stock, or thing in action subject to a trust, may be made on the application of any person beneficially interested in the land, stock, or thing in action, whether under disability or not, or on the application of any person duly appointed trustee thereof.

(2) An order under this Act concerning any interest in land, stock, or thing in action subject to a mortgage may be made on the application of any person beneficially interested in the equity of redemption, whether under disability or not, or of any person interested in the money secured by the mortgage.

60. Power to charge costs on trust estate   [412]

The court may order the costs and expenses of and incident to any application for an order appointing a new trustee, or for a vesting order, or of and incident to any such order, or any conveyance or transfer in pursuance thereof, to be raised and paid out of the property in respect whereof the same is made, or out of the income thereof, or to be borne and paid in such manner and by such persons as to the court may seem just.

61. Power to relieve trustee from personal liability   [413]

If it appears to the court that a trustee, whether appointed by the court or otherwise, is or may be personally liable for any breach of trust, whether the transaction alleged to be a breach of trust occurred before or after the commencement of this Act, but has acted honestly and reasonably, and ought fairly to be excused for the breach of trust and for omitting to obtain the directions of the court in the matter in which he committed such breach, then the court may relieve him either wholly or partly from personal liability for the same.

62. Power to make beneficiary indemnify for breach of trust   [414]

(1) Where a trustee commits a breach of trust at the instigation or request or with the consent in writing of a beneficiary, the court may, if it thinks fit, . . . make such order as to the court seems just, for impounding all or any part of the interest of the beneficiary in the trust estate by way of indemnity to the trustee or persons claiming through him.

(2) This section applies to breaches of trust committed as well before as after the commencement of this Act.

(The words omitted were repealed by the Married Women (Restraint upon Anticipation) Act 1949.)

Payment into Court

63. Payment into court by trustees   [415]

(1) Trustees, or the majority of trustees, having in their hands or under their control money or securities belonging to a trust, may pay the same into court; . . .

(2) The receipt or certificate of the proper officer shall be a sufficient discharge to trustees for the money or securities so paid into court.

(3) Where money or securities are vested in any persons as trustees, and the majority are desirous of paying the same into court, but the concurrence of the other or others cannot be obtained, the court may order the payment into court to be made by the majority without the concurrence of the other or others.

(4) Where any such money or securities are deposited with any banker, broker, or other depositary, the court may order payment or delivery of the money or securities to the majority of the trustees for the purpose of payment into court.

(5) Every transfer payment and delivery made in pursuance of any such order shall be valid and take effect as if the same had been made on the authority or by the act of all the persons entitled to the money and securities so transferred, paid, or delivered.

(The words omitted were repealed by the Administration of Justice Act 1965.)

PART V
GENERAL PROVISIONS

64. Application of Act to Settled Land Act Trustees   [416]

(1) All the powers and provisions contained in this Act with reference to the appointment of new trustees, and the discharge and retirement of trustees, apply to and include trustees for the purposes of the Settled Land Act 1925, and trustees for the purpose of the management of land during a minority, whether such trustees are appointed by the court or by the settlement, or under provisions contained in any instrument.

(2) Where, either before or after the commencement of this Act, trustees of a settlement have been appointed by the court for the purposes of the Settled Land Acts 1882 to 1890, or of the Settled Land Act 1925, then, after the commencement of this Act—

(a) the person or persons nominated for the purpose of appointing new trustees by the instrument, if any, creating the settlement, though no trustees for the purposes of the said Acts were thereby appointed; or

(b) if there is no such person, or no such person able and willing to act, the surviving or continuing trustees or trustee for the time being for the purposes of the said Acts or the personal representatives of the last surviving or continuing trustee for those purposes,

shall have the powers conferred by this Act to appoint new or additional trustees of the settlement for the purposes of the said Acts.

(3) Appointments of new trustees for the purposes of the said Acts made or expressed to be made before the commencement of this Act by the trustees or trustee or personal representatives referred to in paragraph (b) of the last preceding subsection or by the persons referred to in paragraph (a) of that subsection are, without prejudice to any order of the court made before such commencement, hereby confirmed.

67. Jurisdiction of the "court" [417]

(1) In this Act "the court" means the High Court or the county court, where those courts respectively have jurisdiction.

(2) The procedure under this Act in county courts shall be in accordance with the Acts and rules regulating the procedure of those courts.

68. Definitions [418]

In this Act, unless the context otherwise requires, the following expressions have the meanings hereby assigned to them respectively, that is to say:—

(6) "Land" includes land of any tenure, and mines and minerals, whether or not severed from the surface, buildings or parts of buildings, whether the division is horizontal, vertical or made in any other way, and other corporeal hereditaments; also a manor, an advowson, and a rent and other incorporeal hereditaments, and an easement, right, privilege, or benefit in, over, or derived from land, but not an undivided share in land; and in this definition "mines and minerals" include any strata or seam of minerals or substances in or under any land, and powers of working and getting the same, but not an undivided share thereof; and "hereditaments" mean real property which under an intestacy occurring before the commencement of this Act might have devolved on an heir;

(7) "Mortgage" and "mortgagee" include a charge or chargee by way of legal mortgage, and relate to every estate and interest regarded in equity as merely a security for money, and every person deriving title under the original mortgagee;

(15) "Tenant for life," "statutory owner," "settled land," "settlement," "trust instrument," "trustees of the settlement"..."term of years absolute" and "vesting instrument" have the same meanings as in the Settled Land Act 1925, and "entailed interest" has the same meaning as in the Law of Property Act 1925;

(17) "Trust" does not include the duties incident to an estate conveyed by way of mortgage, but with this exception the expressions "trust" and "trustee" extend to implied and constructive trusts, and to cases where the trustee has a beneficial interest in the trust property, and to the duties incident to the office of a personal representative, and "trustee" where the context admits, includes a personal representative, and "new trustee" includes an additional trustee;

(18) "Trust corporation" means the Public Trustee or a corporation either appointed by the court in any particular case to be a trustee, or entitled by rules made under subsection (3) of section four of the Public Trustee Act 1906, to act as custodian trustee;

(19) "Trust for sale" in relation to land means an immediate binding trust for sale, whether or not exercisable at the request or with the consent of any person, and with or without power at discretion to postpone the sale; "trustees for sale" mean the persons (including a personal representative) holding land on trust for sale;

(20) "United Kingdom" means Great Britain and Northern Ireland.

(21) Any reference in this Act to paying money or securities into court shall be construed as referring to paying the money or transferring or depositing the securities into or in the Supreme Court or into or in any other court that has jurisdiction, and any reference in this Act to payment of money or securities into court shall be construed—

(a) with reference to an order of the High Court, as referring to payment of the money or transfer or deposit of the securities into or in the Supreme Court; and

(b) with reference to an order of any other court, as referring to payment of the money or transfer or deposit of the securities into or in that court.

(New subsection added by the Administration of Justice Act 1965. The words omitted were repealed by the Mental Health Act 1959.)

69. Application of Act   [419]

(1) This Act, except where otherwise expressly provided, applies to trusts including, so far as this Act applies thereto, executorships and administratorships constituted or created either before or after the commencement of this Act.

(2) The powers conferred by this Act on trustees are in addition to the powers conferred by the instrument, if any, creating the trust, but those powers, unless otherwise stated, apply if and so far only as a contrary intention is not expressed in the instrument, if any, creating the trust, and have effect subject to the terms of that instrument.

SETTLED LAND ACT 1925
(15 & 16 Geo. 5. c. 18; 30 Halsbury's Statutes (3rd Edn.) 396)

29. Charitable and public trusts   [420]

(1) For the purposes of this section, all land vested or to be vested in trustees on or for charitable, ecclesiastical, or public trusts or purposes shall be deemed to be settled land, and the trustees shall, without constituting them statutory owners, have in reference to the land, all the powers which are by this Act conferred on a tenant for life and on the trustees of a settlement.

In connexion only with the exercise of those powers, and not so as to impose any obligation in respect of or to affect—

(a) the mode of creation or the administration of such trusts; or

(b) the appointment or number of trustees of such trusts;

the statute or other instrument creating the trust or under which it is administered shall be deemed the settlement, and the trustees shall be deemed the trustees of the settlement, and, save where the trust is created by a will coming into operation after the commencement of this Act, a separate instrument shall not be necessary for giving effect to the settlement.

Any conveyance of land held on charitable, ecclesiastical or public trusts shall state that the land is held on such trusts, and, where a purchaser has notice that the land is held on charitable, ecclesiastical, or public trusts, he shall be bound to see that any consents or orders requisite for authorising the transaction have been obtained.

LAW OF PROPERTY ACT 1925
(15 Geo. 5. c. 20; 27 Halsbury's Statutes (3rd Edn.) 372)

20. Infants not to be appointed trustees   [421]

The appointment of an infant to be a trustee in relation to any settlement or trust shall be void, but without prejudice to the power to appoint a new trustee to fill the vacancy.

23. Duration of trusts for sale   [422]

Where land has, either before or after the commencement of this Act, become subject to an express or implied trust for sale, such trust shall, so far as regards the safety and protection of any purchaser thereunder, be deemed to be subsisting until the land has been conveyed to or under the direction of the persons interested in the proceeds of sale.

This section applies to sales whether made before or after the commencement of this Act, but operates without prejudice to an order of any court restraining a sale.

24. Appointment of trustees of dispositions on trust for sale   [423]

(1) The persons having power to appoint new trustees of a conveyance of land on trust for sale shall be bound to appoint the same persons (if any) who are for the time being trustees of the settlement of the proceeds of sale, but a purchaser shall not be concerned to see whether the proper persons are appointed to be trustees of the conveyance of the land.

(2) This section applies whether the settlement of the proceeds of sale or the conveyance on trust for sale comes into operation before or after the commencement of this Act.

25. Power to postpone sale   [424]

(1) A power to postpone sale shall, in the case of every trust for sale of land, be implied unless a contrary intention appears.

(2) Where there is a power to postpone the sale, then (subject to any express direction to the contrary in the instrument, if any, creating the trust for sale) the trustees for sale shall not be liable in any way for postponing the sale, in the exercise of their discretion, for any indefinite period; nor shall a purchaser of a legal estate be concerned in any case with any directions respecting the postponement of a sale.

(3) The foregoing provisions of this section apply whether the trust for sale is created before or after the commencement or by virtue of this Act.

(4) Where a disposition or settlement coming into operation after the commencement of this Act contains a trust either to retain or sell land the same shall be construed as a trust to sell the land with power to postpone the sale.

26. Consents to the execution of a trust for sale   [425]

(1) If the consent of more than two persons is by the disposition made requisite to the execution of a trust for sale of land, then, in favour of a purchaser, the consent of any two of such persons to the execution of the trust or to the exercise of any statutory or other powers vested in the trustees for sale shall be deemed sufficient.

(2) Where the person whose consent to the execution of any such trust or power is expressed to be required in a disposition is not *sui juris* or becomes subject to disability, his consent shall not, in favour of a purchaser, be deemed to be requisite to the execution of the trust or the exercise of the power; but the trustees shall, in any such case, obtain the separate consent of the parent or testamentary or other guardian of an infant or of the receiver (if any) of a person suffering from mental disorder.

(3) Trustees for sale shall so far as practicable consult the persons of full age for the time being beneficially interested in possession in the rents and profits of the land until sale, and shall, so far as consistent with the general interest of the trust, give effect to the wishes of such persons, or, in the case of dispute, of the majority

(according to the value of their combined interests) of such persons, but a purchaser shall not be concerned to see that the provisions of this subsection have been complied with.

In the case of a trust for sale, not being a trust for sale created by or in pursuance of the powers conferred by this or any other Act, this subsection shall not apply unless the contrary intention appears in the disposition creating the trust.

(4) This section applies whether the trust for sale is created before or after the commencement or by virtue of this Act.

(As amended by the Law of Property Amendment Act 1926, and the Mental Health Act 1959.)

27. Purchaser not to be concerned with the   [426] trusts of the proceeds

(1) A purchaser of a legal estate from trustees for sale shall not be concerned with the trusts affecting the proceeds of sale of land subject to a trust for sale (whether made to attach to such proceeds by virtue of this Act or otherwise), or affecting the rents and profits of the land until sale, whether or not those trusts are declared by the same instrument by which the trust for sale is created.

(2) Notwithstanding anything to the contrary in the instrument (if any) creating a trust for sale of land or in the settlement of the net proceeds, the proceeds of sale or other capital money shall not be paid to or applied by direction of fewer than two persons as trustees for sale, except where the trustee is a trust corporation, but this subsection does not affect the right of a sole personal representative as such to give valid receipts for, or direct the application of, proceeds of sale or other capital money, nor, except where capital money arises on the transaction, render it necessary to have more than one trustee.

28. Powers of management, &c. conferred on   [427] trustees for sale

(1) Trustees for sale shall, in relation to land or to manorial incidents and to the proceeds of sale, have all the powers of a tenant for life and the trustees of a settlement under the Settled Land Act 1925, including in relation to the land the powers of management conferred by that Act during a minority: and where by statute settled land is or becomes vested in the trustees of the settlement upon the statutory trusts, such trustees and their successors in office shall also have all the additional or larger powers (if any) conferred by the settlement on the tenant for life, statutory owner, or trustees of the settlement and (subject to any express trust to the contrary) all capital money arising under the said powers shall, unless paid or applied for any purpose authorised by the Settled Land Act 1925, be applicable in the same manner as if the money represented proceeds of sale arising under the trust for sale.

All land acquired under this subsection shall be conveyed to the trustees on trust for sale.

The powers conferred by this subsection shall be exercised with such consents (if any) as would have been required on a sale under the trust for sale, and when exercised shall operate to overreach any equitable interests or powers which are by virtue of this Act or otherwise made to attach to the net proceeds of sale as if created by a trust affecting those proceeds.

(2) Subject to any direction to the contrary in the disposition on trust for sale or in the settlement of the proceeds of sale, the net rents and profits of the land until sale, after keeping down costs of repairs and insurance and other outgoings shall be paid or applied, except so far as any part thereof may be liable to be set aside as capital money under the Settled Land Act 1925, in like manner as the income of investments representing the purchase money would be payable or applicable if a sale had been made and the proceeds had been duly invested.

(3) Where the net proceeds of sale have under the trusts affecting the same become absolutely vested in persons of full age in undivided shares (whether or not such shares may be subject to a derivative trust) the trustees for sale may, with the

consent of the persons, if any, of full age, not being annuitants, interested in possession in the net rents and profits of the land until sale:—

(a) partition the land remaining unsold or any part thereof; and

(b) provide (by way of mortgage or otherwise) for the payment of any equality money;

and, upon such partition being arranged, the trustees for sale shall give effect thereto by conveying the land so partitioned in severalty (subject or not to any legal mortgage created for raising equality money) to persons of full age and either absolutely or on trust for sale or, where any part of the land becomes settled land, by a vesting deed, or partly in one way and partly in another in accordance with the rights of the persons interested under the partition, but a purchaser shall not be concerned to see or inquire whether any such consent as aforesaid has been given: Provided that—

(i) If a share in the net proceeds belongs to a person suffering from mental disorder the consent of his receiver shall be sufficient to protect the trustees for sale.

(ii) If a share in the net proceeds is affected by an incumbrance the trustees for sale may either give effect thereto or provide for the discharge thereof by means of the property allotted in respect of such share, as they may consider expedient.

(4) If a share in the net proceeds is absolutely vested in an infant, the trustees for sale may act on his behalf and retain land (to be held on trust for sale) or other property to represent his share, but in other respects the foregoing power shall apply as if the infant had been of full age.

(5) This section applies to dispositions on trust for sale coming into operation either before or after the commencement or by virtue of this Act.

(As amended by the Law of Property Amendment Act 1926 and the Mental Health Act 1959.)

29. Delegation of powers of management by trustees for sale [428]

(1) The powers of and incidental to leasing, accepting surrenders of leases and management, conferred on trustees for sale whether by this Act or otherwise, may, until sale of the land, be revocably delegated from time to time, by writing, signed by them, to any person of full age (not being merely an annuitant) for the time being beneficially entitled in possession to the net rents and profits of the land during his life or for any less period: and in favour of a lessee such writing shall, unless the contrary appears, be sufficient evidence that the person named therein is a person to whom the powers may be delegated, and the production of such writing shall, unless the contrary appears, be sufficient evidence that the delegation has not been revoked.

(2) Any power so delegated shall be exercised only in the names and on behalf of the trustees delegating the power.

(3) The persons delegating any power under this section shall not, in relation to the exercise or purported exercise of the power, be liable for the acts or defaults of the person to whom the power is delegated, but that person shall, in relation to the exercise of the power by him, be deemed to be in the position and to have the duties and liabilities of a trustee.

(4) Where, at the commencement of this Act, an order made under section seven of the Settled Land Act 1884, is in force, the person on whom any power is thereby conferred shall, while the order remains in force, exercise such power in the names and on behalf of the trustees for sale in like manner as if the power had been delegated to him under this section.

30. Powers of court where trustees for sale refuse to exercise powers [429]

If the trustees for sale refuse to sell or to exercise any of the powers conferred by either of the last two sections, or any requisite consent cannot be obtained, any person interested may apply to the court for a vesting or other order for giving effect to the proposed transaction or for an order directing the trustees for sale to give effect thereto, and the court may make such order as it thinks fit.

31. Trust for sale of mortgaged property [430]
where right of redemption is barred

(1) Where any property, vested in trustees by way of security, becomes, by virtue of the statutes of limitation, or of an order for foreclosure or otherwise, discharged from the right of redemption, it shall be held by them on trust for sale.

(2) The net proceeds of sale, after payment of costs and expenses, shall be applied in like manner as the mortgage debt, if received, would have been applicable, and the income of the property until sale shall be applied in like manner as the interest, if received, would have been applicable; but this subsection operates without prejudice to any rule of law relating to the apportionment of capital and income between tenant for life and remainderman.

(3) This section does not affect the right of any person to require that, instead of a sale, the property shall be conveyed to him or in accordance with his directions.

(4) Where the mortgage money is capital money for the purposes of the Settled Land Act 1925, the trustees shall, if the tenant for life or statutory owner so requires, instead of selling any land forming the whole or part of such property, execute such subsidiary vesting deed with respect thereto as would have been required if the land had been acquired on a purchase with capital money.

(5) This section applies whether the right of redemption was discharged before or after the first day of January, nineteen hundred and twelve, but has effect without prejudice to any dealings or arrangements made before that date.

32. Implied trust for sale in personalty settlements [431]

(1) Where a settlement of personal property or of land held upon trust for sale contains a power to invest money in the purchase of land, such land shall, unless the settlement otherwise provides, be held by the trustees on trust for sale; and the net rents and profits until sale, after keeping down costs of repairs and insurance and other outgoings, shall be paid or applied in like manner as the income of investments representing the purchase-money would be payable or applicable if a sale had been made and the proceeds had been duly invested in personal estate.

33. Application of Part I to personal representatives [432]

The provisions of this Part of this Act relating to trustees for sale apply to personal representatives holding on trust for sale, but without prejudice to their rights and powers for purposes of administration.

53. Instruments required to be in writing [433]

(1) Subject to the provisions hereinafter contained with respect to the creation of interests in land by parol—

(a) no interest in land can be created or disposed of except by writing signed by the person creating or conveying the same, or by his agent thereunto lawfully authorised in writing, or by will, or by operation of law;

(b) a declaration of trust respecting any land or any interest therein must be manifested and proved by some writing signed by some person who is able to declare such trust or by his will;

(c) a disposition of an equitable interest or trust subsisting at the time of the disposition, must be in writing signed by the person disposing of the same, or by his agent thereunto lawfully authorised in writing or by will.

(2) This section does not affect the creation or operation of resulting, implied or constructive trusts.

56. Persons taking who are not partial [434]

(1) A person may take an immediate or other interest in land or other property, or the benefit of any condition, right of entry, covenant or agreement over or respecting land or other property, although he may not be named as a party to the conveyance or other instrument.

138

60. Abolition of technicalities in regard to [435]
conveyances and deeds

(3) In a voluntary conveyance a resulting trust for the grantor shall not be implied merely by reason that the property is not expressed to be conveyed for the use or benefit of the grantee.

97. Priorities as between puisne mortgages [436]

Every mortgage affecting a legal estate in land made after the commencement of this Act, whether legal or equitable (not being a mortgage protected by the deposit of documents relating to the legal estate affected) shall rank according to its date of registration as a land charge pursuant to the Land Charges Act 1925.

This section does not apply to mortgages or charges to which the Land Charges Act 1972 does not apply by virtue of s. 14 (3) of that Act (which excludes certain land charges created by instruments necessitating registration under the Land Registration Act 1925) or to mortgages or charges of registered land or of land

136. Legal assignments of things in action [437]

(1) Any absolute assignment by writing under the hand of the assignor (not purporting to be by way of charge only) of any debt or other legal thing in action, of which express notice in writing has been given to the debtor, trustee or other person from whom the assignor would have been entitled to claim such debt or thing in action, is effectual in law (subject to equities having priority over the right of the assignee) to pass and transfer from the date of such notice—
  (a) the legal right to such debt or thing in action;
  (b) all legal and other remedies for the same; and
  (c) the power to give a good discharge for the same without the concurrence of the assignor:
Provided that, if the debtor, trustee or other person liable in respect of such debt or thing in action has notice—
  (a) that the assignment is disputed by the assignor or any person claiming under him; or
  (b) of any other opposing or conflicting claims to such debt or thing in action;
he may, if he thinks fit, either call upon the persons making claim thereto to interplead concerning the same, or pay the debt or other thing in action into court under the provisions of the Trustee Act 1925.

137. Dealings with life interests, reversions [438]
and other equitable interests

(1) The law applicable to dealings with equitable things in action which regulates the priority of competing interests therein, shall, as respects dealings with equitable interests in land, capital money, and securities representing capital money effected after the commencement of this Act, apply to and regulate the priority of competing interests therein.

This subsection applies whether or not the money or securities are in court.

163. Validation of certain gifts void for remoteness [439]

(1) Where in a will, settlement or other instrument the absolute vesting either of capital or income of property, or the ascertainment of a beneficiary or class of beneficiaries, is made to depend on the attainment by the beneficiary or members of the class of an age exceeding twenty-one years, and thereby the gift to that beneficiary or class or any member thereof, or any gift over, remainder, executory limitation, or trust arising on the total or partial failure of the original gift, is, or but for this section would be, rendered void for remoteness, the will, settlement, or other instrument shall take effect for the purposes of such gift, gift over, remainder, executory limitation, or trust as if the absolute vesting or ascertainment aforesaid had been made to depend on the beneficiary or member of the class attaining the age of twenty-one years, and that age shall be substituted for the age stated in the will, settlement, or other instrument.

(2) This section applies to any instrument executed after the commencement of this Act and to any testamentary appointment (whether made in exercise of a general or special power), devise, or bequest contained in the will of a person dying after such commencement, whether the will is made before or after such commencement.

(3) This section applies without prejudice to any provision whereby the absolute vesting or ascertainment is also made to depend on the marriage of any person, or any other event which may occur before the age stated in the will, settlement, or other instrument is attained.

Accumulations

164. General restrictions on accumulation of income [440]

(1) No person may by any instrument or otherwise settle or dispose of any property in such manner that the income thereof shall, save as hereinafter mentioned, be wholly or partially accumulated for any longer period than one of the following, namely:—

(a) the life of the grantor or settlor; or

(b) a term of twenty-one years from the death of the grantor, settlor or testator; or

(c) the duration of the minority or respective minorities of any person or persons living or en ventre sa mere at the death of the grantor, settlor or testator; or

(d) the duration of the minority or respective minorities only of any person or persons who under the limitations of the instrument directing the accumulations would, for the time being, if of full age, be entitled to the income directed to be accumulated.

In every case where any accumulation is directed otherwise than as aforesaid, the direction shall (save as hereinafter mentioned) be void; and the income of the property directed to be accumulated shall, so long as the same is directed to be accumulated contrary to this section, go to and be received by the person or persons who would have been entitled thereto if such accumulation had not been directed.

(2) This section does not extend to any provision—

(i) for payment of the debts of any grantor, settlor, testator or other person;

(ii) for raising portions for—

(a) any child, children or remoter issue of any grantor, settlor or testator; or

(b) any child, children or remoter issue of a person taking any interest under any settlement or other disposition directing the accumulations or to whom any interest is thereby limited;

(iii) respecting the accumulation of the produce of timber or wood;

and accordingly such provisions may be made as if no statutory restrictions on accumulation of income had been imposed.

(3) The restrictions imposed by this section apply to instruments made on or after the twenty-eighth day of July, eighteen hundred, but in the case of wills only where the testator was living and of testamentary capacity after the end of one year from that date.

175. Contingent and future testamentary gifts [441]
to carry the intermediate income

(1) A contingent or future specific devise or bequest of property, whether real or personal, and a contingent residuary devise of freehold land, and a specific or residuary devise of freehold land to trustees upon trust for persons whose interests are contingent or executory shall, subject to the statutory provisions relating to accumulations, carry the intermediate income of that property from the death of the testator, except so far as such income, or any part thereof, may be otherwise expressly disposed of.

(2) This section applies only to wills coming into operation after the commencement of this Act.

198. Registration under the Land Charges Act 1925, to be notice   [442]

(1) The registration of any instrument or matter under the provisions of the Land Charges Act 1925, or any enactment which it replaces, in any register kept at the land registry or elsewhere, shall be deemed to constitute actual notice of such instrument or matter, and of the fact of such registration, to all persons and for all purposes connected with the land affected, as from the date of registration or other prescribed date and so long as the registration continues in force.

(2) This section operates without prejudice to the provisions of this Act respecting the making of further advances by a mortgagee, and applies only to instruments and matters required or authorised to be registered under the Land Charges Act 1925.

199. Restrictions on constructive notice   [443]

(1) A purchaser shall not be prejudicially affected by notice of—

(i) any instrument or matter capable of registration under the provisions of the Land Charges Act 1925, or any enactment which it replaces, which is void or not enforceable as against him under that Act or enactment, by reason of the non-registration thereof;

(ii) any other instrument or matter or any fact or thing unless—

    (a) it is within his own knowledge, or would have come to his knowledge if such inquiries and inspections had been made as ought reasonably to have been made by him; or

    (b) in the same transaction with respect to which a question of notice to the purchaser arises, it has come to the knowledge of his counsel, as such, or of his solicitor or other agent, as such, or would have come to the knowledge of his solicitor or other agent, as such, if such inquiries and inspections had been made as ought reasonably to have been made by the solicitor or other agent.

(2) Paragraph (ii) of the last subsection shall not exempt a purchaser from any liability under, or any obligation to perform or observe, any covenant, condition, provision, or restriction contained in any instrument under which his title is derived, mediately or immediately; and such liability or obligation may be enforced in the same manner and to the same extent as if that paragraph had not been enacted.

(3) A purchaser shall not by reason of anything in this section be affected by notice in any case where he would not have been so affected if this section had not been enacted.

(4) This section applies to purchases made either before or after the commencement of this Act.

ADMINISTRATION OF ESTATES ACT 1925
(15 Geo. 5, c. 23; 13 Halsbury's Statutes (3rd. Edn.) 68)

42. Power to appoint trustees of infants property   [444]

(1) Where an infant is absolutely entitled under the will or on the intestacy of a person dying before or after the commencement of this Act (in this subsection called " the deceased ") to a devise or legacy, or to the residue of the estate of the deceased, or any share therein, and such devise, legacy, residue or share is not under the will, if any, of the deceased, devised or bequeathed to trustees for the infant, the personal representatives of the deceased may appoint a trust corporation or two or more individuals not exceeding four (whether or not including the personal representatives or one or more of the personal representatives), to be the trustee or trustees of such devise, legacy, residue or share for

the infant, and to be trustees of any land devised or any land being or forming part of such residue or share for the purposes of the Settled Land Act 1925, and of the statutory provisions relating to the management of land during a minority, and may execute or do any assurance or thing requisite for vesting such devise, legacy, residue or share in the trustee or trustees so appointed.

On such appointment the personal representatives, as such, shall be discharged from all further liability in respect of such devise, legacy, residue, or share, and the same may be retained in its existing condition or state of investment, or may be converted into money, and such money may be invested in any authorised investment.

(2) Where a personal representative has before the commencement of this Act retained or sold any such devise, legacy, residue or share, and invested the same or the proceeds thereof in any investments in which he was authorised to invest money subject to the trust, then, subject to any order of the court made before such commencement, he shall not be deemed to have incurred any liability on that account, or by reason of not having paid or transferred the money or property into court.

LIMITATION ACT 1939
(2 & 3 Geo. 6, c. 21; 19 Halsbury's Statutes (3rd Edn.) 79)

19. Limitation of actions in respect of trust property   **[445]**

(1) No period of limitation prescribed by this Act shall apply to an action by a beneficiary under a trust, being an action—

(a) in respect of any fraud or fraudulent breach of trust to which the trustee was party or privy; or

(b) to recover from the trustee trust property or the proceeds thereof in the possession of the trustee, or previously received by the trustee and converted to his use.

(2) Subject as aforesaid, an action by a beneficiary to recover trust property or in respect of any breach of trust, not being an action for which a period of limitation is prescribed by any other provision of this Act, shall not be brought after the expiration of six years from the date on which the right of action accrued:

Provided that the right of action shall not be deemed to have accrued to any beneficiary entitled to a future interest in the trust property, until the interest fell into possession.

(3) No beneficiary as against whom there would be a good defence under this Act shall derive any greater or other benefit from a judgment or order obtained by any other beneficiary than he could have obtained if he had brought the action and this Act had been pleaded in defence.

20. Limitation of actions claiming personal estate   **[446]**
of a deceased person

Subject to the provisions of subsection (1) of the last foregoing section, no action in respect of any claim to the personal estate of a deceased person or to any share or interest in such estate, whether under a will or on intestacy, shall be brought after the expiration of twelve years from the date when the right to receive the share or interest accrued, and no action to recover arrears of interest in respect of any legacy, or damages in respect of such arrears, shall be brought after the expiration of six years from the date on which the interest became due.

22. Extension of limitation period in case of disability   **[447]**

If on the date when any right of action accrued for which a period of limitation is prescribed by this Act, the person to whom it accrued was under a disability, the action may be brought at any time before the expiration of six years from the date when the person ceased to be under a disability or died, whichever event first occurred, notwithstanding that the period of limitation has expired:

Provided that—
(a) this section shall not affect any case where the right of action first accrued to some person (not under a disability) through whom the person under a disability claims;
(b) when a right of action which has accrued to a person under a disability accrues, on the death of that person while still under a disability, to another person under a disability, no further extension of time shall be allowed by reason of the disability of the second person;
(c) no action to recover land or money charged on land shall be brought by virtue of this section by any person after the expiration of thirty years from the date on which the right of action accrued to that person or some person through whom he claims;
(d) this section, so far as it relates to the disability of infancy or unsoundness of mind, shall not apply to any action to which the last foregoing section applies, unless the plaintiff proves that the person under a disability was not, at the time when the right of action accrued to him, in the custody of a parent;

26. Postponement of limitation period in case of fraud or mistake [448]

26. Where, in the case of any action for which a period of limitation is prescribed by this Act, either—
(a) the action is based upon the fraud of the defendant or his agent or of any person through whom he claims or his agent, or
(b) the right of action is concealed by the fraud of any such person as aforesaid, or
(c) the action is for relief from the consequences of a mistake,
the period of limitation shall not begin to run until the plaintiff has discovered the fraud or the mistake, as the case may be, or could with reasonable diligence have discovered it:
Provided that nothing in this section shall enable any action to be brought to recover, or enforce any charge against, or set aside any transaction affecting, any property which—
(i) in the case of fraud, has been purchased for valuable consideration by a person who was not a party to the fraud and did not at the time of the purchase know or have reason to believe that any fraud had been committed, or
(ii) in the case of mistake, has been purchased for valuable consideration, subsequently to the transaction in which the mistake was made, by a person who did not know or have reason to believe that the mistake had been made.

29. Acquiescence [449]

Nothing in this Act shall affect any equitable jurisdiction to refuse relief on the ground of acquiescence or otherwise.

CHARITABLE TRUSTS (VALIDATION) ACT 1954
(2 & 3 Eliz. 2, c. 58: 3 Halsbury's Statutes (3rd Edn.) 556)

1. Validation and modification of imperfect trust instruments [450]

(1) In this Act, "imperfect trust provision" means any provision declaring the objects for which property is to be held or applied, and so describing those objects that, consistently with the terms of the provision, the property could be used exclusively for charitable purposes, but could nevertheless be used for purposes which are not charitable.

(2) Subject to the following provisions of this Act, any imperfect trust provision contained in an instrument taking effect before the sixteenth day of December,

nineteen hundred and fifty-two, shall have, and be deemed to have had, effect in relation to any disposition or covenant to which this Act applies—

    (a) as respects the period before the commencement of this Act, as if the whole of the declared objects were charitable; and

    (b) as respects the period after that commencement as if the provision had required the property to be held or applied for the declared objects in so far only as they authorise use for charitable purposes.

(3) A document inviting gifts of property to be held or applied for objects declared by the document shall be treated for the purposes of this section as an instrument taking effect when it is first issued.

(4) In this Act, "covenant" includes any agreement, whether under seal or not, and "covenantor" is to be construed accordingly.

2. Dispositions and covenants to which the Act applies [451]

(1) Subject to the next following subsection, this Act applies to any disposition of property to be held or applied for objects declared by an imperfect trust provision, and to any covenant to make such a disposition, where apart from this Act the disposition or covenant is invalid under the law of England and Wales, but would be valid if the objects were exclusively charitable.

(2) This Act does not apply to a disposition if before the sixteenth day of December, nineteen hundred and fifty-two, property comprised in, or representing that comprised in, the disposition in question, or another disposition made for the objects declared by the same imperfect trust provision, or income arising from any such property, has been paid or conveyed to, or applied for the benefit of, the persons entitled by reason of the invalidity of the disposition in question or of such other disposition as aforesaid, as the case may be.

(3) A disposition in settlement or other disposition creating more than one interest in the same property shall be treated for the purposes of this Act as a separate disposition in relation to each of the interests created.

RECREATIONAL CHARITIES ACT 1958
(6 & 7 Eliz. 2, c. 17; 3 Halsbury's Statutes (3rd Edn.) 584)

1. General provision as to recreational and similar trusts, etc. [452]

(1) Subject to the provisions of this Act, it shall be and be deemed always to have been charitable to provide, or assist in the provision of, facilities for recreation or other leisure-time occupation, if the facilities are provided in the interests of social welfare:

Provided that nothing in this section shall be taken to derogate from the principle that a trust or institution to be charitable must be for the public benefit.

(2) The requirement of the foregoing subsection that the facilities are provided in the interests of social welfare shall not be treated as satisfied unless—

    (a) the facilities are provided with the object of improving the conditions of life for the persons for whom the facilities are primarily intended; and

    (b) either—

        (i) those persons have need of such facilities as aforesaid by reason of their youth, age, infirmity or disablement, poverty or social and economic circumstances; or

        (ii) the facilities are to be available to the members or female members of the public at large.

(3) Subject to the said requirement, subsection (1) of this section applies in particular to the provision of facilities at village halls, community centres and women's institutes, and to the provision and maintenance of grounds and buildings to be used for purposes of recreation or leisure-time occupation, and extends to the provision of facilities for those purposes by the organising of any activity.

VARIATION OF TRUSTS ACT 1958
(6 & 7 Eliz. 2, c. 53; 38 Halsbury's Statutes (3rd Edn.) 220)

1. Jurisdiction of courts to vary trusts **[453]**

(1) Where property, whether real or personal, is held on trusts arising, whether before or after the passing of this Act, under any will, settlement or other disposition, the court may if it thinks fit by order approve on behalf of—

(a) any person having, directly or indirectly, an interest, whether vested or contingent, under the trusts who by reason of infancy or other incapacity is incapable of assenting, or

(b) any person (whether ascertained or not) who may become entitled, directly or indirectly, to an interest under the trusts as being at a future date or on the happening of a future event a person of any specified description or a member of any specified class of persons, so however that this paragraph shall not include any person who would be of that description, or a member of that class, as the case may be, if the said date had fallen or the said event had happened at the date of the application to the court, or

(c) any person unborn, or

(d) any person in respect of any discretionary interest of his under protective trusts where the interest of the principal beneficiary has not failed or determined,

any arrangement (by whomsoever proposed, and whether or not there is any other person beneficially interested who is capable of assenting thereto) varying or revoking all or any of the trusts, or enlarging the powers of the trustees of managing or administering any of the property subject to the trusts:

Provided that except by virtue of paragraph (d) of this subsection the court shall not approve an arrangement on behalf of any person unless the carrying out thereof would be for the benefit of that person.

(2) In the foregoing subsection "protective trusts" means the trusts specified in paragraphs (i) and (ii) of subsection (1) of section thirty-three of the Trustee Act 1925, or any like trusts, "the principal beneficiary" has the same meaning as in the said subsection (1) and "discretionary interest" means an interest arising under the trust specified in paragraph (ii) of the said subsection (1) or any like trust.

(3) . . . the jurisdiction conferred by subsection (1) of this section shall be exercisable by the High Court, except that the question whether the carrying out of any arrangement would be for the benefit of a person falling within paragraph (a) of the said subsection (1) shall be determined by order of the authority having jurisdiction under Part VIII of the Mental Health Act 1959, if that person is a patient within the meaning of the said Part VIII.

(6) Nothing in this section shall be taken to limit the powers conferred by section sixty-four of the Settled Land Act 1925, section fifty-seven of the Trustee Act 1925, or the powers of the authority having jurisdiction under Part VIII of the Mental Health Act 1959.

(The words omitted were repealed by the County Courts Act 1959 and the section is printed as amended by the Mental Health Act 1959.)

CHARITIES ACT 1960
(8 & 9 Eliz. 2. Ch. 58; 3 Halsbury's Statutes (3rd Edn.) 589)

1. The Charity Commissioners [455]

(1) There shall continue to be a body of Charity Commissioners for England and Wales, and they shall have such functions as are conferred on them by this Act in addition to any functions under any other enactment not repealed by this Act.

(3) The Commissioners shall (without prejudice to their specific powers and duties under other enactments) have the general function of promoting the effective use of charitable resources by encouraging the development of better methods of administration, by giving charity trustees information or advice on any matter affecting the charity and by investigating and checking abuses.

(4) It shall be the general object of the Commissioners so to act in the case of any charity (unless it is a matter of altering its purposes) as best to promote and make effective the work of the charity in meeting the needs designated by its trusts; but the Commissioners shall not themselves have power to act in the administration of a charity.

(5) The Commissioners shall, as soon as possible after the end of every year, make to the Secretary of State a report on their operations during that year, and he shall lay a copy of the report before each House of Parliament.

3. The official custodian for charities [456]

(1) There shall be an "official custodian for charities", whose function it shall be to act as trustee for charities in the cases provided for by this Act; and the official custodian for charities shall be by that name a corporation sole having perpetual succession and using an official seal, which shall be officially and judicially noticed.

4. Register of charities [457]

(1) There shall be a register of charities which shall be established and maintained by the Commissioners and in which there shall be entered such particulars as the Commissioners may from time to time determine of any charity there registered.

(2) There shall be entered in the register every charity not excepted by subsection (4) below; and a charity so excepted may be entered in the register at the request of the charity, but (whether or not it was excepted at the time of registration) may at any time, and shall at the request of the charity, be removed from the register.

(3) Any institution which no longer appears to the Commissioners to be a charity shall be removed from the register, with effect, where the removal is due to any change in its purposes or trusts, from the date of that change; and there shall also be removed from the register any charity which ceases to exist or does not operate.

(4) The following charities are not required to be registered, that is to say,—

    (a) any charity comprised in the Second Schedule to this Act (in this Act referred to as an "exempt charity");

    (b) any charity which is excepted by order or regulations;

    (c) any charity having neither any permanent endowment, nor any income from property amounting to more than fifteen pounds a year, nor the use and occupation of any land;

and no charity is required to be registered in respect of any registered place of worship.

5. Effect of registration [458]

(1) An institution shall for all purposes other than rectification of the register be conclusively presumed to be or have been a charity at any time when it is or was on the register of charities.

(2) Any person who is or may be affected by the registration of an institution as a charity may, on the ground that it is not a charity, object to its being entered by the Commissioners in the register, or apply to them for it to be removed from the register; and provision may be made by regulations as to the manner in

which any such objection or application is to be made, prosecuted or dealt with.

(3) An appeal against any decision of the Commissioners to enter or not to enter an institution in the register of charities, or to remove or not to remove an institution from the register, may be brought in the High Court by the Attorney General, or by the persons who are or claim to be the charity trustees of the institution, or by any person whose objection or application under subsection (2) above is disallowed by the decision.

(4) If there is an appeal to the High Court against any decision of the Commissioners to enter an institution in the register, or not to remove an institution from the register, then until the Commissioners are satisfied whether the decision of the Commissioners is or is not to stand, the entry in the register shall be maintained, but shall be in suspense and marked to indicate that it is in suspense; and for the purposes of subsection (1) above an institution shall be deemed not to be on the register during any period when the entry relating to it is in suspense under this subsection.

(5) Any question affecting the registration or removal from the register of an institution may, notwithstanding that it has been determined by a decision on appeal under subsection (3) above, be considered afresh by the Commissioners and shall not be concluded by that decision, if it appears to the Commissioners that there has been a change of circumstances or that the decision is inconsistent with a later judicial decision, whether given on such an appeal or not.

6. General Power to institute inquiries [459]

(1) The Commissioners may from time to time institute inquiries with regard to charities or a particular charity or class of charities, either generally or for particular purposes:

Provided that no such inquiry shall extend to any exempt charity.

(2) The Commissioners may either conduct such an inquiry themselves or appoint a person to conduct it and make a report to them.

APPLICATION OF PROPERTY CY-PRÈS, AND ASSISTANCE AND SUPERVISION OF CHARITIES BY COURT AND CENTRAL AUTHORITIES

Extended powers of court, and variation of charters

13. Occasions for applying property cy-près [460]

(1) Subject to subsection (2) below, the circumstances in which the original purposes of a charitable gift can be altered to allow the property given or part of it to be applied *cy-près* shall be as follows:—

(a) where the original purposes, in whole or in part,—
   (i) have been as far as may be fulfilled; or
   (ii) cannot be carried out, or not according to the directions given and to the spirit of the gift; or
(b) where the original purposes provide a use for part only of the property available by virtue of the gift; or
(c) where the property available by virtue of the gift and other property applicable for similar purposes can be more effectively used in conjunction, and to that end can suitably, regard being had to the spirit of the gift, be made applicable to common purposes; or
(d) where the original purposes were laid down by reference to an area which then was but has since ceased to be a unit for some other purpose, or by reference to a class of persons or to an area which has for any reason since ceased to be suitable, regard being had to the spirit of the gift, or to be practical in administering the gift; or
(e) where the original purposes, in whole or in part, have, since they were laid down,—
   (i) been adequately provided for by other means; or

147

(ii) ceased, as being useless or harmful to the community or for other reasons, to be in law charitable; or

(iii) ceased in any other way to provide a suitable and effective method of using the property available by virtue of the gift, regard being had to the spirit of the gift.

(2) Subsection (1) above shall not affect the conditions which must be satisfied in order that property given for charitable purposes may be applied *cy-près*, except in so far as those conditions require a failure of the original purposes.

(3) References in the foregoing subsections to the original purposes of a gift shall be construed, where the application of the property given has been altered or regulated by a scheme or otherwise, as referring to the purposes for which the property is for the time being applicable.

(4) Without prejudice to the power to make schemes in circumstances falling within subsection (1) above, the court may by scheme made under the court's jurisdiction with respect to charities, in any case where the purposes for which the property is held are laid down by reference to any such area as is mentioned in the first column in the Third Schedule to this Act, provide for enlarging the area to any such area as is mentioned in the second column in the same entry in that Schedule.

(5) It is hereby declared that a trust for charitable purposes places a trustee under a duty, where the case permits and requires the property or some part of it to be applied *cy-près*, to secure its effective use for charity by taking steps to enable it to be so applied.

14. Application cy-près of gifts of donors unknown or disclaiming [461]

(1) Property given for specific charitable purposes which fail shall be applicable *cy-près* as if given for charitable purposes generally, where it belongs—

(a) to a donor who, after such advertisements and inquiries as are reasonable, cannot be identified or cannot be found; or

(b) to a donor who has executed a written disclaimer of his right to have the property returned.

(2) For the purposes of this section property shall be conclusively presumed (without any advertisement or inquiry) to belong to donors who cannot be identified, in so far as it consists—

(a) of the proceeds of cash collections made by means of collecting boxes or by other means not adapted for distinguishing one gift from another; or

(b) of the proceeds of any lottery, competition, entertainment, sale or similar money-raising activity, after allowing for property given to provide prizes or articles for sale or otherwise to enable the activity to be undertaken.

(3) The court may by order direct that property not falling within subsection (2) above shall for the purposes of this section be treated (without any advertisement or inquiry) as belonging to donors who cannot be identified, where it appears to the court either—

(a) that it would be unreasonable, having regard to the amounts likely to be returned to the donors, to incur expense with a view to returning the property; or

(b) that it would be unreasonable, having regard to the nature, circumstances and amount of the gifts, and to the lapse of time since the gifts were made, for the donors to expect the property to be returned.

(4) Where property is applied *cy-près* by virtue of this section, the donor shall be deemed to have parted with all his interest at the time when the gift was made; but where property is so applied as belonging to donors who cannot be identified or cannot be found, and is not so applied by virtue of subsection (2) or (3) above,—

(a) the scheme shall specify the total amount of that property; and

(b) the donor of any part of that amount shall be entitled, if he makes a claim not later than twelve months after the date on which the scheme is made, to recover from the charity for which the property is applied a sum equal to that part, less any expenses properly incurred by the charity trustees after that date in connection with claims relating to his gift; and

(c) the scheme may include directions as to the provision to be made for meeting any such claim.

(5) For the purposes of this section, charitable purposes shall be deemed to "fail' where any difficulty in applying property to those purposes makes that property or the part not applicable *cy-près* available to be returned to the donors.

(6) In this section, except in so far as the context otherwise requires, references to a donor include persons claiming through or under the original donor, and references to property given include the property for the time being representing the property originally given or property derived from it.

(7) This section shall apply to property given for charitable purposes, notwithstanding that it was so given before the commencement of this Act.

16. Entrusting charity property to official custodian, and termination of trust [462]

(1) The court may by order vest any property held by or in trust for a charity in the official custodian for charities, or authorise or require the persons in whom any such property is vested to transfer it to him, or appoint any person to transfer any such property to him.

17. Supplementary provisions as to property vested in official custodian [463]

(1) Subject to the provisions of this Act, where property is vested in the official custodian for charities in trust for a charity, he shall not exercise any powers of management, but he shall as trustee of any property have all the same powers, duties and liabilities, and be entitled to the same rights and immunities, and be subject to the control and orders of the court, as a corporation appointed custodian trustee under section four of the Public Trustee Act 1906, except that he shall have no power to charge fees.

18. Concurrent jurisdiction with High Court for certain purposes [464]

(1) Subject to the provisions of this Act, the Commissioners may by order exercise the same jurisdiction and powers as are exercisable by the High Court in charity proceedings for the following purposes, that is to say:—

(a) establishing a scheme for the administration of a charity;

(b) appointing, discharging or removing a charity trustee or trustee for a charity, or removing an officer or servant;

(c) vesting or transferring property, or requiring or entitling any person to call for or make any transfer of property or any payment.

(2) Where the court directs a scheme for the administration of a charity to be established, the court may by order refer the matter to the Commissioners for them to prepare or settle a scheme in accordance with such directions (if any) as the court sees fit to give, and any such order may provide for the scheme to be put into effect by order of the Commissioners as if prepared under subsection (1) above and without any further order of the court.

(3) The Commissioners shall not have jurisdiction under this section to try or determine the title at law or in equity to any property as between a charity or trustee for a charity and a person holding or claiming the property or an interest in it adversely to the charity, or to try or determine any question as to the existence or extent of any charge or trust.

(9) The Commissioners shall not exercise their jurisdiction under this section in any case (not referred to them by order of the court) which, by reason of its contentious character, or of any special question of law or of fact which it may involve,

149

or for other reasons, the Commissioners may consider more fit to be adjudicated on by the court.

19. Further powers to make schemes or alter application of charitable property [465]

(1) Where it appears to the Commissioners that a scheme should be established for the administration of a charity, but also that it is necessary or desirable for the scheme to alter the provision made by an Act of Parliament establishing or regulating the charity or to make any other provision which goes or might go beyond the powers exercisable by them apart from this section, or that it is for any reason proper for the scheme to be subject to parliamentary review, then (subject to subsection (6) below) the Commissioners may settle a scheme accordingly with a view to its being given effect under this section.

(2) A scheme settled by the Commissioners under this section may be given effect by order of the Secretary of State made by statutory instrument, and a draft of the statutory instrument shall be laid before Parliament.

20. Power to act for protection of charities [466]

(1) Where the Commissioners are satisfied as the result of an inquiry instituted by them under section six of this Act—

(a) that there has been in the administration of a charity any misconduct or mismanagement; and
(b) that it is necessary or desirable to act for the purpose of protecting the property of the charity or securing a proper application for the purposes of the charity of that property or of property coming to the charity;

then for that purpose the Commissioners may of their own motion do all or any of the following things:—

(i) they may by order remove any trustee, charity trustee, officer, agent or servant of the charity who has been responsible for or privy to the misconduct or mismanagement or has by his conduct contributed to it or facilitated it;
(ii) they may make any such order as is authorised by subsection (1) of section sixteen of this Act with respect to the vesting in or transfer to the official custodian for charities of property held by or in trust for the charity;
(iii) they may order any bank or other person who holds money or securities on behalf of the charity or of any trustee for it not to part with the money or securities without the approval of the Commissioners;
(iv) they may, notwithstanding anything in the trusts of the charity, by order restrict the transactions which may be entered into, or the nature or amount of the payments which may be made, in the administration of the charity without the approval of the Commissioners.

Establishment of common investment funds

22. Schemes to establish common investment funds [467]

(1) The court or the Commissioners may by order make and bring into effect schemes (in this section referred to as "common investment schemes") for the establishment of common investment funds under trusts which provide—

(a) for property transferred to the fund by or on behalf of a charity participating in the scheme to be invested under the control of trustees appointed to manage the fund; and
(b) for the participating charities to be entitled (subject to the provisions of the scheme) to the capital and income of the fund in shares determined by reference to the amount or value of the property transferred to it by or on behalf of each of them and to the value of the fund at the time of the transfers.

23. Power to authorise dealings with charity property, etc. [468]

(1) Subject to the provisions of this section, where it appears to the Commissioners that any action proposed or contemplated in the administration of a charity is expedient in the interests of the charity, they may by order sanction that action, whether or not it would otherwise be within the powers exercisable by the charity trustees in the administration of the charity; and anything done under the authority of such an order shall be deemed to be properly done in the exercise of those powers.

29. Restrictions on dealing with charity property [469]

(1) Subject to the exceptions provided for by this section, no property forming part of the permanent endowment of a charity shall, without an order of the court or of the Commissioners, be mortgaged or charged by way of security for the repayment of money borrowed, nor, in the case of land in England or Wales, be sold, leased or otherwise disposed of.

(2) Subsection (1) above shall apply to any land which is held by or in trust for a charity and is or has at any time been occupied for the purposes of the charity, as it applies to land forming part of the permanent endowment of a charity; but a transaction for which the sanction of an order under subsection (1) above is required by virtue only of this subsection shall, notwithstanding that it is entered into without such an order, be valid in favour of a person who (then or afterwards) in good faith acquires an interest in or charge on the land for money or money's worth.

Miscellaneous Provisions as to Charities and their Affairs

32. General obligation to keep accounts [470]

(1) Charity trustees shall keep proper books of account with respect to the affairs of the charity, and charity trustees not required by or under the authority of any other Act to prepare periodical statements of account shall prepare consecutive statements of account consisting on each occasion of an income and expenditure account relating to a period of not more than fifteen months and a balance sheet relating to the end of that period.

38. Repeal of law of mortmain [471]

(4) Any reference in any enactment or document to a charity within the meaning, purview and interpretation of the Charitable Uses Act 1601, or of the preamble to it, shall be construed as a reference to a charity within the meaning which the word bears as a legal term according to the law of England and Wales.

45. Construction of references to a "charity" or to particular classes of charity [472]

(1) In this Act, except in so far as the context otherwise requires,—

"charity" means any institution, corporate or not, which is established for charitable purposes and is subject to the control of the High Court in the exercise of the court's jurisdiction with respect to charities.

TRUSTEE INVESTMENTS ACT 1961
(9 & 10 Eliz. 2. c. 62; 38 Halsbury's Statutes (3rd Edn.) 228)

1. New powers of investment of trustees [473]

(1) A trustee may invest any property in his hands, whether at the time in a state of investment or not, in any manner specified in Part I or II of the First Schedule to this Act or, subject to the next following section, in any manner specified in Part III of that Schedule, and may also from time to time vary any such investments.

151

2. Restrictions on wider-range investment [474]

(1) A trustee shall not have power by virtue of the foregoing section to make or retain any wider-range investment unless the trust fund has been divided into two parts (hereinafter referred to as the narrower-range part and the wider-range part), the parts being, subject to the provisions of this Act, equal in value at the time of the division; and where such a division has been made no subsequent division of the same fund shall be made for the purposes of this section, and no property shall be transferred from one part of the fund to the other unless either—

(a) the transfer is authorised or required by the following provisions of this Act, or

(b) a compensating transfer is made at the same time.

In this section "compensating transfer", in relation to any transferred property, means a transfer in the opposite direction of property of equal value.

(3) Where any property accrues to a trust fund after the fund has been divided in pursuance of subsection (1) of this section, then—

(a) if the property accrues to the trustee as owner or former owner of property comprised in either part of the fund, it shall be treated as belonging to that part of the fund;

(b) in any other case, the trustee shall secure, by apportionment of the accruing property or the transfer of property from one part of the fund to the other, or both, that the value of each part of the fund is increased by the same amount.

Where a trustee acquires property in consideration of a money payment the acquisition of the property shall be treated for the purposes of this section as investment and not as the accrual of property to the trust fund, notwithstanding that the amount of the consideration is less than the value of the property acquired; and paragraph (a) of this subsection shall not include the case of a dividend or interest becoming part of a trust fund.

(4) Where in the exercise of any power or duty of a trustee property falls to be taken out of the trust fund, nothing in this section shall restrict his discretion as to the choice of property to be taken out.

3. Relationship between Act and other powers of investment [475]

(1) The powers conferred by section one of this Act are in addition to and not in derogation from any power conferred otherwise than by this Act of investment or postponing conversion exerciseable by a trustee (hereinafter referred to as a "special power").

(3) In relation to property, including wider-range but not including narrower-range investments,—

(a) which a trustee is authorised to hold apart from—

(i) the provisions of section one of this Act or any of the provisions of Part I of the Trustee Act 1925, or any of the provisions of the Trusts (Scotland) Act 1921, or

(ii) any such power to invest in authorised investments as is mentioned in the foregoing subsection, or

(b) which became part of a trust fund in consequence of the exercise by the trustee, as owner of property falling within this subsection, of any power conferred by subsection (3) or (4) of section ten of the Trustee Act 1925, or paragraph (o) or (p) of subsection (1) of section four of the Trusts (Scotland) Act 1921,

the foregoing section shall have effect subject to the modifications set out in the Second Schedule to this Act.

(4) The foregoing subsection shall not apply where the powers of the trustee to invest or postpone conversion have been conferred or varied—

(a) by an order of any court made within the period of ten years ending with the passing of this Act, or

(b) by any enactment passed, or instrument having effect under an enactment made, within that period, being an enactment or instrument relating specifically to the trusts in question; or

(c) by an enactment contained in a local Act of the present Session;
but the provisions of the Third Schedule to this Act shall have effect in a case falling
within this subsection.

4. Interpretation of references to trust property [476]
and trust funds

(1) In this Act " property " includes real or personal property of any description, including money and things in action:

Provided that it does not include an interest in expectancy, but the falling into possession of such an interest, or the receipt of proceeds of the sale thereof, shall be treated for the purposes of this Act as an accrual of property to the trust fund.

(2) So much of the property in the hands of a trustee shall for the purposes of this Act constitute one trust fund as is held on trusts which (as respects the beneficiaries or their respective interests or the purposes of the trust or as respects the powers of the trustee) are not identical with those on which any other property in his hands is held.

(3) Where property is taken out of a trust fund by way of appropriation so as to form a separate fund, and at the time of the appropriation the trust fund had (as to the whole or a part thereof) been divided in pursuance of subsection (1) of section two of this Act, or that subsection as modified by the Second Schedule to this Act, then if the separate fund is so divided the narrower-range and wider-range parts of the separate fund may be constituted so as either to be equal, or to bear to each other the same proportion as the two corresponding parts of the fund out of which it was so appropriated (the values of those parts of those funds being ascertained as at the time of appropriation), or some intermediate proportion.

5. Certain valuations to be conclusive for purposes [477]
of division of trust fund

(1) If for the purposes of section two or four of this Act or the Second Schedule thereto a trustee obtains, from a person reasonably believed by the trustee to be qualified to make it, a valuation in writing of any property, the valuation shall be conclusive in determining whether the division of the trust fund in pursuance of subsection (1) of the said section two, or any transfer or apportionment of property under that section or the said Second Schedule, has been duly made.

(2) The foregoing subsection applies to any such valuation notwithstanding that it is made by a person in the course of his employment as an officer or servant.

6. Duty of trustees in choosing investments [478]

(1) In the exercise of his powers of investment a trustee shall have regard—
(a) to the need for diversification of investments of the trust, in so far as is appropriate to the circumstances of the trust;
(b) to the suitability to the trust of investments of the description of investment proposed and of the investment proposed as an investment of that description.

(2) Before exercising any power conferred by section one of this Act to invest in a manner specified in Part II or III of the First Schedule to this Act, or before investing in any such manner in the exercise of a power falling within subsection (2) of section three of this Act, a trustee shall obtain and consider proper advice on the question whether the investment is satisfactory having regard to the matters mentioned in paragraphs (a) and (b) of the foregoing subsection.

(3) A trustee retaining any investment made in the exercise of such a power and in such a manner as aforesaid shall determine at what intervals the circumstances, and in particular the nature of the investment, make it desirable to obtain such advice as aforesaid, and shall obtain and consider such advice accordingly.

(4) For the purposes of the two foregoing subsections, proper advice is the advice of a person who is reasonably believed by the trustee to be qualified by his ability in and practical experience of financial matters; and such advice may be given by a person notwithstanding that he gives it in the course of his employment as an officer or servant.

(5) A trustee shall not be treated as having complied with subsection (2) or (3) of this section unless the advice was given or has been subsequently confirmed in writing.

(6) Subsections (2) and (3) of this section shall not apply to one of two or more trustees where he is the person giving the advice required by this section to his co-trustee or co-trustees, and shall not apply where powers of a trustee are lawfully exercised by an officer or servant competent under subsection (4) of this section to give proper advice.

(7) Without prejudice to section eight of the Trustee Act 1925 or section thirty of the Trusts (Scotland) Act 1921 (which relate to valuation, and the proportion of the value to be lent, where a trustee lends on the security of property) the advice required by this section shall not include, in the case of a loan on the security of a freehold or leasehold property in England and Wales or Northern Ireland or on heritable security in Scotland, advice on the suitability of the particular loan.

FIRST SCHEDULE

MANNER OF INVESTMENT

PART I

NARROWER-RANGE INVESTMENTS NOT REQUIRING ADVICE [479]

1. In Defence Bonds, National Savings Certificates, Ulster Savings Certificates, [Ulster Development Bonds and National Development Bonds]. [British Savings Bonds].

2. In deposits in the National Savings Bank, ordinary deposits in a trustee savings bank and deposits in a bank or department thereof certified under subsection (3) of section nine of the Finance Act, 1956.

PART II

NARROWER-RANGE INVESTMENTS REQUIRING ADVICE [480]

1. In securities issued by Her Majesty's Government in the United Kingdom, the Government of Northern Ireland or the Government of the Isle of Man, not being securities falling within Part I of this Schedule and being fixed-interest securities registered in the United Kingdom or the Isle of Man, Treasury Bills or Tax Reserve Certificates.

2. In any securities the payment of interest on which is guaranteed by Her Majesty's Government in the United Kingdom or the Government of Northern Ireland.

3. In fixed-interest securities issued in the United Kingdom by any public authority or nationalised industry or undertaking in the United Kingdom.

4. In fixed-interest securities issued in the United Kingdom by the government of any overseas territory within the Commonwealth or by any public or local authority within such a territory, being securities registered in the United Kingdom. References in this paragraph to an overseas territory or to the government of such a territory shall be construed as if they occurred in the Overseas Service Act, 1958.

5. In fixed-interest securities issued in the United Kingdom by the International Bank for Reconstruction and Development, being securities registered in the United Kingdom [and in fixed-interest securities issued in the United Kingdom by the Inter-American Development Bank, the European Investment Bank or the European Coal and Steel Community, being securities registered in the United Kingdom].

6. In debentures issued in the United Kingdom by a company incorporated in the United Kingdom, being debentures registered in the United Kingdom.

7. In stock of the Bank of Ireland [in Bank of Ireland 7 per cent. Loan Stock 1968/91].

8. In debentures issued by the Agricultural Mortgage Corporation Limited or the Scottish Agricultural Securities Corporation Limited.

9. In loans to any authority to which this paragraph applies charged on all or any of the revenues of the authority or on a fund into which all or any of those revenues are payable, in any fixed-interest securities issued in the United Kingdom by any such authority for the purpose of borrowing money so charged, and in deposits with any such authority by way of temporary loan made on the giving of a receipt for the loan by the treasurer or other similar officer of the authority and on the giving of an undertaking by the authority that, if requested to charge the loan as aforesaid, it will either comply with the request or repay the loan.

This paragraph applies to the following authorities, that is to say—
(a) any local authority in the United Kingdom;
(b) any authority all the members of which are appointed or elected by one or more local authorities in the United Kingdom;
(c) any authority the majority of the members of which are appointed or elected by one or more local authorities in the United Kingdom, being an authority which by virtue of any enactment has power to issue a precept to a local authority in England and Wales, or a requisition to a local authority in Scotland, or to the expenses of which, by virtue of any enactment, a local authority in the United Kingdom is or can be required to contribute;
(d) the Receiver for the Metropolitan Police District or a combined police authority (within the meaning of the Police Act 1946);
(e) the Belfast City and District Water Commissioners.
[(f) the Great Ouse Water Authority.]

10. In debentures or in the guaranteed or preference stock of any incorporated company, being statutory water undertakers within the meaning of the Water Act, 1945, or any corresponding enactment in force in Northern Ireland, and having during each of the ten years immediately preceding the calendar year in which the investment was made paid a dividend of not less than five per cent. on its ordinary shares.

11. In deposits by way of special investment in a trustee savings bank or in a department (not being a department certified under subsection (3) of section nine of the Finance Act 1956) of a bank any other department of which is so certified.

12. In deposits in a building society designated under section one of the House Purchase and Housing Act 1959.

13. In mortgages of freehold property in England and Wales or Northern Ireland and of leasehold property in those countries of which the unexpired term at the time of investment is not less than sixty years, and in loans on heritable security in Scotland.

14. In perpetual rent-charges charged on land in England and Wales or Northern Ireland and fee-farm rents (not being rent-charges) issuing out of such land, and in feu-duties or ground annuals in Scotland.

Part III

Wider-Range Investments   **[481]**

1. In any securities issued in the United Kingdom by a company incorporated in the United Kingdom, being securities registered in the United Kingdom and not being securities falling within Part II of this Schedule.

2. In shares in any building society designated under section one of the House Purchase and Housing Act 1959.

3. In any units, or other shares of the investments subject to the trusts, of a unit trust scheme in the case of which there is in force at the time of investment an order of the Board of Trade under section seventeen of the Prevention of Fraud (Investments) Act 1958, or of the Ministry of Commerce for Northern Ireland under section sixteen of the Prevention of Fraud (Investments) Act (Northern Ireland) 1940.

PERPETUITIES AND ACCUMULATIONS ACT 1964
(1964, c. 55; 25 Halsbury's Statutes (3rd End.) 17)

Accumulations

13. Amendment of s. 164 of Law of Property Act 1925   **[482]**

(1) The periods for which accumulations of income under a settlement or other disposition are permitted by section 164 of the Law of Property Act 1925 shall include—

(a) a term of twenty-one years from the date of the making of the disposition, and

(b) the duration of the minority or respective minorities of any person or persons in being at that date.

(2) It is hereby declared that the restrictions imposed by the said section 164 apply in relation to a power to accumulate income whether or not there is a duty to exercise that power, and that they apply whether or not the power to accumulate extends to income produced by the investment of income previously accumulated.

MATRIMONIAL HOMES ACT 1967
(1967, c. 75; 17 Halsbury's Statutes (3rd Edn.) 139)

1. Protection against eviction, etc., from matrimonial home   **[484]**
of spouse not entitled by virtue of estate, etc.,
to occupy it.

(1) Where one spouse is entitled to occupy a dwelling house by virtue of any estate or interest or contract or by virtue of any enactment giving him or her the right to remain in occupation, and the other spouse is not so entitled, then, subject to the provisions of this Act, the spouse not so entitled shall have the following rights (in this Act referred to as "rights of occupation") :—

(a) if in occupation, a right not to be evicted or excluded from the dwelling house or any part thereof by the other spouse except with the leave of the court given by an order under this section;

(b) if not in occupation, a right with the leave of the court so given to enter into and occupy the dwelling house.

(2) So long as one spouse has rights of occupation, either of the spouses may apply to the court for an order declaring, enforcing, restricting or terminating those rights or regulating the exercise by either spouse of the right to occupy the dwelling house.

(3) On an application for an order under this section the court may make such order as it thinks just and reasonable having regard to the conduct of the spouses in relation to each other and otherwise, to their respective needs and financial resources, to the needs of any children and to all the circumstances of the case, and, without prejudice to the generality of the foregoing provision,—

   (a) may except part of the dwelling house from a spouse's rights of occupation (and in particular a part used wholly or mainly for or in connection with the trade, business or profession of the other spouse);

   (b) may order a spouse occupying the dwelling house or any part thereof by virtue of this section to make periodical payments to the other in respect of the occupation;

   (c) may impose on either spouse obligations as to the repair and maintenance of the dwelling house or the discharge of any liabilities in respect of the dwelling house.

(4) Orders under this section may, in so far as they have a continuing effect, be limited so as to have effect for a period specified in the order or until further order.

(5) Where a spouse is entitled under this section to occupy a dwelling house or any part thereof, any payment or tender made or other thing done by that spouse in or towards satisfaction of any liability of the other spouse in respect of rent, rates, mortgage payments or other outgoings affecting the dwelling house shall, whether or not it is made or done in pursuance of an order under this section, be as good as if made or done by the other spouse; and a spouse's occupation by virtue of this section shall for purposes of the Rent Acts 1968 (other than Part VI thereof) and of the Landlord and Tenant (Rent Control) Act 1949 be treated as possession by the other spouse.

Where a spouse entitled under this section to occupy a dwelling house or any part thereof makes any payment in or towards satisfaction of any liability of the other spouse in respect of mortgage payments affecting the dwelling house, the person to whom the payment is made may treat it as having been made by that other spouse, but the fact that that person has treated any such payment as having been so made shall not affect any claim of the first-mentioned spouse against the other to an interest in the dwelling house by virtue of the payment.

(6) The jurisdiction conferred on the court by this section shall be exercisable by the High Court or by a county court, and shall be exercisable by a county court notwithstanding that by reason of the amount of the net annual value for rating of the dwelling house or otherwise the jurisdiction would not but for this subsection be exercisable by a county court.

(7) In this Act "dwelling house" includes any building or part thereof which is occupied as a dwelling, and any yard, garden, garage or outhouse belonging to the dwelling house and occupied therewith.

(8) This Act shall not apply to a dwelling house which has at no time been a matrimonial home of the spouses in question; and a spouse's rights of occupation shall continue only so long as the marriage subsists and the other spouse is entitled as mentioned in subsection (1) above to occupy the dwelling house, except where provision is made by section 2 of this Act for those rights to be a charge on an estate or interest in the dwelling house.

2. Effect of statutory rights of occupation as charge   **[485]**   on dwelling house.

(1) Where, at any time during the subsistence of a marriage, one spouse is entitled to occupy a dwelling house by virtue of an estate or interest, then the other spouse's rights of occupation shall be a charge on that estate or interest, having the like priority as if it were an equitable interest created at whichever is the latest of the following dates, that is to say,—

   (a) the date when the spouse so entitled acquires the estate or interest;

   (b) the date of the marriage; and

   (c) the commencement of this Act.

(2) Notwithstanding that a spouse's rights of occupation are a charge on an estate or interest in the dwelling house, those rights shall be brought to an end by—

(a) the death of the other spouse, or

(b) the termination (otherwise than by death) of the marriage,

unless in the event of a matrimonial dispute or estrangement the court sees fit to direct otherwise by an order made under section 1 above during the subsistence of the marriage.

(3) Where a spouse's rights of occupation are a charge on the estate or interest of the other spouse—

(a) any order under section 1 above against the other spouse shall, except in so far as the contrary intention appears, have the like effect against persons deriving title under the other spouse and affected by the charge; and

(b) subsections (2) to (5) of section 1 above shall apply in relation to any person deriving title under the other spouse and affected by the charge as they apply in relation to the other spouse.

(4) Where a spouse's rights of occupation are a charge on an estate or interest in the dwelling house, and that estate or interest is surrendered so as to merge in some other estate or interest expectant thereon in such circumstances that, but for the merger, the person taking the estate or interest of the other spouse would be bound by the charge, then the surrender shall have effect subject to the charge and the persons thereafter entitled to the other estate or interest shall, for so long as the estate or interest surrendered would have endured if not so surrendered be treated for all purposes of this Act as deriving title to the other estate or interest under the other spouse by virtue of the surrender.

(5) Where a spouse's rights of occupation are a charge on the estate or interest of the other spouse, and the other spouse—

(a) is adjudged bankrupt or makes a conveyance or assignment of his or her property (including that estate or interest) to trustees for the benefit of his or her creditors generally; or

(b) dies and his or her estate is insolvent;

then, notwithstanding that it is registered under s. 2 of the Land Charges Act, 1972, or subsection (7) below, the charge shall be void against the trustee in bankruptcy, the trustees under the conveyance or assignment or the personal representatives of the deceased spouse, as the case may be.

(6) At the end of section 10 (1) of the Land Charges Act 1925 (which lists the classes of charges on, or obligations affecting, land which may be registered as land charges) there shall be added the following paragraph:—

"Class F: A charge affecting any land by virtue of the Matrimonial Homes Act 1967";

and in the enactments mentioned in the Schedule to this Act there shall be made the consequential amendments provided for by that Schedule.

(7) Where the title to the legal estate by virtue of which a spouse is entitled to occupy a dwelling house is registered under the Land Registration Act 1925 or any enactment replaced by that Act, registration of a land charge affecting the dwelling house by virtue of this Act shall be effected by registering a notice or caution under that Act, and a spouse's rights of occupation shall not be an overriding interest within the meaning of that Act affecting the dwelling house notwithstanding that the spouse is in actual occupation of the dwelling house.

(8) Where a spouse's rights of occupation are a charge on the estate or interest of the other spouse, and that estate or interest is the subject of a mortgage within the meaning of the Law of Property Act 1925, then if, after the date of creation of the mortgage, the charge is registered under s. 2 of the Land Charges Act 1972, the charge shall, for the purposes of section 94 of that Act (which regulates the rights of mortgagees to make further advances ranking in priority to subsequent mortgages), be deemed to be a mortgage subsequent in date to the first-mentioned mortgage.

3. Restriction on registration where spouse entitled to more than one charge.   [486]

Where one spouse is entitled by virtue of section 2 above to a charge on the estate or interest of the other spouse in each of two or more dwelling houses, only one of the charges to which that spouse is so entitled shall be registered under s. 2 of the Land Charges Act 1972, or s. 2 (7), above at any one time, and if any of those charges is registered under either of those provisions the Chief Land Registrar, on being satisfied that any other of them is so registered, shall cancel the registration of the charge first registered.

4. Contract for sale of house affected by registered charge to include term requiring cancellation of registration before completion.   [487]

(1) Where one spouse is entitled by virtue of section 2 above to a charge on an estate or interest in a dwelling house and the charge is registered under s. 2 of the Land Charges Act 1972 or s. 2 (7) above, it shall be a term of any contract for the sale of that estate or interest whereby the vendor agrees to give vacant possession of the dwelling house on completion of the contract that the vendor will before such completion procure the cancellation of the registration of the charge at his expense :

Provided that the foregoing provision shall not apply to any such contract made by a vendor who is entitled to sell the estate or interest in the dwelling house freed from any such charge.

(2) If, on the completion of such a contract as is referred to in subsection (1) above, there is delivered to the purchaser or his solicitor an application by the spouse entitled to the charge for the cancellation of the registration of that charge, the term of the contract for which subsection (1) above provides shall be deemed to have been performed.

(3) This section applies only if and so far as a contrary intention is not expressed in the contract.

(4) This section shall apply to a contract for exchange as it applies to a contract for sale.

(5) This section shall, with the necessary modifications, apply to a contract for the grant of a lease or underlease of a dwelling house as it applies to a contract for the sale of an estate or interest in a dwelling house.

5. Cancellation of registration after termination of marriage, etc.   [488]

(1) Where a spouse's rights of occupation are a charge on the estate or interest of the other spouse in a dwelling house and the charge is registered under s. 2 of the Land Charges Act 1972 or s. 2 (7) above, the Chief Land Register shall, subject to subsection (2) below, cancel the registration of the charge if he is satisfied—

(a) by the production of a certificate or other sufficient evidence, that either spouse is dead, or
(b) by the production of an official copy of a decree of a court, that the marriage in question has been terminated otherwise than by death, or
(c) by the production of an order of the court, that the spouse's rights of occupation constituting the charge have been terminated by the order.

(2) Where—
(a) the marriage in question has been terminated by the death of the spouse entitled to an estate or interest in the dwelling house or otherwise than by death, and
(b) an order affecting the charge of the spouse not so entitled had been made by virtue of section 2 (2) above,

then if, after making of the order, registration of the charge was renewed or the charge registered in pursuance of subsection (3) below, the Chief Land

Registrar shall not cancel the registration of the charge in accordance with subsection (1) above unless he is also satisfied that the order has ceased to have effect.

(3) Where such an order has been made, then, for the purposes of subsection (2) above, the spouse entitled to the charge affected by the order may—

(a) if before the date of the order the charge was registered under s. 2 of the Land Charges Act 1972, or s. 2 (7) of this Act, renew the registration of the charge, and

(b) if before the said date the charge was not so registered, register the charge under s. 2 of the Land Charges Act 1972, or s. 2 (7) of this Act.

(4) Renewal of the registration of a charge in pursuance of subsection (3) above shall be effected in such manner as may be prescribed, and an application for such renewal or for registration of a charge in pursuance of that subsection shall contain such particulars of any order affecting the charge made by virtue of section 2 (2) above as may be prescribed.

(5) The renewal in pursuance of subsection (3) above of the registration of a charge shall not affect the priority of the charge.

(6) In this section "prescribed" means prescribed by rules made under section 16 of the Land Charges Act 1972 or section 144 of the Land Registration Act 1925, as the circumstances of the case require.

6. Release of rights of occupation and postponement   [489]
of priority of charge.

(1) A spouse entitled to rights of occupation may by a release in writing release those rights or release them as respects part only of the dwelling house affected by them.

(2) Where a contract is made for the sale of an estate or interest in a dwelling house, or for the grant of a lease or underlease of a dwelling house, being (in either case) a dwelling house affected by a charge registered under s. 2 of the Land Charges Act 1972, or s. 2 (7) of this Act, then, without prejudice to subsection (1) above, the rights of occupation constituting the charge shall be deemed to have been released on the happening of whichever of the following events first occurs, that is to say, the delivery to the purchaser or lessee, as the case may be, or his solicitor on completion of the contract of an application by the spouse entitled to the charge for the cancellation of the registration of the charge or the lodging of such an application at Her Majesty's Land Registry.

(3) A spouse entitled by virtue of section 2 above to a charge on an estate or interest of the other spouse may agree in writing that any other charge on, or interest in, that estate or interest shall rank in priority to the charge to which that spouse is so entitled.

WILLS ACT 1968
(1968, c. 28; 39 Halsbury's Statutes (3rd Edn.) 895)

1. Restriction of operation of Wills Act 1837, s. 15   [490]

(1) For the purposes of section 15 of the Wills Act 1837 (avoidance of gifts to attesting witnesses and their spouses) the attestation of a will by a person to whom or to whose spouse there is given or made any such disposition as is described in that section shall be disregarded if the will is duly executed without his attestation and without that of any other such person.

(2) This section applies to the will of any person dying after the passing of this Act, whether executed before or after the passing of this Act.

MATRIMONIAL PROCEEDINGS AND PROPERTY ACT 1970
(1790, c. 45; 40 Halsbury's Statutes (3rd Edn.) 802)

4. Orders for transfer and settlement of property and for   [491]
variation of settlements in cases of divorce, etc.

On granting a decree of divorce, a decree of nullity of marriage or a decree of judicial separation, or at any time thereafter (whether, in the case of a decree of divorce or of nullity of marriage, before or after the decree is made absolute), the court may, subject to the provisions of sections 8 and 24 (1) of this Act, make any one or more of the following orders, that is to say—

(a) an order that a party to the marriage shall transfer to the other party, to any child of the family or to such person as may be specified in the order for the benefit of such a child such property as may be so specified, being property to which the first-mentioned party is entitled, either in possession or reversion;

(b) an order that a settlement of such property as may be so specified, being property to which a party to the marriage is so entitled, be made to the satisfaction of the court for the benefit of the other party to the marriage and of the children of the family or either or any of them;

(c) an order varying for the benefit of the parties to the marriage and of the children of the family or either or any of them any ante-nuptial or post-nuptial settlement (including such a settlement made by will or codicil) made on the parties to the marriage;

(d) an order extinguishing or reducing the interest of either of the parties to the marriage under any such settlement;

and the court may make an order under paragraph (c) above notwithstanding that there are no children of the family.

37. Contributions by spouse in money or money's worth   [492]
to the improvement of property

It is hereby declared that where a husband or wife contributes in money or money's worth to the improvement of real or personal property in which or in the proceeds of sale of which either or both of them has or have a beneficial interest, the husband or wife so contributing shall, if the contribution is of a substantial nature and subject to any agreement between them to the contrary express or implied, be treated as having then acquired by virtue of his or her contribution a share or an enlarged share, as the case may be, in that beneficial interest of such an extent as may have been then agreed or, in default of such agreement, as may seem in all the circumstances just to any court before which the question of the existence or extent of the beneficial interest of the husband or wife arises (whether in proceedings between them or in any other proceedings).

38. Rights of occupation under Matrimonial Homes Act 1967   [493]
of spouse with equitable interest in home, etc.

There shall be inserted in section 1 of the Matrimonial Homes Act 1967 (which protects against eviction from the home the spouse not entitled by virtue of any estate or interest, etc., to occupy it) a new subsection—

" (9) It is hereby declared that a spouse who has an equitable interest in a dwelling house or in the proceeds of sale thereof, not being a spouse in whom is vested (whether solely or as a joint tenant) a legal estate in fee simple or a legal term of years absolute in the dwelling house, is to be treated for the purpose only of determining whether he or she has rights of occupation under this section as not being entitled to occupy the dwelling house by virtue of that interest.

39. Extension of s. 17 of Married Women's   **[494]**
    Property Act 1882

An application may be made to the High Court or a county court under section 17 of the Married Women's Property Act 1882 (powers of the court in disputes between husband and wife about property) (including that section as extended by section 7 of the Matrimonial Causes (Property and Maintenance) Act 1958) by either of the parties to a marriage notwithstanding that their marriage has been dissolved or annulled so long as the application is made within the period of three years beginning with the date on which the marriage was dissolved or annulled; and references in the said section 17 and the said section 7 to a husband or a wife shall be construed accordingly.

LAND CHARGES ACT 1972
(1972, c. 61; 42 Halsbury's Statutes (3rd Edn.) 1593)

2. The register of land charges   **[495]**

(1) If a charge on or obligation affecting land falls into one of the classes described in this section, it may be registered in the register of land charges as a land charge of that class.

(2) A Class A land charge is—

(a) a rent or annuity or principal money payable by instalments or otherwise, with or without interest, which is not a charge created by deed but is a charge upon land (other than a rate) created pursuant to the application of some person under the provisions of any Act of Parliament, for securing to any person either the money spent by him or the costs, charges and expenses incurred by him under such Act, or the money advanced by him for repaying the money spent or the costs, charges and expenses incurred by another person under the authority of an Act of Parliament; or   .

(b) a rent or annuity or principal money payable as mentioned in paragraph (a) above which is not a charge created by deed but is a charge upon land (other than a rate) created pursuant to the application of some person under any of the enactments mentioned in Schedule 2 to this Act.

(3) A Class B land charge is a charge on land (not being a local land charge within the meaning of the Land Charges Act 1925) of any of the kinds described in paragraph (a) of subsection (2) above, created otherwise than pursuant to the application of any person.

(4) A Class C land charge is any of the following, namely—

  (i) a puisne mortgage;

  (ii) a limited owner's charge;

  (iii) a general equitable charge;

  (iv) an estate contract;

and for this purpose—

  (i) a puisne mortgage is a legal mortgage which is not protected by a deposit of documents relating to the legal estate affected;

  (ii) a limited owner's charge is an equitable charge acquired by a tenant for life or statutory owner under the Finance Act 1894 or any other statute by reason of the discharge by him of any death duties or other liabilities and to which special priority is given by the statute;

  (iii) a general equitable charge is any equitable charge which—

      (a) is not secured by a deposit of documents relating to the legal estate affected; and

      (b) does not arise or affect an interest arising under a trust for sale or a settlement; and

      (c) is not a charge given by way of indemnity against rents equitably apportioned or charged exclusively on land in exoneration of other land and against the breach or non-observance of covenants or conditions; and

(d) is not included in any other class of land charge;

(iv) an estate contract is a contract by an estate owner or by a person entitled at the date of the contract to have a legal estate conveyed to him to convey or create a legal estate, including a contract conferring either expressly or by statutory implication a valid option to purchase, a right of pre-emption or any other like right.

(5) A Class D land charge is any of the following, namely—

(i) an Inland Revenue charge;

(ii) a restrictive covenant;

(iii) an equitable easement;

and for this purpose—

(i) an Inland Revenue charge is a charge on land, being a charge acquired by the Board under any enactment (including an enactment passed after this Act) for death duties leviable or payable on any death occurring on or after 1st January 1926;

(ii) a restrictive covenant is a covenant or agreement (other than a covenant or agreement between a lessor and a lessee) restrictive of the user of land and entered into on or after 1st January 1926;

(iii) an equitable easement is an easement, right or privilege over or affecting land created or arising on or after 1st January 1926, and being merely an equitable interest.

(6) A Class E land charge is an annuity created before 1st January 1926 and not registered in the register of annuities.

(7) A Class F land charge is a charge affecting any land by virtue of the Matrimonial Homes Act 1967.

(8) A charge or obligation created before 1st January 1926 can only be registered as a Class B land charge or a Class C land charge if it is acquired under a conveyance made on or after that date.

(9) Neither a redemption annuity charged by section 3 of the Tithe Act 1936 nor a substituted annuity within the meaning of that Act shall be deemed to be a land charge of any class.

4. Effect of land charges and protection of purchasers **[496]**

(1) A land charge of Class A (other than a land improvement charge registered after 31st December 1969) or of Class B shall, when registered, take effect as if it had been created by a deed of charge by way of legal mortgage, but without prejudice to the priority of the charge.

(2) A land charge of Class A created after 31st December 1888 shall be void as against a purchaser of the land charged with it or of any interest in such land, unless the land charge is registered in the register of land charges before the completion of the purchase.

(3) After the expiration of one year from the first conveyance occurring on or after 1st January 1889 of a land charge of Class A created before that date the person entitled to the land charge shall not be able to recover the land charge or any part of it as against a purchaser of the land charged with it or of any interest in the land, unless the land charge is registered in the register of land charges before the completion of the purchase.

(4) If a land improvement charge was registered as a land charge of Class A before 1st January 1970, any body corporate which, but for the charge, would have power to advance money on the security of the estate or interest affected by it shall have that power notwithstanding the charge.

(5) A land charge of Class B and a land charge of Class C (other than an estate contract) created or arising on or after 1st January 1926, shall be void as against a purchaser of the land charged with it, or of any interest in such land, unless the land charge is registered in the appropriate register before the completion of the purchase.

163

(6) An estate contract and a land charge of Class D created or entered into on or after 1st January 1926 shall be void as against a purchaser for money or money's worth of a legal estate in the land charged with it, unless the land charge is registered in the appropriate register before the completion of the purchase.

(7) After the expiration of one year from the first conveyance occurring on or after 1st January 1926 of a land charge of Class B or Class C created before that date the person entitled to the land charge shall not be able to enforce or recover the land charge or any part of it as against a purchaser of the land charged with it, or of any interest in the land, unless the land charge is registered in the appropriate register before the completion of the purchase.

(8) A land charge of Class F shall be void as against a purchaser of the land charged with it, or of any interest in such land, unless the land charge is registered in the appropriate register before the completion of the purchase.

GLOSSARY

OF LATIN AND OTHER WORDS
AND PHRASES

Abatement. Testamentary gifts of specific property take effect before general legacies; if there is not enough money left to pay the general legacies in full, they "abate", *i.e.* are all reduced in equal proportions.

Ab initio. From the beginning.

Absolute. An estate which is not conditional nor determinable nor defeasible, but will continue for ever.

Ademption. A legacy is adeemed, *i.e.* destroyed wholly or partly where the specific property comprised in the legacy has been destroyed or disposed of before the testator's death; where the testator having given a legacy to a creditor later pays the debt; where a gift or portion made by a testator to a child is presumed to have been intended to replace a prior legacy to the child.

Ad hoc. Arranged for this purpose; special; a settlement or trust for sale created specially in order to overreach certain equitable rights under Settled Land Act 1925, s. 21, or Law of Property Act, 1925, s. 2.

Ad litem. For the purpose of the law suit.

Administrator. Person authorised by the Probate Division of the High Court to wind up or deal with the estate of a deceased where there are no executors in existence, or while the executors are infants (Durante Minore Aetate) or abroad (Durante Absentia), or while an action concerning the will or estate is pending (Pendente Lite), or where an executor or administrator has died after commencing to administer the estate an administrator may be appointed to deal with the property which has not already been administered (De Bonis non Administratis). Where a will exists in which no execu-

tors have been appointed, or where the executors die before the testator or refuse to act, an administrator is appointed by letters of administration "with the will annexed" (Cum Testamento Annexo). *See also* De Son Tort.

Ad opus. For the benefit of: on behalf of.

Ad valorem. Calculated in proportion to the value or price of the property.

Advancement. (1) When property is purchased by husband and transferred or given to his wife or child, it is presumed to be intended to be a gift, and not to be held on resulting trust for the donor; (2) a payment of capital made by trustees from a trust fund to an infant beneficiary contingently entitled to establish him in life or in a career.

A fortiori. For a stronger reason; it follows necessarily; much more so.

Alio intuitu. For a different motive; for a secret and improper motive.

Aliter. Otherwise; the situation would be different if . . .; (also used of a judge who thinks otherwise or dissents).

Aliud est celare; aliud est tacere; neque enim id est celare quicquid reticeas. Mere silence is one thing but active concealment is quite another thing; for it is not disguising something when you say nothing about it.

Aliunde. From elsewhere; from other sources.

Animo revocandi. With the intention of revoking.

Animus. Intention (**donandi**—of giving; **revocandi** of revoking a will; **testandi**—of making a will.)

Ante. Before; referred to previously on a page or in a book.

Ante-nuptial. Made before marriage.

A priori. From previous assumptions or reasoning; in view of the initial assumption; from a preconceived theory; by deduction.

Assensus ad idem. Agreement as to the same terms.

Assent. A document by which personal representatives having completed the administration of the estate transfer part of the estate to the beneficiary entitled to it.

Assignment. A document by which property (esp. a lease) is transferred by one party to another.

Assumpsit (super se). A form of action in which the plaintiff pleaded that the defendant "undertook" to do something.

Assurance. A document by which property is transferred by one party to another; insurance against death.

Bare trustee. One who holds property in trust for the absolute benefit of beneficiaries who are all of full age and capacity and has no duties to perform except to transfer the property to them or as they may direct.

Base fee. The estate created when a tenant in tail in remainder barred the entail without the consent of the protector; it lasted only as long as the entail would have lasted, and therefore ended on the failure of the issue of the tenant in tail.

Beneficial owner. A person entitled to enjoy property for his own benefit who does not hold it as trustee for the benefit of someone else.

Beneficiary. A person entitled to benefit under a trust or will.

Bis dat qui cito dat. He gives doubly who gives swiftly; a quick gift is worth two slow ones.

Bona fide. In good faith; honest.

Bona vacantia. Goods of which no one claims the ownership.

Cestui(s) que trust (use). Person(s) for whose benefit property is held in trust; beneficiary (ies).

Cestui que vie. Person for the duration of whose life an estate is granted to another person.

Chose in action. Intangible personal property or right, which can be enjoyed or enforced only by legal action, not by taking physical possession.

Collateral. Blood relations descended from a common ancestor.

Colore officii. Under the pretext of his official position.

Commorientes. Persons who die at the same time.

Condition precedent. A condition which delays the vesting of an estate or right until a specified event has happened.

Condition subsequent. A condition which on the happening of a specified event destroys an estate or right which had previously vested.

Consolidation. The right of a mortgagee who holds two mortgages made by the same mortgagor to refuse to allow him to redeem the one without also redeeming the other.

Constructive trust. Where a trustee or person in a fiduciary position makes a profit from his position, or someone knowingly receives trust property, equity obliges him to hold the profit or the property in trust for the beneficiaries.

Contingent interest. An interest or right which a person cannot enjoy unless or until an event which may or may not happen has occurred.

Contra. To the contrary: (used of a case decided contrary to the doctrine or cases previously cited; also of a person who holds a contrary opinion.)

Contra bonos mores. Contrary to good morals.

Conversion. Where in a trust there is a direction that land should be sold and turned into money or that money should be used in the purchase of land, equity "looks on that as done which ought to be done" and notionally treats the land (whether it has been sold or not) as though it had been converted into money (*i.e.* personalty), and the money as though it had been converted into land.

Corpus. Capital; physical substance; physical possession.

Coup de grace. Mortal blow; complete destruction.

Covenant. An agreement contained in a deed.

Coverture. Marriage: the status of a married woman; the period during which her husband is alive.

Cum div. Sold together with the right to receive the dividend payable on or near the date of sale.

Cum onere. Together with the burden.

Cum testamento annexo. *See* ADMINISTRATOR.

Curtesy. A husband enjoyed a life estate in the land of his deceased wife, provided that she had borne him a child who was alive at birth and capable of inheriting the land.

Cy-près. For a purpose resembling "as nearly as possible" the purpose originally proposed.

Damnum emergens. A loss which arises.

Debitor non praesumitur donare. A debtor is presumed to give a legacy to a creditor to discharge his debt and not as a gift.

De bonis non. *See* ADMINISTRATOR.

De bonis testatoris. Awarding execution against the property of the testator.

De donis conditionalibus. "Concerning conditional gifts": the opening words of the statute which established the estate in fee tail.

Deed. A document which has been signed, sealed and delivered.

De facto. In fact; actual.

Defeasible. An estate or interest which has vested in someone but is liable to be "defeated" or terminated if or when a specified event occurs.

Dehors. Outside (the matter or document in question); irrelevant; extraneous.

De jure. In accordance with the law; rightful; legitimate.

Delegatus non potest delegare. He who is entrusted with a duty to perform has no power to appoint someone else to perform it instead of himself.

De minimis non curat lex. The law does not care about trivial matters.

Demise. Transfer or devolution of a right; the grant of a lease.

Deodand. A chattel which caused the death of a human and was forfeited to the Crown.

De son tort. He who without having been appointed an executor or trustee deals with property of the deceased or of the trust as though he were an executor or trustee and is therefore "through his own fault" held to be subject to all the duties and obligations of an executor or trustee.

Determine. Terminate; come or bring to an end.

Devastavit. The action brought against an executor who has "squandered" or misapplied the deceased's estate.

Devise. Gift of real property in a will.

Dictum. Remark. *See* OBITER.

Discretionary trust. A trust under which the trustees have a complete discretion as to the amount of income (if any) which they decide to pay to any member of a class of beneficiaries, and no beneficiary has any right to claim any part of the income.

Disentailing assurance. A document by which a tenant in tail barred his estate tail so as to convert it (1) into a fee simple if the protector consented or there was no protector or (2) without the protector's consent into a base fee.

Donatio mortis causa. Gift made in contemplation of death but conditional on its occurrence.

Dower. The right of a widow to a life interest in one-third of any realty owned by her deceased husband during the marriage, unless it was disposed of by a deed or will containing a declaration barring dower.

Dramatis personae. Cast: list of characters in a drama.

Dum casta (et sola) fuerit (vixerit). For as long as she remains chaste and unmarried).

Durante absentia. During an executor's absence abroad.

Durante minore aetate. While an executor remains an infant.

Durante viduitate. During widowhood.

Ejusdem generis. Of the same type; a rule of construction which implies that where a list of specific things which are of the same type or have a common characteristic is followed by general words which would normally have a wide meaning, the general words are construed as describing only things "of the same type" as the specific things.

Election. He who takes a benefit under an instrument must elect, *i.e.* choose whether to accept or reject the instrument as a whole: he cannot accept part only. If X.'s will contains a gift to E. and also a gift of property belonging to E. to Z., E. must choose either (1) to take his gift and allow Z. to have his (E.'s) property or its value, or (2) to reject the gift but keep his own (E.'s) property.

Enceinte. Pregnant.

Entail. Estate or interest which descends only to the issue of the grantee ascertained under the pre-1926 rules; since 1925 entails cannot exist as legal estates but only as equitable interests.

En ventre sa mère. Conceived but not yet born.

Eo instanti. At that instant; simultaneously.

Equity. An equitable right enforceable by equitable remedies in a court of equity.

Equity of redemption. The equitable right of a mortgagor to redeem the mortgaged property on payment of the loan with interest and costs even after the legal or contractual right to redeem has beeen lost by failure to repay the loan with interest on the date when repayment was due under the terms of the mortgage. Also the equitable interest held by the mortgagor in his mortgaged property while an equitable right to redeem exists.

Escrow. Document delivered subject to a condition which must be fulfilled before it becomes a deed.

Estoppel. Rule of evidence which ops a man from denying the truth of (ı) a statement previously made by him to and relied on by another person who is induced to change his position on the faith of it, or (ii) an issue decided by the Court in previous litigation between the same parties.

Et seq. And subsequent pages.

Ex abundanti cautela. From an abundance of caution.

Ex aequo et bono. On the basis of reasonableness and fairness.

Ex cathedra. From his seat of office: an authoritative statement made by someone in his official capacity.

Ex concessis. In view of what has already been assumed.

Ex converso. Conversely.

Ex debito justitiae. As of right; which the court has no discretion to refuse.

Ex div. Sold without the right to receive the dividend payable on or near the date of sale.

Executor(s). Person(s) appointed by a testator in his will to administer or wind up his estate. See also DE SON TORT.

Executory trust. A trust which is outlined in one document but which is intended to be set forth in greater detail in a later document.

Ex gratia. Out of kindness; voluntary; without accepting legal liability.

Ex hypothesi. In view of what has already been assumed.

Ex officio. By virtue of his official position.

Ex parte. An application made to the court by one party without giving notice to the other party, where the court has not heard argument from the other party; one sided; biased.

Ex relatione. An action instituted by the Attorney General on behalf of the Crown on the information of a member of the public who is interested in the matter (the relator).

Ex turpi causa non oritur actio. No action can be brought arising out of illegal or immoral conduct.

Falsa demonstratio non nocet cum de corpore constat. Where the substance of the property in question is clearly identified, the addition of an incorrect description of the property does no harm.

Feme covert. Married woman.

Feme sole. Unmarried woman.

Feoffee to uses. Person to whom property has been transferred which is to be held to the use of another; a trustee.

Fieri facias de bonis. Writ addressed to the sheriff: "that you cause to be made from the defendant's goods" the sum due to the plaintiff under the judgment.

Fi. fa. *See above.*

Foreclosure. Proceedings by a mortgagee which put an end to the mortgagor's right to redeem the property.

Forum domesticum. Private jurisdiction.

Functus officio. Having discharged his duty: having exhausted its powers.

General power of appointment. A power given by deed or will which empowers the donee of the power to appoint any person (including himself) to take an interest in property.

Hotchpot. A clause in a will or settlement which requires a beneficiary who has received prior payments or benefits from the testator or settlor to add these benefits to a fund (so as to enable each beneficiary to receive an equal share) before he can receive any part of the fund.

Ibid. In the same place, book or source.

Id certum est quod certum reddi potest. Anything which can be reduced to a certainty is as good as a certainty.

Ignorantia juris haud (neminem) (non) excusat, Ignorantia facti excusat. A man is excused for mistaking facts, but not for mistaking the law. Ignorance of the law is no excuse.

In aequali jure melior est conditio possidentis. Where the legal rights of the parties are equally matched, the party with possession is in the better position.

In articulo mortis. On the point of death.

In capite. In chief; holding as tenant directly under the Crown.

In consimili casu. In a similar case: by the Statute of Westminster a new type of writ could only by issued if there already existed a writ covering a similar type of case.

Indebitatus assumpsit. A form of action in which the plaintiff alleged that the defendant "being already indebted to the plaintiff" undertook to pay him the money for which he now sues.

In delicto. At fault.

Indicium (-a). Mark(s); sign(s); characteristic(s).

In esse. In existence.

In expeditione. On active military service.

In extenso. At length; fully.

In fieri. In the course of being performed or established.

Infra. Below; lower down on a page; later in a book.

In futuro. In the future.

In hac re. In this matter; in this particular aspect.

Injunction. An order of a court requiring a person to do, or refrain from doing, a particular thing.

In limine. On the threshold; at the outset.

In lieu. In place of,

In loco parentis. In the position of a parent.

In odium spoliatoris. See OMNIA PRAESUMUNTUR.

Inops consilii. Lacking facilities for legal advice.

In pari delicto potior est conditio defendentis (possidentis). Where both parties are equally at fault, the defendant (or the party in possession) is in the better position.

In pari materia. Concerned with similar subject matter: analogous.

In personam. Against the person of the defendant. See also JUS IN PERSONAM.

In praesenti. At the present time.

In re. In the matter of.

In rem. Against the property which is the subject of the action. See also JUS IN REM.

In specie. In kind: property in its original form; not converted into anything else.

In statu quo ante. In the same state in which it was before: in its existing situation.

Inter alia (-os). Amongst other things (persons).

Inter mercatores. See JUS ACCRESCENDI.

Inter partes. Between the parties: made between two or more parties.

In terrorem. As a warning: treated by the Courts as a mere threat or penalty inserted to ensure compliance and therefore void in law.

Inter se. As between themselves; amongst themselves.

Intestacy. Where a man dies having failed to dispose of all or part of his property by will.

In toto. In its entirety.

Intra vires. Within the powers recognized by law as belonging to the person or body in question: fully authorized.

In vacuo. In the abstract; without considering the circumstances.

Ipsissima verba. Very words: authoritative statement.

Ipso facto. By that very fact: automatically.

Issue. Descendants (including children, grandchildren and descendants of subsequent generations).

Ius. See JUS.

Jointure. Provision made by a

husband for his widow in a settlement.

Jura. Rights. *See also under* Jus.

Jure mariti. By virtue of his rights as husband.

Jus. A right which is recognized in law.

Jus accrescendi. The right of survivorship; the right of joint tenants to have their interests in the joint property increased by inheriting the interests of deceased joint tenants until the last survivor inherits the entire property **(Inter mercatores locum non habet pro beneficio commercii**—does not apply as between partners in a business, so that the growth of commerce may be fostered).

Jus in personam. A right which can be enforced against a particular person or a limited number of persons only.

Jus in rem. A right which can be enforced against the property in question.

Jus neque in re neque ad rem. A right which is enforceable neither over the property in question against all the world nor against specific persons only.

Jus quaesitum tertio. A right vested in a third party (who is not one of the parties to the contract).

Jus regale. Right belonging to the state.

Laches. Delay in taking action which disqualifies a party from obtaining a remedy in equity.

Laesio fidei. Breach of faith.

Lapse. When a person to whom property is given in a will dies before the testator, the gift if of specific property lapses and falls into residue and if of a share of residue lapses and devolves as on intestacy.

Lapsus linguae. Slip of the tongue.

Legacy. A gift of personalty by will.

Legitim (-a portio). The fraction of the deceased's estate which under certain legal systems, *e.g.* in Scotland could not be disposed of away from the family by will but passed by operation of law to the deceased's widow and children.

Letters of administration. The document which is evidence of the appointment of Administrators by the court and of their authority to administer the deceased's estate.

Lex domicilii. The law of the country where the deceased was domiciled at his death.

Lex situs. The law of the country in which the land is situated.

Lien. The right to retain possession of goods, deeds or other property belonging to another as security for payment of money.

Limitation. Words in a document which limit or declare the nature of the estate given to a person and the period during which it is to continue, *e.g.* to the purchaser "and his heirs", or "in fee simple".

Lis pendens. Pending action.

Loc. cit. In the case, page or book previously mentioned.

Locus poenitentiae. Opportunity for repentance: where a party has a limited time within which he is allowed to withdraw from an illegal undertaking.

Locus standi. Standing: right to appear and be heard by a court on a matter.

Lucrum cessans. A benefit which is terminated.

Mala fide(s). (In) bad faith.

Malum in se. An act which in itself is morally wrong, *e.g.* murder.

Malum prohibitum. An act which is wrong because it is prohibited by human law but is not morally wrong.

Malus animus. Evil intent.

Mobilia sequuntur personam. The domicile of movable property follows its owners personal domicile.

Mortmain. A grant of land to the "dead hand" of a corporation which never died (*e.g.* to a monastery).

Mutatis mutandis. With the necessary changes of detail being made.

Nemo est haeres (heres) viventis. No one can be the "heir" of a person who is still living (since the identity of a man's heir is not ascertained until the man dies).

Nemo heres est. *See* NEMO EST.

Next-of-kin. The closest blood relations.

Nisi. Unless; (used of a decree or order which will later be made absolute "unless" good cause be shown to the contrary); provisional.

Nomen collectivum. A collective name, noun or description; a word descriptive of a class.

Non compos mentis. Not of sound mind and understanding.

Non est factum. See SCRIPTUM.

Nonne. Why not? (Introduces a question expecting the answer: "Yes").

Non sequitur. It does not follow: an illogical argument.

Nudum pactum. A bare agreement (not supported by consideration).

Obiter dictum (-a). Thing(s) said by the way; opinion(s) expressed by the judge(s) in passing on issues which do not form part of the essential reasoning of the decision in the case, and carry little authority as precedents.

Omnia praesumuntur contra spoliatorem. Every presumption is made against a wrongdoer.

Onus probandi. The burden of proving.

Op. cit. In the book or source referred to previously.

Orse. Otherwise.

Overreach. To free land from rights which are thereafter exercised over the capital moneys representing the proceeds of sale of the land.

Parens patriae. The King in his capacity as "Father of the Nation" exercises guardianship jurisdiction over persons under legal disability or in need of protection, *e.g.* infants and mental patients.

Pari passu. On an equal footing (with); in step with; equally.

Pari ratione. By a similar process of reasoning; by analogy.

Parol. By word of mouth, or unsealed document.

Part performance. Where an oral contract for the purchase of land would normally be unenforceable for lack of a written agreement (which has been pleaded) by virtue of s. 40, L.P.A. 1925, equity will order specific performance (where applicable) if the plaintiff relying on an oral contract has with the consent of the defendant done acts exclusively in fulfilment of his obligations under the contract and has thereby been prejudiced.

Participes criminis. Accomplices in the crime.

Particular estate. An estate which is only a part of (*i.e.* less than) the fee simple; an estate which is followed by a reversion or a remainder.

Passim. Generally; referred to throughout the book or source in question.

Patrimonium. Beneficial ownership.

Pendente lite. *See* ADMINISTRATOR. While a law suit is pending.

Per. By; through; in the opinion or judgment of a judge.

Per capita. One share per head; divided equally between all the persons fulfilling the description.

Per curiam. In the opinion of the court.

Per formam doni. Through the form of wording of the gift or deed.

Performance. When a man having covenanted to do an act does not fully perform the act but does something which could be a step towards the fulfilment of the covenant, equity treats that step as having been taken in performance of the covenant. Thus where there is a covenant (1) to purchase and settle land and land is purchased but not settled, the land will be bound by the terms of the covenant; (2) to leave a sum of money to A. by will, if the covenantor dies intestate and A. inherits money on his intestacy, A. cannot recover a second sum of money under the covenant.

Per incuriam. Through lack of care; where a court gives a mistaken decision through overlooking relevant authorities.

Perpetuity. A disposition of property under which an interest does not or can not vest until after the expiry of a life or lives in being and a further period of 21 years thereafter, or after a specified period not exceeding 80 years, is void as being a perpetuity.

Per se. By itself; in itself; considered alone.

Persona(e) designata(e). A person(s) specified as an individual(s), not identified as a member(s) of a class nor as fulfilling a particular qualification.

Personal representative. The person who winds up the deceased's estate, *i.e.* his executor or administrator.

Personalty. Movable property, goods, money, choses in action and leaseholds.

Per stirpes. According to the stocks of descent; one share for each line of descendants; where the descendants of a deceased person (however many they may be) inherit between them only the one share which the deceased would have taken if alive.

171

Plene administravit. A plea by an executor "that he has fully administered" all the assets which have come into his hands and that no assets remain out of which the plaintiffs claim could be satisfied (**Praeter**—"except" certain assets insufficient to meet the claim).

Portions. Provisions for establishing children in life, especially lump sums provided for the younger children under a will or settlement.

Post. After; mentioned in a subsequent passage or page.

Post-nuptial. Made after marriage.

Post obit bond. Agreement or bond by which a borrower agrees to pay the lender a sum larger than the loan on or after the death of a person on whose death he expects to inherit property.

Power of appointment. *See* GENERAL POWER or SPECIAL POWER.

Prima facie. At first sight; which has the appearance of being valid.

Probate. An official copy of a will which has been proved in the Probate Division of the High Court. It is sealed by the Court and is confirmation of the appointment of an executor in the will, and evidence of his authority to administer the deceased's estate.

Profit à prendre. The right to enter the land of another and take part of its produce.

Pro rata. In proportion.

Pro tanto. Only so far; to that extent; to the extent of the interest held by a person; proportionately; partially.

Protective trust. A trust under which the principal beneficiary has a life interest which is determined in the event of his bankruptcy or attempting to sell or charge his life interest, and thereupon the trust income is to be applied by the trustees at their discretion for the maintenance of the beneficiary and his family or any of them.

Protector. The person whose consent was required by a tenant in tail who wished to completely bar the entail: normally he was the tenant for life in possession, unless the settlement named one or more persons as Special Protectors.

Puisne. Inferior; legal mortgage not secured by deposit of title deeds; junior; High Court judge.

Punctum temporis. Point of time; moment.

Pur autre vie. During the life of another person.

Purchase. Words which confer an interest upon the person to whom they refer.

Purchaser. A person who takes an estate in land by act of parties (*e.g.* by gift or sale), and not by operation of law (*e.g.* on intestacy).

Q.v. Which should be referred to.

Qua. As; in the capacity of.

Quaere. Consider whether the statement is correct.

Quantum. How much; extent; amount (*e.g.* of damages).

Quantum meruit. An action for reasonable remuneration for work done by the plaintiff, *i.e.* "for what he has earned".

Quantum valebant. An action for a fair price for goods supplied by the plaintiff, *i.e.* "for what they were worth".

Quia timet. Because he fears what he will suffer in the future.

Quicquid plantatur solo solo cedit. Whatever is planted in the soil belongs to the soil.

Qui prior est tempore potior est jure. He who is earlier in point of time is in the stronger position in law.

Quoad. As far as; until; as to; as regards.

Quoad hoc. As far as this matter is concerned.

Quo animo. With what intention.

Quot judices tot sententiae. There were as many different opinions as there were judges.

Quousque. Until the time when.

Quo warranto. A writ brought by the Crown against anyone who claimed or usurped an office or franchise enquiring "by what authority" he justified his claim.

Ratio decidendi. Reason for deciding; the principle of law on which a case is decided.

Ratione domicilii. By reason of domicile.

Re. In the matter of.

Realty. Land.

Reconversion. Where property which was formerly subject to notional conversion into a different type of property (*e.g.* where land was directed to be sold and converted into money) passes into the possession of an absolute owner before it has actually been converted, the owner may elect to keep the property in its existing form (*i.e.* as land) instead of actually converting it. The property is thereupon "reconverted" into its original form (*i.e.* realty).

Relator. *See* EX RELATIONE.

Religio sequitur patrem. A child's religion follows that of his father.

Remainder. An estate granted to a person other than the settlor which vests in possession on the determination of a prior particular estate (*e.g.* after the death of a tenant for life).

Renvoi. Reference to or application of the rules of a foreign legal system in a different country's courts.

Res. Property; thing.

Res integra. A question not covered by the authority of a decided case, which must therefore be decided on principle.

Res judicata. An issue which a court has decided in an action between two parties is binding and cannot be questioned in a later action between the same parties. Fresh evidence which could have affected the decision in the first action cannot be introduced in a second action.

Res nova. *See* RES INTEGRA.

Respondeat superior. Let the man who has authority answer for the acts of his servant or agent.

Restitutio in integrum. Restoration of a party to his original position.

Resulting trust. A trust which is implied by equity whereby the beneficial interest in property which is transferred into the name of a person other than a purchaser "results" or comes back to the person who provided the purchase price or transferred the property.

Reversion. Where the owner of an estate in land grants an estate or interest which is less than his own estate but retains the residue of his own estate, he has a reversion, as the land will revert into his possession on the determination of the particular estate which he has granted. The owner of the fee simple who grants a term of years by a lease retains a reversion expectant on the expiry of the lease.

Rex est procurator fatuorum. The King is the protector of the simple minded.

Rigor aequitatis. The hardness of equity.

Satisfaction. (1) Where a debtor in his will gives a creditor a legacy equal to or exceeding an existing debt, the legacy is presumed to be intended to pay off the debt. The creditor cannot claim both. (2) Where a testator gives two legacies of the same amount to the same person he is presumed to have intended to give only one of them. (3) Where a father or person in *loco parentis* covenants to give a child a portion and later makes the child a gift in the nature of a portion inter vivos or by will, the gift is presumed to replace the covenant wholly or in part. Where a father after making a will containing a legacy of a portion later gives or covenants to give the child a portion, the legacy is adeemed wholly or in part.

Sc.(-ilicet). Namely; that is to say.

Scintilla. Spark; trace; (**Temporis.** Moment of time).

Scriptum praedictum non est factum suum. A plea that "the aforesaid document is not his deed".

Secundum formam doni. In accordance with the form of wording of the gift or deed.

Secus. Differently; it is otherwise; the legal position is different (also used of a case decided to the contrary).

Sed quaere. But consider whether the statement is correct.

Semble. It appears; apparently.

Sentit commodum et periculum rei. He both enjoys the benefit of the thing and bears the risk of its loss.

Seriatim. In series; one by one; point by point.

Settlement. A document (deed or will) by which property is limited upon trust for persons who take successive interests, *e.g.* to A. for life with remainder to B. in fee simple.

Sic. Thus; (to show wording or spelling copied from another source) this was the actual wording (or spelling) of the original.

Sic utere tuo ut alienum non laedas. Use your own property in such a way as not to injure your neighbour's property.

Simpliciter. Simply; standing alone; by itself; without any qualification; in the absence of any additional factors.

Sine animo revocandi. Without any intention of revoking.

Special power of appointment. A power given by deed or will which empowers the donee of the power to appoint any member of a specified class of persons to take an interest in property.

Special protector. *See* PROTECTOR.

Specific performance. Where damages would be an inadequate remedy for a breach of contract, the defendant may be compelled to perform what he has agreed to do by a decree of specific performance which the court may grant in its discretion.

Spes successionis. The hope of inheriting property on the death of another person.

Status quo (ante). Existing situation; situation in which things were before; unchanged situation.

Statutory owners. The persons who under a settlement within the Settled Land Act 1925, have the powers of a tenant for life while there is no tenant for life, or the tenant for life is an infant—*i.e.* usually the trustees of the settlement.

Statutory trusts. Trusts which are imposed by statute, *e.g.* the trusts for sale which are imposed where (1) land is conveyed to persons as joint tenants or tenants in common, or (2) the property of an intestate is administered by his administrators.

Stricto sensu. In the strict sense.

Sub modo. Within limits; to a limited extent.

Sub nom. Under the name or title of.

Sub tit. Under the title of.

Suggestio falsi. The putting forward of something which is untrue; active misrepresentation.

Sui generis. Of its own special kind; unique.

Sui juris. Of his own right; of full age and legal capacity.

Sup. *See* SUPRA.

Suppressio veri (est suggestio falsi). The suppression or concealment of the truth (is equivalent to active misrepresentation).

Supra. Above: referred to higher up the page, or on a previous page.

Tabula in naufragio. Tacking was for a mortgagee like "a plank in a shipwreck" for a drowning man, as it gave his mortgage priority over earlier equitable mortgages.

Tam . . . quam. As well . . . as.

Testator. The maker of a will.

Timeo. I am afraid.

Toties quoties. As often as occasion shall arise.

Trust for sale. A trust which imposes on the trustees a duty to sell the property and convert it into money, but allows them to postpone the sale in their discretion for as long as they all agree.

Tu quoque. You also (are in the wrong).

Turpis causa. Disgraceful immoral or illegal conduct.

Uberrimae fidei. A contract which requires "most abundant good faith" from a party who is in a specially advantageous position.

Ubi supra. In the passage or reference quoted previously.

Ultimus heres. The ultimate heir who is last in order of priority of those who may be entitled to claim the estate of an intestate.

Ultra vires. Outside the powers recognized by law as belonging to the person or body in question; without authority; unauthorized.

Vest. Clothe with possession: confer an unconditional legally enforceable right; fall into the absolute ownership of someone.

Vested. Owned absolutely and unconditionally.

Vested in interest. Where the owner has an existing absolute right to possess the property in the future.

Vested in possession. Where the owner has an absolute right to possess the property at present.

Vice versa. The other way round; in turn.

Vide. See

Videlicet. (*See* VIZ.).

Vigilantibus et non dormientibus jura subveniunt (or Jus succurrit or Aequitas subvenit). The law(s) (or equity) assist(s) those who are watchful, not those who sleep.

Virtute officii. By virtue of a person's official position.

Vis-à-vis. In relation to; compared with.

Viz. Namely: that is to say.

Volunteer. A person who takes the benefit of a gift or settlement without having given any valuable consideration.

INDEX

All references are to paragraph numbers.

175

All references are to paragraph numbers.

All references are to paragraph numbers.

All references are to paragraph numbers.

All references are to paragraph numbers.

All references are to paragraph numbers.